THE
50
GREATEST
Yankee
GAMES

THE
50
GREATEST
Yankee
GAMES

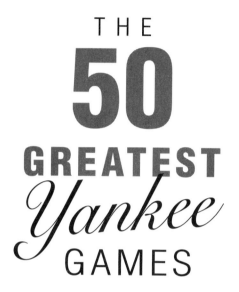

CECILIA TAN

WILEY

John Wiley & Sons, Inc.

Library of Congress Cataloging-in-Publication Data:

Tan, Cecilia, 1967–
    The 50 greatest Yankee games / Cecilia Tan.
        p. cm.
    Includes bibliographical references and index.
    ISBN 0-471-65938-X (cloth : alk. paper)
    1. New York Yankees (Baseball team) I. Title: Fifty greatest Yankee games.
    II. Title
    GV875.N4T36 2005
    796.357'64'097471—dc22

                                                                                    2004015425

Printed in the United States of America

10   9   8   7   6   5   4   3   2   1

To my family, who made baseball something to cherish

Contents

Introduction

My first experience of major league baseball—or at least the first I remember—came when I was five years old. My grandparents had come to visit on their annual summer trip, and one night my father suggested we go to a game. For some reason my mother and grandmother decided to stay behind, but my grandfather, dad, and I took off for Yankee Stadium. We lived not far from the George Washington Bridge on the Jersey side, so going to a game was an easy thing.

We went up to the ticket window and my father, perhaps hoping to impress his father-in-law, asked for the best seats they could give us. We were seated behind home plate, maybe twenty rows back, behind the protective screen. These were probably team tickets that no one claimed—players' wives seats or something. I was so small that most of what I saw of the game was the shoulders of the adults around me, but that didn't really detract from my experience. The noise, the excitement, the lights, the cheering—I found it much more exciting than the circus or some "kiddie" entertainment.

I remember only one detail from that game. At one point Bobby Murcer came to the plate with the bases loaded. I felt all the adults around me suddenly focus their attention—for a child like me it was akin to those mysterious moments in church when all the people seemed to know when to get ready to sing. Something was about to happen. Shortly thereafter, everyone began jumping up and down and screaming. Murcer had hit a home run, and my dad then taught me the words "grand slam." From that moment, I was hooked. We made a lot of trips to the Stadium after that, and as I got older, I got more involved with the game. I learned to keep a scorecard when I was ten years old, and started collecting and trading baseball cards a year or so after that. I guess you could say I started writing about baseball around then, as well. If I had to do a book report for school, I'd try to work baseball into it somehow. A biography? How about Willie Mays? Gee, Cecilia, what do you want to do for your thirteenth birthday? Other girls were having hair-and-makeup parties. I made my parents take two carloads of teenage girls to the Stadium.

My passion for baseball took a hiatus when I went to college and started my adult life, but it returned even stronger in 1998, when the country was caught up in the Mark McGwire/Sammy Sosa home run race, and I with it. I started to write about baseball when I could, began making annual pilgrimages to spring training, and returned to my childhood love of the Yankees. I was soon writing a column for the Yankees' Web site (long-since dismantled by the centralization of MLB.com) and writing historical feature pieces for *Yankees Magazine*, the team's official scorecard magazine.

As a baseball historian now, I can tell you that the date of my first game had to have been August 4, 1972, when Murcer's slam sealed a 9–5 victory over the Brewers (who were in the American League back then). That would have been the "old" Yankee Stadium, since renovated, but still the same park where Ruth, Gehrig, DiMaggio, and Mantle played, and the site of so many incredible moments and so many history-making games. My family and I were there on July 4, 1983, when Dave Righetti threw his no-hitter against the Boston Red Sox. I was there for Hideki Matsui's game-winning grand slam in his first game at Yankee Stadium in 2003. My brother was there six months later for Aaron Boone's liberating pennant-winner into the left-field seats.

Every baseball fan has a story of the greatest game he or she has ever seen. We each have a story that starts "I was there when . . ." Every time you go to the park there is always the chance to see something historic, a milestone reached, a record set, or even something that has never been done before. It was while wishing I could have been at even more of the great moments in Yankees history that the urge to write this book took hold of me. "What do you think the top 50 games in Yankees history are?" Once I had heard the question, I set about trying to answer it for myself.

The first criterion I used to consider whether a game might make the list was this: if I were a fan in the stands on that day, would I tell an "I was there" story about it? Trying to narrow the field to 50 was tricky, though. After all, since my subject is the Yankees, I could have limited the list to World Series games only and still had more than enough to choose from. I decided, though, that the regular season had to be given serious consideration. After all, these are the games that the majority of fans attend year in and year out, while only an elite few attend the World Series. (I have yet to be so lucky.) There would definitely be World Series and playoff candidates on the list, but regular season games as well. After all, one of the magical things about baseball is that on any given day at the park, you may see something you have never seen before; history may be made in front of your very eyes.

Certainly the perfect games and no-hitters had to be included. I also knew I wanted to include some epic pennant race games, such as the showdown between the Ted Williams Red Sox and the Joe DiMaggio Yankees in 1949.

The intensity of every regular season game played between these old rivals makes almost any contest between the teams a possible contender.

I also wanted to honor some incredible individual achievements, such as Lou Gehrig's four-homer game, and each time a Yankee hit for the cycle. I still haven't seen a player hit for the cycle. Only one Yankee has done it since the renovation of the Stadium, in fact (Tony Fernandez in 1995, see pages 184–188). In the more than 15,000 games the Yankees have played since their birth in 1903, a Yankee has achieved this feat only 14 times. That makes it something that happens in fewer than one in a thousand games.

I also knew that my list would not be complete without some losses. The Yankees have racked up more triumphs than any other professional sports team on planet Earth, but for all the turns of Yankee luck that have contributed to the trophies and rings, there are also those times when the story's end was a tragedy. The heartbreakers.

Still sharp in my mind is game seven of the 2001 World Series. That was an autumn of heartbreak and grief, after the destruction of the World Trade Center and the wounds dealt to New York City and the nation. For me, and many others, baseball and the Yankees became the one uplifting thing buoying us through those incredibly rocky months. To have them win the World Series again would have perhaps restored a modicum of order to the universe; the Yankees winning would have signified that not everything had changed.

But the world had changed, irrevocably. The glee that followed Alfonso Soriano's golf-swing home run off a Curt Schilling splitter was quickly replaced by anxiety as Mariano Rivera looked spent and exhausted in the dugout, his head hanging after striking out the side. Mariano was the horse the team had ridden to so many victory circles, but he, like all of us by that point, was fatigued. The game and the Series were lost. I cried for a week.

I'm still too close to that day and that game to be able to look at it objectively, so I have left it out of the 50 greatest, for now. Instead I chose the turning point game of that October, the "Jeter flip" game, where Mike Mussina outdueled Barry Zito to a 1–0 victory, to represent the 2001 postseason. And besides, the Yankee annals have other game seven losses to choose from. I have included three of them, as well as an early exit from the playoffs that presaged the Torre dynasty and some pennant races that were lost—the very first one dating back to 1904.

When my initial list was completed, it ran to exactly 100 games, some of historical significance, some unforgettable for individual achievement, others for their level of drama and excitement. I narrowed it to 50 games, but eliminating half of them meant I left out many great contests. It pains me to say

Ron Guidry's 18-strikeout game is not here. The Yankees have won 26 World Series, yet games from only 14 would fit. (I do, however, give summaries of the "other" 50 greatest games in the back of this book.) And although the games that made the cut are presented chronologically, I have also ranked them 1–50; look in the back of the book to see if you agree.

I have tried, as much as possible, to re-create the suspense or excitement of each game. I still love the noise and the cheering, after all. I have based my research on newspaper game stories, history books, interviews with players, video- and audiotapes of the games—anything I could get my hands on to fill out the detail of what each event was like. Most of these games were played before my lifetime, but there have been nights when I staggered out of the public library, bug-eyed from staring at microfilm, when I felt as if the streets should have been full of Model-T Fords. After all, hadn't I just been reading yesterday's newspaper? For the vast majority of these games, I cannot say I was there. But I feel like I was. And I hope you will feel that way, too, as you are reading.

October 10, 1904: Boston at New York

Throwing It All Away

In which Happy Jack Chesbro pitches his team to the brink of a pennant

The Yankees have always had an expectation of greatness. That expectation today is built on a championship tradition, but turn the clock back a century and you will find the roots of Yankee greatness in the plan of one man, American League founder and president Ban Johnson.

When the American League came into being, Johnson knew that if he planned to compete successfully with the National League, he would need a premier franchise in New York. The American League easily horned in on National League territory in cities such as Boston and Chicago, but New York City was a much tougher nut to crack. Giants owner Andrew Freedman was not about to allow his team's fan base to be undercut, and using his contacts in the city government, Freedman blocked Johnson at every turn in his search for land to build a ballpark. While thwarted on the isle of Manhattan, Johnson stepped up his raids on National League talent. To stop the escalation of salaries and loss of star players, the owners in the National League sued for peace. The price for the truce was the right to place a team in New York City.

Although the owners of the team were Big Bill Devery and Frank Farrell, Ban Johnson was not going to leave the league's new prize franchise in the hands of amateurs, and he continued to pull the strings behind the scenes. Johnson's plan for New York was to create a powerhouse team, as he had done in Boston, that would demolish the National League competition and make the city into another jewel in the American League crown. Although the team itself began life as the dregs of the Baltimore Orioles, Johnson had stockpiled talent for his New York franchise, including Wee Willie Keeler (who "hit 'em where they ain't") and the "Old Fox," Clark Griffith. Griffith had jumped to the American League in 1901, and player-managed the White Sox to their first pennant; Johnson pried Griffith out of Charles Comiskey's grip with the argument that it was in the best interests of the league to send him to New York. In that one move Johnson acquired both an able manager and a hurler who could take the mound at least once a week. A stadium site was found some 13 blocks north of where the Giants played, and a grandstand was erected.

And so as Opening Day arrived in 1903 in New York, the sportswriters quickly dubbed the team the Highlanders, or Hilltoppers, thanks to the rocky perch their ballpark, Hilltop Park, occupied in northern Manhattan. (Freedman had used his numerous political connections to ensure that though he acquiesced to the American League, their home was still less than ideal.) On the mound that day was another former National League star, "Happy Jack" Chesbro, a spitballer who had been an important part of the Pirates' 1902 pennant run, in which they outpaced their nearest competitor by 27½ games. Johnson had "packed the court" with winners, and he expected great things of the new club. But in 1903, the Yankees (as headline writers and sportswriters alike would come to prefer calling them before the year was out) failed to contend.

John Dwight "Jack" Chesbro

The 1904 season was a different story, in large part because Happy Jack hit his stride.

Jack Chesbro was born in 1874 in North Adams, Massachusetts. He had pitched three undistinguished years in the minor leagues before he reeled off a 40–19 record and was snatched up by the Pirates in July 1899. In 1901 he led the National League in winning percentage at 21–10, with six shutouts. Then he discovered the spitball, and again led the league, at 28–6, with eight shutouts, in 1902. In 1903 he racked up decent numbers for the Yankees, going 21–15. But no one could have predicted the year he was about to have.

It began on April 14, 1904, Opening Day, when the Boston Americans (now known as the Red Sox) came to town as the defending champs. Their starter was no slouch, a righthander of some distinction named Cy Young. Chesbro pitched masterfully that day, though, while Young gave up five runs in the first, leading to a final score of 8–2 New York.

Chesbro beat Boston again a few weeks later, but the defending champion Bostons were otherwise manhandling league pitching, including some of the other Yankee starters. Ban Johnson wanted the balance of power evened, and arranged for several midseason trades to boost the Yankees' lineup. One of these, the acquisition of formidable slugger Patsy Dougherty from Boston in exchange for a bag of used balls (actually the trade was for Bob Unglaub, who was too sick to play), was a blatant blow to Boston's domination. By midsummer, a bona fide pennant race between the two rivals was under way.

Chesbro continued to chug along, winning 14 in a row after May 14 before facing Boston in early July. The Bostons managed to beat him twice, but hardly slowed down his record pace. Chesbro was on his way to compiling what may be the greatest single season a pitcher has had in the modern era. He pitched two or three times a week—and usually won. When all was tallied, Chesbro started 51 games, appeared in 4 others, and finished with a 41–12 record. He pitched complete games in 48 of his 51 starts, racking up a total of 454⅔ innings. Of all the great pitchers in the Hall of Fame—Christy Mathewson, Walter Johnson, Sandy Koufax—none has ever had a season like Chesbro's 1904. The only thing that kept Happy Jack from winning the Cy Young Award was that the award was not created until 1956.

The summer of 1904, the American League blossomed. Interest in the pennant race only sharpened when the Giants, firmly in first place in the National League in August, declared that they would not deign to meet the American League champion in the "world's series," preferring to "rest on their laurels." The pennant became the final prize, and fans in both Boston and New York hungered for it. The teams continued to battle, exchanging blows, separated in the standings by mere percentage points. New York traveled to Boston's Huntington Avenue Grounds in mid-September. Chesbro pitched three times in five days, beating Boston twice, but the clubs remained essentially even.

Chesbro entered the final three weeks of the season as the Yankees' best and healthiest starter. In the final 20 days of the season, he started nine games and made a relief appearance in a doubleheader (earning the win in both games). Thanks to previous rainouts, the final five games of the season were all against Boston, including two doubleheaders. Originally all five games would have been played in New York, but the October 7 games had to be moved to Boston to accommodate a previously planned Columbia University football game at Hilltop Park.

Chesbro pitched the first game in New York and beat Boston 3–2 in a hard-fought game. Afterward, fans hoisted Chesbro onto their shoulders and paraded him around the field. New York needed to win only two of the remaining four games to clinch the pennant. But then the teams boarded trains to Boston for the doubleheader the next day.

Manager Griffith's plan had been to leave Chesbro behind in New York, to rest up for the doubleheader that awaited the teams on their return to the city. But Chesbro caught up with Griffith at the train station and insisted he be given the ball. Griffith agreed. Unfortunately, Chesbro's arm began to show the wear and tear of more than 400 innings pitched, and he unraveled in the fourth inning of the game the next day. Boston took both games of the doubleheader in their home park, prompting this wordy but informative slug line in the *Boston Sunday Globe*: "With Dineen in the Box, 13 to 2—With [Cy] Young Pitching, 1 to 0—The Mighty Chesbro Driven to the Bench."

After a day off (no baseball was allowed on Sundays in New York or Boston then), hostilities resumed in Manhattan. The Yankees would have to win both games. More than thirty thousand fans arrived at Hilltop Park (which seated half that number) in anticipation of something great. And who else was on the mound in game one but John Dwight Chesbro? Happy Jack was pitching for the fourth time in eight days, and tired or not, there was no one the New York fans would have preferred to see.

He started off well, retiring the side in order in the first and striking out Freddy Parent. But though the Yankees threatened, they did not score in their half of the inning. Chesbro gave up two base hits in the second, but bore down to escape the jam without giving up a run, as he induced a comebacker off the bat of light-hitting catcher Lou Criger to end the inning.

The game underwent a curious pause in the third, when Chesbro himself came to the plate. Some North Adams rooters, from Chesbro's hometown, ran onto the field, presenting him with hugs and a seal fur coat and hat. Their lauding of their hero was supported by a standing ovation from the crowd. Thus buoyed, Chesbro, when he was finally allowed to step into the batter's box, tripled. But Bill Dineen, who had his share of wins against the Yanks, struck out both his former teammate Dougherty (on three pitches) and the notoriously hard-to-fan Willie Keeler.

The Yankees eventually put a tally on the board, and again Chesbro was in the thick of it. In the fifth inning, catcher Red Kleinow, a 25-year-old rookie in 1904, singled to right with two out. Chesbro hit a ball up the middle that Dineen reached for with his bare hand. He succeeded only in slowing the ball down, and Chesbro was safe at first on the late throw. Patsy Dougherty then singled in the game's first run. Dineen then gave Keeler an intentional pass to load the bases, perhaps figuring his previous strikeout on the diminutive contact hitter was as much as he could hope for. But the next batter was Kid Elberfeld, who worked out a walk, driving in the second run.

Chesbro protected the two-run lead jealously until the seventh, when second baseman Jimmy Williams came unglued. Williams had earned the nickname "Home Run" when he broke into the majors in 1899 with nine homers. He also led the National League and later the American League in triples. Although he had started out as a third baseman, he played most of his career at second. In 1904 he made 40 errors, which was at the time not considered awful. (Elberfeld made 48. Boston's shortstop, Freddy Parent, made 63.)

Unfortunately for Williams, three of those forty E's came in a flurry. Candy LaChance, Boston's big first baseman, hit a slow hopper that Williams booted. The next batter, Hobe Ferris, hit a hard liner between Williams's legs. Criger sacrificed the runners to second and third, which brought pitcher Bill Dineen to the plate. He grounded right to Williams, who chose to throw home to get the slow-footed LaChance. His throw was in the dirt, got past Kleinow, and two runs scored.

With the game tied at two apiece, Chesbro finally admitted he was getting tired. Griffith stuck with him anyway, sending him out for the eighth. Boston smacked three singles, but Kid Elberfeld made a terrific relay throw to cut down Chick Stahl at the plate. In the bottom of the inning, the Yankees still could not score. So it was that Chesbro took the mound with the score tied in the ninth.

Elberfeld, who had saved the game with the great relay just an inning before, got a grounder off Criger's bat but threw short. Dineen bunted Criger to second. Then another grounder to Elberfeld—Kid threw to first for the second out of the inning but was unable to hold the runner. With Criger perched on third, Chesbro needed just one more out to send it to the bottom of the ninth.

Freddy Parent stepped in. Chesbro had owned Parent that day, notching two strikeouts already. Two more strikes followed, both spitters, putting Parent in an 0–2 hole. Chesbro needed just one more dancing, dipping spitball to escape the inning. He wetted his fingers and delivered the ball. Maybe, in his tired state, desperate for one more good one, he overthrew? The pitch sailed high and wide of Kleinow, far out of his reach and to the backstop. Criger easily scored, and the Yankees had been stabbed through the heart. Manager Griffith fell to his knees while Chesbro turned away from the plate, unable to look. Parent was eventually retired, on a force-out at second, but with the score 3–2, the Yankees had only three outs left to make a miracle.

They almost did. Chesbro collapsed in tears on the bench, but the Yankee batters went to work on Dineen. John Ganzel struck out, but Dineen walked the next man, "Wid" Conroy. Kleinow popped up. With one out to go, Chesbro was due to bat, but Griffith knew the exhausted pitcher was in no shape to go up there. He sent Deacon McGuire in, and he worked a walk. With the tying run at second and the go-ahead run on first, the batter was once again the former Boston Patsy Dougherty. The big slugger now waved his bat for New York. He took a strike. Then a ball. Then he swung at a pitch and missed, and looked at another ball. Ernest Lawrence Thayer's classic poem "Casey at the Bat" had appeared in 1888, and must have been on the minds of many New York spectators in the stands that day as they watched their last hope flare, and then die, as Dougherty struck out. The pennant belonged to Boston.

It was the original heartbreaker for the Yankees, who would not contend again until another slugger from Boston came to change their fortune in 1920: Babe Ruth. Chesbro's great season landed him in the Hall of Fame, but he regretted the pitch for the remainder of his days.

◄ Extra Innings

- Chesbro's widow fought unsuccessfully for years after his death to have the scoring of "the pitch" changed from a wild pitch to a passed ball.

- More than two hundred of Boston's "Royal Rooters," accompanied by a brass band, took the train to New York to support their team. They paraded uptown to the ballpark, creating quite a spectacle, and kept up a continuous racket during the games, including repeated renditions of their good-luck song, "Tessie."

- In 1908 another spitballer, Ed Walsh, had a similar (some would say better) season than Chesbro's 1904. He went 40–15, pitching 464 innings with a 1.42 ERA (good for third that season, as forty-one-year-old Cy Young came in at 1.26 and Addie Joss at 1.16). The White Sox also fell just short of a pennant, but not in quite as heartbreaking a fashion.

- **How the Yankees Became the Yankees**
  In the early days of baseball (the late 1800s to early 1900s), teams were officially known only by their city and league name. As such, the team we now know as the Yankees were the "New York Americans," their rivals, the "Boston Americans." The Giants were the "New York Nationals." In newspaper stories, writers often shortened these appellations to just the "New Yorks" or the "Bostons." But the need for entertaining writing and catchy headlines spurred many newspapermen to coin nicknames for the teams. Nicknames could come from any source, including mascots, the manager or team owner's name, local traditions, news references, or political puns. In a given game recap, a single writer might toss off several nicknames.

  One of the Yankees' initial nicknames, "Highlanders," was both a reference to their ballpark, Hilltop Park, which was built on a rocky plateau, and to the heritage of team owner Frank Farrell. Sometimes they were dubbed the "Griff-men" in honor of manager Clark Griffith. But of all their early nicknames, "Yankees" was the one that stuck.

  Although no definitive resource identifies the origin of "Yankees" as a nickname, the nickname makes perfect sense in the context of the times. "Yankee" as a term has evolved in American slang to mean "the folks to the North." In South America, anyone from the United States or Canada is a

"Yankee." Within the United States, to southerners, anyone from north of the Mason-Dixon line is a "Yankee." And within the North, it is the denizens of New England, the northernmost of all, who are the Yankees.

In all likelihood, the application of the term "Yankees" to the American League team in New York was a tongue-in-cheek reference to the fact that Hilltop Park was just north of the Polo Grounds, home of the Giants. Since the Giants were the center of the baseball universe in New York at the time, it made sense to refer to the newcomers as northerly. They also might have been punning on the fact that if you can take "Yankees" to mean "Americans," then that was a snappier way to refer to the "American League club" as well. It also could have been a subtle reference to the fact that the franchise was moved to New York from Baltimore, and hence the former southerners were now "Yankees." The headline writers especially favored anything shorter than "Highlanders," and their repeated use of the name "Yankees" ensured that it stuck. The team officially adopted the name in 1913, and would later build up the association of "Yankees" with "Americans" with the creation of the team's red, white, and blue "Uncle Sam" top hat logo.

◆**2**

July 25, 1912: Chicago at New York

A Yankee First

In which Bert Daniels and the Highlanders enter the record books

One of the first Yankees to enter the record books played not only before the Yankees were good, but also before they were officially the Yankees. By 1912, the newspapers had long been using the "Yankee" nickname, but the name wouldn't be adopted officially by the club until the following year, when they would move to the Polo Grounds. Although the "Highlanders" played on the elevated plateau known to fans as Hilltop Park, they were cellar-dwellers in the American League standings.

The great stars of the game were the likes of Ty Cobb, who batted .409 for the Detroit Tigers in 1912, and "Shoeless" Joe Jackson, then with Cleveland, not far behind at .395. The two great hitters each knocked 226 hits. Tris Speaker in Boston swatted 222. Eddie Collins and Frank "Home Run" Baker led the offensive assault for the Philadelphia Athletics, Baker belting a league-leading 10 home runs. (You can see why it was called the "Deadball Era.")

That year Bert Daniels was in his third season in the majors with New York.

He was a bit of an athletic nomad, having played for three different colleges (Bucknell, Villanova, and Notre Dame) and for various semipro and minor league teams (under assumed names to keep from voiding his college status) before joining the Highlanders. A speedy outfielder, Daniels joined the great stars of the day for his stolen base prowess. He swiped 37 bases in 1912, good for eighth on the list.

Bert also got himself into the record books by leading the league in being hit by pitch in 1910, 1912, and 1913. In fact, he set a new record in 1913 by getting hit with three pitches in one day, during a doubleheader in Washington. (Senators pitching hit six men that day, three in the first inning!)

But on July 25, 1912, Daniels did something that no hitter expects to do. Babe Ruth never did it, Ty Cobb never did either. Daniels hit for the cycle, hitting a single, double, triple, and home run in a single game. Averaged over the past hundred years of baseball, the cycle is a rare occurrence, about as rare as the no-hitter. In Daniels's day, the home run alone was relatively rare. In five big league seasons, Daniels himself hit only five round-trippers total.

How emblematic of the early Highlanders' struggles that on the day when Daniels had his four history-making hits, the team lost 6–4 to the White Sox. Ban Johnson's upstart American League scored a coup when they placed a team in New York City, but the team itself was in a struggle for legitimacy. In 1912 they drew the second-lowest attendance in the league and committed the most errors. Hilltop Park was a rickety wooden structure with rocky depressions in the outfield. Since the near-miss of 1904, the Yankees were gaining a reputation as a second-rate team, never quite able to make the jump into the top tier.

Daniels scored the first run of the game in the top of the first, singling, stealing second, moving to third on a hit by Hal Chase, and scoring on a sac fly off the bat of Dutch Sterrett. He tripled in the third, was stranded and the score remained 1–0. But New York starter Ray Caldwell, after cruising through three innings, surrendered a triple to Shano Collins in the fourth, who tied the score at one, scoring on a Ping Bodie sacrifice.

Daniels came through the next inning. With two out, Sweeney walked, Caldwell reached on an infield hit, and Daniels came to the plate. Chicago starter Joe Benz got two strikes on the left fielder, but then Daniels connected to send the ball over the fence in right center.

Caldwell took that three-run lead and handed it right back. The Yankee hurler came apart, giving up four hits, hitting a batter, and failing to field a bunt. "They resolved him into his component parts," was how the *New York Tribune* described Caldwell's collapse. Manager Harry Wolverton replaced him with Jack Warhop, who held the White Sox at four runs right through nine innings. Daniels doubled in the eighth but was stranded. With the score tied, the game moved on to the tenth.

Warhop went out for the tenth, and the Sox jumped on him for four hits and two runs. The Highlanders had a chance to win, though, when Chicago manager Jimmy Callahan argued an umpire's call so vociferously he was ejected. When he took too long to vacate the premises, field umpire Jack Sheridan almost awarded the game to the home team.

Instead, they had to try to earn the victory in the bottom of the inning. Ed Sweeney singled and Wolverton put himself in to pinch-hit. Although the player-manager singled, he also injured himself running to first. After replacing himself with a pinch runner, Wolverton was so vocal from the coaches' box that he, too, was ejected. The Sox finally lifted Benz and replaced him on the mound with Ed Walsh, a consummate control pitcher. Perhaps Walsh was nervous to face Bert, having seen Daniels smack four hits already. He walked him to load the bases. Unfortunately, Hal Chase then hit a high fly to right and Ping Bodie nailed Sweeney tagging up and trying to come home. Sterrett struck out to end the game. In 1912 the Highlanders finished dead last in the standings, winning only 50 of 152 games.

Extra Innings

- Accomplishing the feat of hitting a single, double, triple, and home run in the same game was not called "hitting for the cycle" until the 1930s.
- Of all the players who have hit for the cycle, Bert Daniels hit the fewest career home runs (only five).
- In 1912, Daniels led the Yankees in runs scored (68), doubles (25), and tied for the team lead in triples (11).
- Ping Bodie, who later played for the Yankees (1918–1921), reportedly said, when asked what it was like to room with Babe Ruth, "I don't know. I room with his suitcase."

April 24, 1917: New York at Boston

Like Barn Doors

In which George Mogridge hurls the first Yankee no-hitter

In 1917 the Boston Red Sox were the reigning world champions, while the Yankees were still trying to find the winning formula. Lefty pitcher Babe Ruth went 24–13 with a 2.01 ERA for the Bostons, while Carl Mays was 22–9, 1.74. In this early season contest at Fenway Park, 28-year-old George Mogridge for the Yankees was matched against fellow lefty Dutch Leonard. Leonard had pitched a no-hitter against the St. Louis Browns the previous year, but Mogridge was no slouch himself. "[Mogridge] is always good when he is pitted against the Red Sox," opined the *Boston Daily Globe.*

Five years earlier, the White Sox had given up on Mogridge after he had posted a 3–4 record in eight starts, and the southpaw went to the Minneapolis Millers of the minor league American Association. In 1913 he posted a 13–10 record for the Millers, pitching 202 innings in 36 games. By 1915 he was with the Yankees, where he established his reputation for being stingy with bases on balls and runs allowed. In 1916 he posted a 2.31 ERA, and in 1917 he looked to match his earlier success.

Only 3,219 fans showed up at Fenway Park that day, but the few who turned out were treated to a pitchers' duel. Leonard held the Yankees scoreless for five innings, and Mogridge matched him pitch for pitch, mixing speeds effectively and using a curve that "had the . . . Red Sox swinging like barn doors in a gale" (*New York Tribune*). Even though the Sox got only four balls out of the infield all day, they still must have anticipated a victory, especially when the Yankees' fielding proved to be less than stellar. Errors by both shortstop Roger Peckinpaugh and second baseman Fritz Maisel let runners on in the early innings, but both were stranded. The Yankees made up for Peck's bobble by foiling a double-steal attempt in the second inning that kept the Sox scoreless.

In the sixth, Leonard finally showed a crack in his armor. Angel Aragon was one of the first Cuban-born players to play in the major leagues. Strictly a bench player who batted .067 that year, he was at third base for the Yanks that day because Frank "Home Run" Baker was feeling under the weather. Aragon doubled to lead off the inning, one of only three hits he would get all season. Lee Magee, another scrub, singled him in immediately, but was cut down at the plate after a hit by Peckinpaugh.

Meanwhile, Mogridge cruised. "So seldom was Mogridge distressed that there was no occasion for any exceptional play on the part of those supporting him," reported the *New York Tribune.* After the errors, "[Wally Pipp] was a perfectly lonesome first baseman. He had nobody to talk to but the Red Sox coacher [*sic*] and the base umpire. The world champions were either tapping weakly to the infield and outfield or dribbling easy chances down the infield lanes."

In the seventh Mogridge issued his second walk of the day to Jack Barry, the

Sox player-manager, to lead off the inning. Del Gainer followed with a rip that looked like a double-play ball. But Maisel's throw pegged Peckinpaugh in the glove a bit too sharply, and the ball dropped, leaving both runners safe on the error. Duffy Lewis sacrificed the runners over, recording one out. Mogridge then intentionally walked slugger Tilly Walker to set up the force play at any base or the double play. Jimmy Walsh came in to pinch-hit for "the ancient and honorable Larry Gardner" (*New York Tribune*) and managed a sacrifice fly that brought in one run. The score was tied at one, but still no Sox hits were recorded. Mogridge bore down, escaping the inning without further trouble and keeping the score tied. In the eighth he turned the Sox back again, still tied at one run apiece.

The Yankees seized their chance at victory in the ninth when Peck smacked a ball at third baseman Mike McNally, who stopped it but couldn't get it out of his glove in time. Peck stole second, moved to third when the throw from Hick Cady scooted into center, then came home with the go-ahead run on an easy ground out from Les Nunamaker.

With the score then 2–1 in his favor, Mogridge closed the door on the world champions for the complete-game no-hitter.

◢ Extra Innings

- George Mogridge went on to win a World Series with the Washington Senators, the only year the franchise did (1924). The Yankees gave up on him in 1920, and in 1924 he won 16 games for the Senators, who edged the Yankees for the pennant by two games. He won game four of the Series, and then pitched 4⅔ innings of excellent relief in the deciding game seven.

- There have been two pitchers named Dutch Leonard. Hubert Benjamin Leonard, born in 1892 in Birmingham, Ohio, pitched for the Red Sox and Tigers in an 11-year career. The lefthander posted a career 2.76 ERA and racked up 1,160 strikeouts. In 1933 another "Dutch," Emil Leonard, no relation to Hubert, came along. This Dutch was a right-handed knuckleballer with the Dodgers, Senators, Phillies, and Cubs who was one of the first pitchers to truly rely on the knuckler.

- George Mogridge was born and raised in Rochester, New York. Upon retiring from Major League Baseball, the hometown hero went on to manage the minor league Rochester Red Wings.

- Some other pitchers who gave up a run while pitching a no-hitter:

  Earl Hamilton, August 30, 1912
  Browns 5, Detroit 1

Joe Benz, May 31, 1914
   White Sox 6, Cleveland 1
Bob Feller, July 1, 1951
   Indians 2, Tigers 1
Don Nottebart, May 17, 1963
   Houston 4, Phillies 1
Joe Cowley, September 19, 1986
   White Sox 7, Angels 1
Darryl Kile, September 8, 1993
   Astros 7, Mets 1

July 6, 1920: New York at Washington

Bombers Away

In which the Yankees set a new record by tallying 14 runs in a single inning

Independence Day is an excellent time to visit the nation's capital, as the city brims over with patriotic celebrations, fireworks, and festivities. Perhaps the holiday left the Washington "Nationals" (also nicknamed the "Griffs," for owner Clark Griffith, and the "Senators," for their D.C. location) with a bit of a hangover. The Yankees came into town for a four-game series over the holiday weekend, and the Senators had jubilantly taken the first three games, knocking the Yankees back into second place behind Cleveland. But the finale turned out to be no party for the home team.

The game got under way with Carl Mays on the hill for the Yankees. Mays was one of a slew of star players the Yankees had acquired from the Red Sox, including, of course, Babe Ruth. Mays's name has mostly been remembered by history not as a world champion, but as the unfortunate pitcher who delivered the fatal pitch to Ray Chapman of the Indians on August 16 later in the year. Mays had a wicked underhand motion that allowed him to sling the ball with great force upward at the batter, a deceptive motion that made the ball's flight difficult for the batter to pick up. In Chapman's case, the muddy ball, poor light, and tricky motion conspired against him fatally. The pitch caught him in the head, and he later died at the hospital.

But on that July day Mays's underhand was merely dangerous to the Griffs' egos, not their health. He was opposed by Olaf Erickson, who was the early victim of some sloppy play. The Yanks played small ball and scored in the second on a Bob Meusel single, Ping Bodie sacrifice, and Del Pratt hit to center. But in the third they should have been held scoreless. Ruth came up with Sammy Vick on second and grounded easily to second baseman Bucky Harris, who booted the ball. Meusel then singled Vick home to put the Yanks up by two.

The lead would soon balloon. On that afternoon the home team was "not bad outside of the fifth," the *Washington Post* reported with some irony, because what a fifth it was.

Erickson gave up three hits and a walk, while his team made three errors behind him before he was sent to the showers. Bill Snyder followed and pitched to five batters, all of whom reached base. "He struck the bats of two of them, stuck the ball in the ribs of another, and passed the other pair. Also he turned in a wild pitch, but he missed a balk. How he overlooked that is a mystery," wrote J. V. Fitz Gerald miserably in the *Post*. A rookie "fork hander" (lefty) named Harry Courtney then followed, giving up another two hits,

George Herman "Babe" Ruth

including a home run to Pratt, which capped the slapstick comedy of the inning by getting past outfielder Braggo Roth and rolling through a hole in the wall, allowing all three runs to score. When the dust cleared, the Yankees had scored fourteen runs, a new American League record for total runs in an inning. Never before had so many runs been scored on so few hits—seven. Only one of the runs was earned, and every Yankee batted twice.

Amazingly, Ruth did not homer as part of the onslaught, which left other clubs wondering what kind of powerhouse the Yankees had built for themselves in the era of the rabbit ball. "Those cork centers were certainly playing tricks on the Griffs all afternoon," Fitz Gerald wrote. With the 17–0 win, the Yankees regained first place in the standings. In the eighth, Courtney fanned Ruth, but there was not much else for Washington fans to cheer about, as the proud Griffs were held scoreless. They were the last team in the league that year to be shut out, but "when it arrived the shut out was the most decisive of the year" (*New York Times*).

The headline on the box score in the *Post* read simply: PLAIN MURDER.

How the 14 runs scored:

Vick reached on Ellerbe's throwing error.

Pipp doubled Vick to third.

Ruth intentionally walked to load the bases.

Meusel's sac fly scored Vick. [1]

Bodie singled to left, scoring Pipp. [2]

Ruth then scored on a bad throw from Milan, and Bodie moved to third. [3]

Pratt flied to Roth, who dropped the ball, and Bodie scored. [4]

Ruel doubled, sending Pratt to third.

Snyder relieved Erickson.

Mays singled, scoring both Pratt and Ruel. [5, 6]

Fewster then was hit by pitch.

A wild pitch followed, allowing the runners to move up.

Then Vick and Pipp both walked, the latter forcing in Mays. [7]

Ruth singled, scoring Fewster and Vick. [8, 9]

Meusel singled Pipp home. [10]

Harris let Bodie reach on another error, and Ruth scored. [11]

Pratt homered by hitting a ball under the fence, scoring three. [12, 13, 14]

Picinich retired Ruel on slow roller at the plate.

Rice then erred, dropping a fly ball from Mays.

Fewster struck out to end the inning.

◄Extra Innings

- After Ray Chapman's death, a rule was instituted that dirty baseballs had to be replaced by clean ones throughout the course of the game. Today an average of 60 baseballs will be used during a big league game.

- The Yankees' offense, which included Pratt, Bodie, Fewster, and Pipp before Ruth arrived, was referred to as "Murderers' Row" as early as 1918 and the nickname was cemented by a 1919 cartoon by Robert Ripley.

October 5, 1921: New York at New York

In the Company of Giants

In which the Yankees play their first World Series game

Baseball is a game of adages and folk wisdom, a game that both delights us with the way any ordinary game can turn extraordinary and pleases us when it falls into familiar and expected patterns. Here is an adage one cannot help but apply when looking at the 1921 World Series: the more things change, the more they stay the same. New York City in the grip of World Series fever then looked much the same as it has in many Octobers since.

The Babe Ruth Yankees entered their first World Series facing their hometown rivals, John McGraw and the Giants, who also happened to be their landlords. The Yankees had given up playing in rocky, swampy Hilltop Park in 1912 and arranged to share the Polo Grounds instead. So it was that every game in the '21 Series was a "home" game for both teams, as well as a be-seen event for New York City's upper crust and celebrities. Then as today, politicians, business leaders, and "sportsmen" occupied many of the best boxes—"reserved" seating was sold out well in advance of the game. Both the commissioner of baseball, Judge Kenesaw Mountain Landis, and Mayor James J. Hylan of New York City entertained visitors in their boxes prior to the game. Mayor Hylan threw out the first pitch but declined to reveal his rooting interest.

And then as today, the common fan resorted to extreme measures to ensure a seat. "Mr. and Mrs. Fan in Line All Night," read a *New York Times* headline.

"Women Join Cheerful Crowds That Argue, Eat, and Sleep in the Rain and Chill." Despite the ardent attitude of these baseball lovers, only 30,203 actually paid to see the game, as overeager press reports led thousands more to believe that unreserved tickets would be too difficult to get on the day of the game. Some 4,000 seats sat empty in the upper grandstand, while more than 13,000 fans turned up in Times Square to watch the mechanical reproduction of the game on a giant board operated from a balcony. Ten thousand more watched a similar mechanical re-creation at Madison Square Garden. Although the upper-crust crowd at the Polo Grounds was reported to be sedate, applauding for both teams, the masses on the Times Square streets were partisan. "Judged by the earsplitting outbursts which greeted every favorable chronicle of Yankee doings, [the crowd] was solidly back of the Huggins warriors' first World Series effort," the *Times* reported.

The opening game of the Series was the first time the Yankees had risen to such a height, while McGraw's Giants were perennial favorites to make it to October. Manager Miller Huggins, the "mighty mite," elected to pitch submariner Carl Mays in the opener. "The ball he served upward from the height of his ankle seemed no bigger than a fleck of shimmering sunlight on a gnat's wing," the *Times* lyrically reported. McGraw went with Phil Douglas, whom the same paper described as a "big spitball twirler who employs not only his arms and head, but also his salivary glands." Disparate though the hurlers' styles were, they were evenly matched, each giving up only five hits. Four of the five knocks on Mays were off the bat of Frankie Frisch, third baseman for the Giants. This meant a great line in the box score for Frisch, but his hits were harmlessly scattered over Mays's outing.

Babe Ruth, meanwhile, provided the difference. In the first inning, Elmer Miller singled, then Peckinpaugh sacrificed him to second to put him in scoring position for the big slugger. A hush of anticipation fell over the crowd, which quickly turned to a roar as Ruth, "home run king of the world," strode to the plate. Ruth swung at the first pitch from Douglas and lashed it into center field, scoring Miller. That one run would prove to be the difference in the game, as Mays continued to set down the Giants.

The Yankees got an insurance run in the fifth when Mike McNally hit a double down the third-base line. Wally Schang sacrificed him to third. Mays then came to the plate and looked at three strikes in a row for the second out. Miller was at the plate when Douglas wound up and threw a high fastball that Giants catcher Frank Snyder had to come up to snag. McNally had broken for the plate on the pitch and slid in just under Snyder's tag. Thus McNally was the first player to steal home in a World Series since Ty Cobb on October 9, 1909. "At this stage of the game supporters of the Yankees . . . settled more comfortably in their seats and learned that their chairs had backs," the *Times* wrote. The Yankees got yet a third run in the sixth, on a Peckinpaugh hit followed by a long drive from Bob Meusel, who would have had a triple except that he missed first base and had to double back to touch up. The Yankees had nailed down their first World Series victory ever.

Of course, the Giants eventually went on to win the best-of-nine series in eight games, despite Ruth's .313 batting average. (McGraw instructed his pitchers to throw Ruth nothing but curves; the Babe mustered only one extra-base hit in the Series.) But the seeds of Yankee greatness and the love affair of the city for the team in pinstripes had begun to grow. A few years later they would be in full flower, and a few decades after that, the Giants would abandon the city for San Francisco, following the Dodgers into the American frontier. A new status quo had been established.

Extra Innings

- The scoreboard in centerfield read "N. York" versus "N. York"—the only distinguishing factor being the Giants' sign was white, the Yankees' yellow.

- After six games the Series stood tied at three games each. "Scalpers' Holiday" read one *Times* headline. "Prices Soar to $10." "Pasteboards for the world's series, which were available yesterday for the sixth game at the new low level of [only] 50 cents or a dollar above their face value, yesterday skyrocketed like one of Babe Ruth's foul flies." The average face value per ticket was three dollars.

- New York State Supreme Court justice George V. Mullan reported the score to his courtroom after the third inning, during a break in the legal proceedings. While the lawyers were conferring among themselves, His Honor enjoyed the view out an open window and overheard a newspaperman making an announcement of the score with a "sound amplifying device." He immediately passed a note with the score to the witness on the stand—apparently a Yankees fan, given his happy reaction. "In order that you may know what the court has handed to the witness," the judge then announced the score to the room at large.

- Two brothers played in the Series, one for each team, as Irish Meusel patrolled left field for the Giants, and Bob Meusel right field for the Yankees.

6

September 4, 1923: New York at Philadelphia

Philadelphia Un-Athletic

In which "Sad Sam" Jones shines

Sam Jones was a nine-year veteran of the major leagues when he made his way into the record books for good. He had a distinguished career in Boston, where he had racked up a 16–5 record in 1918, leading the league in win percentage and the Red Sox to a world championship. In 1921, though the Sox finished fifth, he won 23 games and pitched five shutouts, making him an easy target for the cash-rich Yankees, who acquired him that December along with short-stop Everett Scott and pitcher "Bullet" Joe Bush in exchange for three players and $50,000. Jones would be the Yankees' Opening Day starter the following spring. Although the Yankees won the American League pennant for the second straight year in 1922, they didn't win even one game in their rematch with the Giants in the World Series. In 1923 they would fare better, with a sizable lead in the standings over Detroit and Cleveland as the season drew to a close.

In early September of that year, the Yankees traveled to Philadelphia for a four-game series. The heat of August had carried over, and the weather was "hot as blazes and sultry" (*New York Tribune*).

It did not at first appear that Jones was going to shine that day when he walked the second batter of the game, Chick Galloway, in the first inning. The Athletics were putting the ball in play, but "the Yankees gave their pitcher wonderful support," reported the *New York Times*, "and many stops and throws were made that were of a spectacular nature." Buoyed by the defense, Jones settled into a zone where his control was good and "his arm was lashing free and rhythmic," in the words of *Tribune* reporter W. B. Hanna. He had the "usual accoutrement of no-hit pitching, change-of-pace, a clipping curve . . . and the snappiest sort of fastball."

The Yankees, for their part, put up a crooked number in the third inning. Fred Hofmann led off the inning with a walk and advanced to third on a scratch hit by Scott. Jones himself put the bat on the ball but did not get it out of the infield. His grounder moved Scott to second. Both men scored on the next hit from Whitey Witt, to make the score 2–0. Not a commanding lead, but one that held up fine when you consider that no other Athletic reached base until there was one out in the eighth, when shortstop Scott got a grounder off the bat of Frank Welch in his glove but fumbled it. Welch was safe on the error. Jimmy Dykes then reached on a fielder's choice as Welch was forced at second. The threat was rendered harmless when Cy Perkins flew out to end the inning.

"Round about the fourth or fifth inning you begin to realize nobody's got a hit yet," Jones later told Larry Ritter, "and then you start to get a little tense." As the game progressed and the Philadelphia crowd also realized they could be witnesses to history, the fans began rooting for Jones, cheering every out.

In the ninth, Galloway came to the plate with two outs and heard his own fans imploring him to strike out. Jones, in fact, had not struck out a batter all day. "I'm going to break it up if I can," Jones said Galloway called out to him before dropping a bunt down the third-base line. Joe Dugan nipped him with a good throw to end the game. Jones's was the second no-hitter in Yankees history and the first in the major leagues in 1923.

Extra Innings

- Tom Hughes almost became the first Yankee to pitch a no-hitter, on August 30, 1910, pitching nine hitless innings. But in extra innings the Cleveland Indians touched him for seven hits and five runs and won 5–0.

- Sam Jones would end the season with a 21–8 record and also come into the sixth and final game of the World Series in relief, nailing down the Yankees' first world championship.

- "Sad" Sam got his nickname from wearing his hat low over his eyes, which made him look downcast to Bill McGeehan, a writer for the *New York Herald Tribune*. As Sam explained it, "The sportswriters were more used to fellows like Waite Hoyt, who'd always wear their caps way up so they wouldn't miss seeing any pretty girls."

October 10, 1926: St. Louis at New York

Crime Doesn't Pay

In which Babe Ruth puts an odd finale on the Series

In 1926 the Yankees entered the World Series as an emergent superpower in Major League Baseball. They had brought home the pennant in 1921 and

1922, and the world championship in 1923, and in 1924 were edged into second place, winning 89 games. In 1925 both the club and Babe Ruth had bad years, Ruth's season beginning with the "bellyache heard 'round the world" on the train trip back from spring training (modern reports conclude he was suffering from syphilis). Ruth played in only 98 games, and the Yankees finished seventh. But the nucleus of the championship clubs was still there, and despite expectations to the contrary by columnists and "experts," in 1926 the Babe rebounded to lead the league in almost every offensive category, including 146 RBI and 144 walks. The Yankee powerhouse was rolling once again.

The Yankees' opposite number from the National League, the St. Louis Cardinals, is currently the National League franchise that has won the most World Series titles (nine). But back in 1926, the Cardinals were first-timers in the Series. The two teams were so closely matched in ability that bookies and oddsmakers had them at almost even odds, and an epic Series was predicted. Wilbert Robinson, manager of the Brooklyn Robins, wrote in the *New York Times* that he expected both clubs to drive in a lot of runs. "Their power at the bat is too great to risk losing scoring chances . . . on steals and taking the extra base."

For once, predictions were correct as the two teams played an action-packed Series, trading blows, homers, and wins. Public sentiment swelled in favor of Rogers Hornsby, the player-manager of the Redbirds, whose mother's last instructions—from her deathbed in Austin, Texas—were to stay with the team and win the championship. The fact that this World Series was broadcast "instantaneously" on the radio to listeners on loudspeakers across the country was front-page news.

The curtain went up in Yankee Stadium on a cloudy Saturday afternoon as Colonel Jacob Ruppert, the Yankee owner, and his canny staff shoehorned well over the announced 61,658 in attendance into the big ballpark in the Bronx. Though the spotlight was on Ruth, it was Lou Gehrig who drove in both runs in the 2–1 victory. The next day the announced record-breaking crowd swelled to 63,600 as Grover Cleveland Alexander held the Yankees to four hits. The Cardinals won 6–2, thanks to a tie-breaking homer in the seventh off the bat of former Giant Billy Southworth.

The Series then shifted to Sportsman's Park in St. Louis, with the teams, along with hordes of fans, traveling all day and all night by train to "the West." The modern fan may have difficulty appreciating the fact that in 1926 (and for decades afterward) St. Louis was the major-league franchise that was the farthest west and the farthest south. The Cardinals were greeted by fireworks, confetti, and 100,000 fans. Businesses throughout St. Louis closed for the day, and the hometown heroes were treated to a parade. The sedan carrying Hornsby came last and was met with the most thunderous applause and cheers.

The Cardinal crowds buoyed their boys to a win in the third game, 4–0, as "Jess" Haines blew blazing fastballs by the Yankee batters and also hit his first Series homer. But the Yankees brought the Series even in game four, as Ruth's bat led them to a 10–5 victory. "Contrary to reports, the king is not dead," wrote James B. Harrison in the *Times*. "Long live the king, for he hit three home runs and broke six series records [today]. . . . When [the Yankees] were going down for the third and . . . last time, Ruth tossed them the rope of three homers. He took personal charge of the world's series [*sic*], and made the game his greatest single triumph."

The Yankees also took the fifth game, in extra innings, winning 3–2 in ten, after Gehrig tied the game in the ninth. Mark Koenig, who had led the league in errors that year (52), was the game's hero, as his defense this time kept the Yanks in the game, and he sparked the rally in the tenth with a single and scored the winning run. Thus it was that the Series shifted back to Yankee Stadium, with the Yankees needing only one more win to take the championship.

Cold weather kept some fans away from the ballpark for game six, but it was the pitching of Grover Cleveland Alexander that chilled the Yankees' bats. The wily veteran held the Hugmen to two runs while the Cardinals' bats exploded for 10 runs to even the series at three-all and set the stage for the deciding game seven.

Robinson summarized the game in the *Times* thus: "To baseball history can be added one more chapter where the seventh game of the big series was decided not by skill or courage, but by fate."

Waite Hoyt took the hill for the Yankees, facing Haines, who had held the Yanks scoreless once already in the Series. Hoyt looked sharp throughout the game, and when Ruth muscled a home run in the third off of Haines's "slow ball," it looked like Hoyt might be able to make the slim lead stand. Hoyt had once before pitched a near-shutout in a World Series; in 1921, errors in the field led to a 1–0 loss. And 1926 must have seemed like déjà vu all over again. Hoyt himself made the first put out of the fourth inning, fielding an easy grounder in front of the mound. Jim Bottomley singled, but the next ball, off the bat of Les Bell, looked to be a tailor-made double-play ball to Koenig.

The young shortstop muffed it, putting men on first and second. With two strikes on Chick Hafey, Hoyt induced a pop fly, but it fell in no-man's-land between Koenig and Bob Meusel, loading the bases. Koenig's error was then compounded by another fly ball, a can of corn to the veteran Meusel, who waved off Earle Combs, thinking he had the stronger arm and might have a play on Bottomley, who would tag up and go for home. That thinking may have cost the Yankees the Series, as Meusel tried to throw before making the catch and dropped the ball. Bottomley scored easily, and the game was tied. The next batter, light-hitting shortstop Tommy Thevenow, capped the inning with a two-run single, giving the Cardinals a sudden 3–1 lead.

The Yankees were not out of it yet, though. In the sixth they scratched another run off Haines, to make it a one-run game. Ruth, Gehrig, any number of sluggers could have tied it with one swing of the bat. In the seventh, the Yankees rose once again. Combs started them off with a single over Thevenow's head. Koenig sacrificed him to second, and Ruth was walked intentionally with first base open. Up came Meusel, with a chance to redeem himself for the dropped fly. But he bounced into a force-out, putting men on the corners with two out.

Haines had been in hot water the whole game, troubled by a bleeding blister that formed when he threw the knuckleball, and he seemed to weaken further after taking a hit off his hand. During Gehrig's at-bat he seemed to lose his mechanics completely. Though he started Columbia Lou off with two strikes, after that he could not come close to the plate, which brought Hornsby out from the Cardinals' dugout. With the bases loaded and only a one-run lead, Hornsby was not about to let a wild pitch or another walk jeopardize the game. Control was called for. Tony Lazzeri, one of the great San Francisco Bay Italians to play for the Yankees and then in his rookie year, stepped into the batter's box, but it would not be Haines he would face. Hornsby gave the ball to the man who had proved to be the Yankees' nemesis, Grover Cleveland Alexander.

Alexander remains one of the most baffling characters in baseball history, both to biographers and to batters. An alcoholic and epileptic, Alexander was partially deafened by combat action in World War I and even had suffered from double vision in the minor leagues as a result of catching a double-play throw in the head while on the basepaths, though this condition seemed to clear in time. He shambled when he walked, and his uniform never seemed to fit him. And yet he won 190 games between 1911 and 1917 with the Phillies (nearly a third of all the team's wins) and dominated the league. By the time of his appearance in this World Series he was 39 years old. He had landed with the Cardinals that season after Joe McCarthy shipped him from the Chicago Cubs for the waiver price of $6,000.

But he could still pitch. He had a live fastball that, with his three-quarters overhand motion, seemed to explode out of the light-colored chest of his uniform. Always a control pitcher, he walked few, and struck out many who tried to sit on a pitch over the plate.

Lazzeri had come to the Yankees after tearing up the Pacific Coast League in 1925. Playing in the thin air of Salt Lake City, Lazzeri established himself as a power-hitting second baseman, setting then-records for home runs (60), RBI (222), and runs scored (202). In his rookie season in New York he was a sensation, playing in 155 games and earning the name "Poosh 'Em Up" Tony by legions of Italian American fans. And here he stood, twenty-two years old, facing the veteran of a world war and the National League, with a chance to turn the tide of the game and the Series. Three Yankees filled the bases—even a small poke, a bloop into the outfield, could put the Yankees ahead. Would Alexander be tired from having pitched nine innings in the previous game? Or from celebrating his victory?

If he was, the final result did not show it. Lazzeri tagged one pitch deep but foul, and "Alexander the Great" did not let him get ahold of another. He struck out Lazzeri and snuffed the threat.

Alexander's poise and control, and the Yankees' helplessness against him, remained the same as it had been the day before. He sat them down one-two-three in the eighth, and induced two easy grounders to start the ninth. He then faced Ruth. Alex was not going to give Ruth a chance to tie the score with a mighty clout. He pitched carefully to the big slugger, taking the count full, and then missing. Ruth trotted down to first base, the winning run at the plate in the person of Bob Meusel, his last chance for redemption.

Unfortunately, Meusel never got to swing the bat. Ruth broke for second but could not beat the throw from Bob O'Farrell, which Hornsby received to tag the big man out. Thus the Series ended, with Ruth on the ground and Alexander triumphant on the hill. "To Ruth as well as to Hoyt should go the heartfelt condolences of Yankee rooters," wrote Harrison in the *Times*. If not for the errors in the field, Ruth's homer would have been the defining moment of the Series. Instead, the Yankees found themselves dividing up the losers' share in the Series while Rogers Hornsby went home to Texas having fulfilled his mother's deathbed wish.

Extra Innings

- The Yankees set a new record during the Series—this one for the fastest trip ever taken by train from New York to St. Louis. The "Yankees' Special" took only 23 hours, 25 minutes to arrive, and beat the Cardinals' train by 10 minutes into the station. "Well, we are ahead of the Cardinals now anyway," Ruth told reporters.

- The part of Grover Cleveland Alexander in the movie *The Winning Team* was played by a young actor whose name would later become presidential as well: Ronald Reagan.

---

⑧

July 26, 1928: Game One, New York at Detroit

Thrice He Routed All His Foes

In which Bob Meusel sets a new American League record

There is an old saw in baseball that a team is only as good as its starting pitching. Like many baseball aphorisms, the phrase stands in for the fact that there is no way to explain how a team can get blown out one day, and then win a blowout the next. On July 26, 1928, the Yankees faced the Tigers in Detroit for a doubleheader and didn't even have to wait until the next day to experience both extremes.

The day didn't begin as a blowout—in fact, it began as a pitchers' duel of epic proportions. On the hill the Yankees' Waite Hoyt faced Vic Sorrell, and both pitchers were still on the mound through 11 innings. Hoyt was a pillar of the Yankees' rotation of the twenties and by this time had established himself as one of the toughest World Series pitchers since Christy Mathewson. Sorrell was a rookie from North Carolina. In the first eight innings of the game only one run was scored, a home run for the Yankees off the bat of Bob Meusel.

Meusel was the younger brother of Irish Meusel, who had been a star in the National League. At six-three "Long Bob" was the tallest Yankee on Murderers' Row and also sported a tremendous throwing arm. He could run and could hit for power, and he might have stood as the sole hero on that day thanks to his homer. But Meusel would enter the record books for more than that, as he was about to get a chance to increase his offensive output.

With the Hugmen leading 1–0 into the bottom of the ninth, Red Hargrave was sent in to pinch-hit for Jackie Warner and evened the score with a circuit clout of his own off Hoyt. That was the only run the Tigers would tally, sending the game into extra innings, with both starters still in the game. Hoyt and Sorrell matched each other out for out through eleven.

"Hargrave's home run that looked to be Sorrell's savior worked with reverse English," wrote Sam Greene in the *Detroit News*. "Without the Hargrave smash, the game would have ended 1 to 0 in favor of the Yankees and Sorrell would have been the subject of many laudatory paragraphs dealing with this great but unsuccessful battle, against Hoyt, one of the leading pitchers in the American League. As it is, Sorrell will be remembered as the victim of one of the fiercest one-inning rallies of the current base ball year." In the top of the twelfth, Sorrell imploded. When the dust cleared, the Yankees had sent fifteen men to the plate, hitting five singles, three doubles, and two triples. The Tigers were unable to overcome the sudden 11-run deficit and went down 12–1.

And to think Long Bob had gone into the game not only overshadowed (and understandably so) by Babe Ruth and Lou Gehrig, but also in a slump. The day before, he had eight chances at bat and struck out in three, never once reaching first base. On this day, he struck out his first two times at bat before hitting the homer in the sixth. He doubled in the ninth but was stranded, and had a single in the eleventh. But his was one of the two triples in the 11-run twelfth, completing the cycle with the hit that was the hardest to achieve. Perhaps even more amazing is the fact that this was the third time in his career that Meusel pulled off the feat!

The second game was no pitchers' duel at all, as the Yankees continued to slug, and the Tigers slugged back. Both teams used three pitchers apiece. "Judging from the scores," wrote an appalled James B. Harrison in the *Times*, "you might think it was football, and maybe you're right at that. Certainly it wasn't baseball." Final score, 13–10 Tigers.

Extra Innings

- Bob Meusel is the only player in American League history to hit for the cycle three times. (Babe Herman also did it three times, in the National League.)

⬥ 9

June 3, 1932: New York at Philadelphia

The Hits Keep on Coming

In which the Iron Horse and Poosh 'Em Up Tony have memorable days

In this era of pumped-up offense, baseball curmudgeons sometimes paint a picture of past eras that would make one think that in "the old days" every game was a one-run affair, with victory scratched out by a suicide squeeze in the ninth. But there always have been blowouts, and there always have been slugfests, and in 1932, the height of the "lively ball" era, double-digit scores excited fans in ballparks all around the country. Sometimes the offensive fireworks were provided by one player's big day. At other times, the ball simply flew for everyone.

Take, for example, June 3, 1932. The Yankees faced the Philadelphia Athletics at Shibe Park. George "Moose" Earnshaw was on the mound for the hometown A's, while Johnny Allen pitched for the Yanks. Both pitchers had reasonably distinguished records versus their opponents, but the A's touched up the tough Allen for eight runs. Allen, though, could easily retort, "Oh, yeah? Ya shoulda seen the other guy," as the Yankees came out on the winning end of the record-breaking barrage.

"Records fell like raindrops in an April shower," recounted Richards Vidmer in the *New York Herald Tribune*. The trouble began in the very first inning, when Lou Gehrig homered—a two-run shot, off Earnshaw. In the bottom of the inning Mickey Cochrane answered with a two-run shot of his own. Both pitchers tried valiantly to restore order for a few innings, but in the fourth Gehrig homered again, sparking a rally that led to a fourth run.

The A's were not about to let a two-run deficit deter them, and they were helped in their cause by three walks and three errors in the answering frame. It was not a good day for pitchers. Earnshaw came to the plate with the bases loaded and no one out but popped up a bunt. Allen tried to catch it, got ahold of it, but then dropped it. Once the ball fell to the grass, he had a chance to make a triple play. He threw to Lazzeri (playing third that day), who cycled the ball to second, but umpire Harry Geisel ruled that Allen had held the ball and only Earnshaw was out. Philadelphia's four hits, though, were what drove Allen from the game, as the score seesawed to 8–4 A's. The incident riled the Yankee bench such that "the whole Yankee team seemed out for vengeance and they attacked with their bats" (*New York Herald Tribune*).

Now, there are slugfests and there are slugfests. Down four going into the fifth, Babe Ruth and Earle Combs began plastering Earnshaw, each knocking a solo shot off him before Gehrig came to the plate for this third try of the day. This one sailed over the wall in left-center field and gave Gehrig another line in the record books: he became the first man to hit three home runs in a game on four separate occasions. This dinger also put the Yankees within one of their opponent, at 8–7.

Tony Lazzeri's offensive day was about to become very interesting as well. In the sixth he and Frank Crosetti, hitting at the bottom of the order, sparked a two-run rally, and the Yanks took the lead. Although he played a position largely populated by light-hitting defensive specialists, Lazzeri displayed incongruous power, proving that his minor-league slugging feats were not a fluke. He continued his hard-hitting ways in all his years with the Yankees.

Gehrig came to bat for the fourth time in the seventh. Hitting three home runs in a game was a nice feat; Lazzeri himself had done it in 1927. But up until that point, only two men in big-league baseball had ever hit four homers in a game. Robert Lowe and Ed Delahanty had both done it back in the 1890s. But this was a moment for Columbia Lou.

In the 1930s, the baseball writers did not crowd around the lockers of baseball players, collecting platitudes to spice their game stories with. There was no SportsCenter, no nightly telecasts of clubhouse interviews. So we don't know what Lou would have said when a reporter asked him the inevitable: "What was it like hitting four home runs in a game?" or "What were you thinking about when you went to the plate?" When Gehrig did talk to the media, he was the model of today's self-deprecating ballplayer. In this he was the opposite of the gregarious, myth-making Ruth. One can almost imagine Gehrig saying, "I was just looking for a good pitch to hit."

He got it. This time the ball went to right center and gone, the first time in the twentieth century that a player had hit four home runs in a game. The Yankees did not stop there, though. They continued to apply the pressure to the A's pitching staff, as Lazzeri tripled in the inning as well.

The A's weren't about to stop swinging, however, not with the way the ball was flying that day. They even took the lead again, but although Gehrig was retired in his final at-bat—a long drive into the corner that might have carried a little farther and made Lou the only man to hit five in a game, as even the yelping Philly crowd seemed to hope—Lazzeri was not.

The fleet infielder, who had notched a single, double, and triple already on the day, came to bat in the ninth with the bases loaded and did the only thing he could do to put the Yankee offensive performance over the top—he hit a grand slam, bringing the Yankee tally to 20 and ensuring himself a place in the record books as well for "making a complete set" (*New York Herald Tribune*).

Jimmie Foxx hit an answering shot for the Athletics in the bottom of the ninth, adding to the total offensive records amassed on the day, but the gesture was too little, too late, as the final score stood 20–13 in favor of the Yankees.

Extra Innings

Records set or tied:

- 4 home runs, Gehrig (tied)
- 16, most total bases by a Yankee player in a game
- 7 home runs by a single club, Yankees (tied with the A's record of 1921)
- 41 extra bases by a single club, Yankees

- 50 total bases by a single club, Yankees (former record 46)

- 77 total bases in a nine-inning game

- The Yankees would later beat their own record for home runs in a game, clouting 8 on June 28, 1939. The victimized team was again Philadelphia.

10

October 1, 1932: New York at Chicago

Two Balls in the Corner Pocket

In which Babe Ruth performs the most debated gesture in sports history

In 1932 the Yankees returned to the World Series after a three-year absence. The "Murderers' Row" of 1927 and 1928 was mostly gone, with only Ruth, Gehrig, Lazzeri, and Earle Combs carrying over from the lineup. There had been some lean years at the end of the decade as the Depression hit the country, and the Yankees had suffered both the death of manager Miller Huggins and the surging of Connie Mack's Philadelphia Athletics. But in 1932, a new era was beginning in the Bronx for two reasons. One was the addition of players such as Frank Crosetti, Bill Dickey, Red Ruffing, and Lefty Gomez. The other was the new man at the helm, Joe McCarthy.

McCarthy's presence with the Yankees turned the World Series against the Chicago Cubs into a grudge match. "Marse Joe" had led the Cubs to a pennant in 1929, then was fired in 1930 for finishing second. To return to Wrigley flying the American League pennant with a chance to deny Chicago a world title was the best revenge.

Animosity between the two clubs festered for other reasons as well. The Cubs at the time were led by player-manager Charlie Grimm, who had been thrust into the post on August 2 when the former Cardinal Rogers Hornsby was canned after a disagreement with club president William Veeck Sr., despite the club's first-place standing. Grimm had held them at the top of the league under much stress. That month the Cubs also picked up a former Yankee, Mark Koenig, to fill a hole at shortstop. Koenig batted .353 and was instrumental in their pennant drive. He "gives [the club] pennant wings," reported the *Sporting News*. But the Cub players voted Koenig only half a share of the World Series winnings, which the Yankees thought was bush, and which they let the Cubs know at every opportunity.

Initially, the fans of Chicago were quite welcoming to the Yankees when the team arrived in town for game three of the Series. The Yankees had already manhandled the Cubs in the first two games in New York, winning 12–6 behind a complete game from Red Ruffing, and 5–2 behind Lefty Gomez. In truth, Chicago had hit both Ruffing and Gomez fairly well, but did not come close to the run production of the Yankee offense. Somehow the maltreatment of their team on the field did not harden the hearts of Chicago's baseball fans against the Yankees, but made them all the more eager to see them play. The Yankees were greeted by thousands of cheering Chicagoans at the train station "in a reception quite unlike any for a visiting team in a world's series," wrote John Drebinger in the *New York Times*. "As the Yanks arrived aboard their special train they were greeted by a throng that jammed the La Salle Street Station and at once a great roar went up for Babe Ruth who was almost swallowed up by the crowd the moment he alighted from his car."

Thousands more jammed the streets outside, and the assistance of police on motorcycles was needed to clear the way for the motorcade of taxicabs to the hotel. The Cubs expected to sell 51,000 tickets to the game, including seats in two temporary wooden stands erected just for the occasion. Determined spectators slept overnight on the streets of Wrigleyville, waiting for unreserved tickets to go on sale at 10 in the morning. And manager Grimm chirped hopeful words in the papers, assuring all that the Cubs had the advantage because Wrigley was a foreign ballpark to the Yankees.

What Charlie Grimm seemed to forget was that the quirks of a field hardly matter when the ball flies completely out of it. "Yankee Power Will Smash Cubs' Defense Most of Experts Say," ran one headline in the *Sporting News* prior to the Series. "New York's Left-Handed Sluggers Figured to Make Merry at the Expense of the Cubs' Right-Handed Pitching Staff." The day dawned warm and sunny with a steady west wind, all conditions in Wrigley that favor power hitting. The outpouring of love for Ruth and the Yankees from the train station glory seekers was now replaced by the derision of the diehard fans. Ruth and his wife were spat upon while leaving their hotel and from the stands. Some threw lemons. Ruth, at age 37, was rotund and supposedly in decline, though that year he had hit .341 with 137 RBI and 41 homers. He doffed his cap to his detractors and let a steady stream of invective fly at the Cubs' bench.

Taking the hill for the Yankees that day was one more holdover from the championship teams of the twenties, George Pipgras. Though a veteran of World War I, as a baseball rookie Pipgras came to the Yankees in 1923, in a preseason trade with the Red Sox. That year the Yankees had gone on to win their first World Series title, though the young hurler did not play in it. He did win his starts in the '27 and '28 sweeps, though, and he and the Yankees looked to repeat the feat in Chicago.

Facing him was Charlie Root, a hard-throwing righthander who had also made his debut in 1923. In 1927 he had gone 26–15 and threw a one-hitter against the Pirates. In 1932 his strikeout totals dipped a bit. After topping 120 K's a season for six straight years, in '32 he mustered only 96 while going 15–10 with a 3.58 ERA.

The Yankees pounced on Root right away. Earle Combs led off the game with a grounder that shortstop Billy Jurges threw into the Yankee dugout, allowing Combs to reach second. Joe Sewell walked, putting two ducks on the pond for the Babe. Ruth deposited the ball into the right-center-field bleachers for three runs. Root gave up two more hits after that but got out of the inning before further damage could be done.

Pipgras, for his part, was not perfect at the start. He walked Billy Herman to lead off the game, and after getting a fly ball out from Woody English, gave up a long double over left fielder Ben Chapman's head, which scored Herman. After that he got Riggs Stephenson and Grimm to hit the ball on the ground for outs, neutralizing his walk of Johnny Moore.

Pipgras himself led off the second with a strikeout, but the other Yankees continued to hit the ball hard. Perhaps after seeing the way the ball was flying that day, both clubs swung for the fences. Combs hit a long fly to deep left center, but it was hauled in by Moore. Sewell walked again, and up came Ruth. Ruth put a charge in another ball, but this one was caught by Kiki Cuyler with his back against the right-field bleachers. Chicago went down harmlessly in the bottom of the inning, bringing the Yankees back to the plate.

Lou Gehrig wasted no time in continuing the long-ball derby, homering into the right-field bleachers Ruth had narrowly missed in his previous turn, but that would be the only tally the Yankees got. Cuyler would answer with a solo shot for the Cubs in their half, also to right. The Cubs would add another on an RBI double to right by Grimm, making the score 4–3 Yankees.

In the fourth, the Cubs looked like they might take the lead. Jurges hit a liner to right. Ruth lunged for the ball and almost took it off his shoetops. As it was, the Babe nearly gunned Jurges out at second. Root then grounded out harmlessly, and Herman flew out to short center. But English then hit a slow roller in the infield, beat out the throw from Lazzeri, and Jurges scored from second. The Cubs might have had more but the rally was squelched when English tried to steal second and was gunned down by Bill Dickey.

Still, the score stood tied at four, and the Yankees did not appreciate the threat to their dominance. Sewell tried to whack a ball hard in the shortstop hole but Jurges was able to make a brilliant play to nip him at first. So here came Ruth. A volley of heckling flew to and from the Cubs' dugout. Ruth gesticulated and jawed at Root before and after every pitch. Root blew a fastball by Ruth for a called strike, and Ruth held up a finger. Then came another, and Ruth held up two fingers.

What happened next has been discussed, written about, and retold so many times it has entered the realm of American folklore. Even the nonbaseball fan knows what supposedly happened next. Ruth pointed to the flagpole in deep center—and deposited the very next pitch at the base of the pole with the go-ahead run. Radio announcer Quin Ryan, calling the game for the Cubs, saw the ball fly and burst out, "That ball went out to almost the exact spot that Babe had been pointing to!"

Babe Ruth was always "good copy" for the newspapermen. With his outsize personality, childlike enthusiasm, outrageous appetites, and unmatched athletic prowess on the baseball field, he was a perfect folk hero, a Paul Bunyan that they could write a new story about every day. Did Ruth ever hit a homer for a sick kid in a hospital? Yes, but perhaps not as often as the newspaper accounts might tell so. (Johnny Sylvester was one well-documented case, but reports of Ruth performing the feat in various cities throughout his career invariably cropped up.) Ruth was a figure of such stature in the American imagination that even stories about other ballplayers were mistakenly attributed to him. "Common wisdom" made it easy to believe that Ruth could call his shot like a pool shark.

Most of the newspapers the next day included lengthy, dramatic accounts of the fifth-inning homer, all mentioning the tremendous bravado Ruth displayed. "On . . . other occasions in his glamorous career he has hit three home runs in the course of a single World Series game, but never with the arrogance and showmanship he displayed today," wrote Richards Vidmer in the *New York Herald Tribune*. The *New York Times* had a similar account, describing the Babe's arm-waving and pointing as a "pantomime." As John Drebinger put it in the *Times*, then "Ruth set aside his buffoonery, smashing one of the longest home runs ever seen at Wrigley Field. It was an amazing demonstration by baseball's outstanding figure, who a few weeks ago was ill and confined to his bed." The wallop was reportedly the longest home run hit at Wrigley up to that point, 436 feet. But some were more brazen in labeling it a "called shot." Joe Williams in the *New York World-Telegram* described it thus: "Ruth pointed to center and punched a screaming liner to a spot where no ball had been hit before." The headline was even bolder: RUTH CALLS SHOT AS HE PUTS HOMER NO. 2 IN SIDE POCKET.

Even the *Chicago Tribune* story interpreted it in the most dramatic way. "Babe Calls His Shots" read a subheadline in the body of the story by Westbrook Pegler. "Then with a warning gesture on his hand to [the Cubs], he sent the signal for the customers to see. 'Now,' it said, 'this is the one.' And that one went riding in the longest home run ever hit in the park." A legend was born. And Ruth, ever the showman, cagily encouraged the legend to grow.

What really happened? There are as many interpretations of Ruth's gestures as there are eyewitnesses, and even home movies made by fans have been used by both camps, those who say he did, and those who say he didn't. Some believe he was pointing at the Chicago bench. Some think he pointed at Chicago pitcher Guy Bush, and then at the mound as if to say, "Why don't you get out here next?" But as the legend grew, most of the Yankees defended it, or at least avoided it. McCarthy was known to say he wasn't looking just then. Charlie Root, for his part, denied Ruth could have pointed as if to say he meant to hit a home run, because he "would have drilled him in the ear with the very next pitch" if it were so. Root's own catcher, Gabby Hartnett, told interviewer Lawrence Ritter years later that Ruth's words before the fateful pitch were: "It only takes one to hit it." A brazen, Ruthian statement—Ruth's bravado is never in question in any eyewitness account—but can Hartnett be trusted any more than any of the other participants in the event? There are as many who want to deny he did it, as say with all surety that they know what they saw—the greatest player of all time performing a feat that has never been equaled.

In baseball we are always prepared to see something unbelievable, something we've never seen before. It is one of the things that makes the game so special. Magnified by the World Series stage and by Ruth's involvement, an action that might have been an obscure footnote is instead the subject of ongoing debate more than 70 years after the fact. Had Mark Koenig, for example, gone through the same motions, would anyone but trivia buffs remember? At this point in the 21st century, the "truth" we must accept is that Ruth could have done it, might indeed have done it, and is believed to have done it by multitudes of fans who were at the ballpark that day, who were listening on the radio, and who are still debating the point today. Ruth himself sometimes bragged, sometimes demurred, when asked whether he had "really" done it. Whatever the intended significance of his pointing and gestures at the time, it is because he was Babe Ruth, with his prodigious home run history and penchant for boasts, that so many observers in the media and in the stands came to the instant conclusion that Ruth had called his shot—and also why so many naysayers sprang up to try to tear down the "myth." But Ruth's is a figure of such mythic proportions that mere facts barely apply to his story, and the called shot falls under the category of "apocryphal truth." This much we know: the home run put the Yankees ahead in the game.

After Ruth circled the bases, exchanging insults with each Chicago player he passed, Lou Gehrig stepped to the plate and homered as well: 6–4 Yankees. That was it for Root. Pat Malone came in to pitch and walked Lazzeri and Dickey in succession. Chapman hit a slow roller to third, and though he was out, both runners advanced. The Cubs elected to walk Frank Crosetti intentionally to get to Pipgras, and lucky for them the Yankee myth-making was over for the moment. Pipgras did what pitchers then and now so commonly do: he struck out looking. But he faced only three Cubs in the bottom of the inning, aided by a double play. He would repeat the act in the seventh, taking a called third strike with two out and two on, and then coming back to retire the side with no damage.

Jakie May, Chicago's only lefty, took the hill in the eighth and kept the Yankees in check. In the ninth he might have done so again if not for some miscues in the field. The inning began with Lou Gehrig popping up to the mound, where catcher Hartnett reeled it in. Tony Lazzeri then popped one up as well, but May tried to take it himself and failed, allowing Lazzeri to reach. Bill Dickey followed suit, popping a ball into right, which Herman muffed. Ben Chapman exploited the opportunity, doubling over third and scoring Lazzeri. Grimm pulled May in favor of Bud Tinning, who induced yet another pop-up, this one from Crosetti—an out—bringing up Pipgras, who actually swung the bat this time. Maybe he expected to pop up, too. Instead he struck out, setting a World Series record with five in one game.

Perhaps he should have looked at that third strike and saved his energy for pitching the last of the ninth. Up came Hartnett, who led off the inning with a home run, igniting the crowd. Jurges followed quickly with a single, and Mark Koenig was inserted to pinch-hit for Tinning. McCarthy decided Pipgras had done enough and produced Herb Pennock out of the bullpen.

Hartnett's home run merely "provided a setting that added still further to the glamour of the Yankees triumph. For it brought on the scene one of the greatest world's series pitchers of all time . . . who started pitching in these classes back in 1914," gushed the *Times*. With a man on and the score now 7–5, every batter who came to the plate represented the tying run. But "the famous Squire of Kennett Square sharply halted the belated Cub rally . . . smothering the desperate bid with consummate ease and skill." Koenig was lifted in favor of Rollie Hemsley, and Pennock struck him out. He got a soft, infield dribbler out of Herman, which he fielded himself for the assist. Jurges moved to second on the play and then stole third. But he was still standing there when Pennock got another gentle roller off the bat of English to Gehrig to end the game.

The Yankees completed the sweep of the Cubs the next day. But, noted the *Times*, "[Ruth and Gehrig] produced no homers . . . and this in itself may be considered some sort of moral victory for the opposition." The Yankees trounced them, 13–6, winning not only their fourth world championship but also setting another world record. After the sweeps of the Pirates and Cardinals in 1927 and 1928, and now the Cubs in 1932, they had won 12 World Series games in a row.

◄Extra Innings

- After he retired from pitching, George Pipgras became a major-league umpire.

- The six home runs hit by the combined Yankees and Cubs in one game was a new record for a single World Series game.

- The wind at Wrigley Field has always been a tremendous factor. When blowing in, the ball is nearly impossible to hit out. When blowing out, it makes pitchers wish they were hitters. "I wish I was in there today," Lefty Gomez told reporters after feeling the stiff breeze at the Yankees' lakeside hotel. "I bet I could hit one into those bleachers. Babe and Lou ought to hit a dozen."

- The "called shot" home run was the last one Ruth would hit in a World Series, setting the record for a single player at 15.

11

August 1, 1937: St. Louis at New York

Pride of the Yankees

In which Columbia Lou makes another mark in the record books

Perhaps it was Lou Gehrig's fate to always live in the shadow of others. The quiet, unassuming son of German immigrant parents, Lou was raised in New York and attended Columbia University, where his mother worked as a cleaning woman. Lou played baseball at Columbia in the spring of 1923, where he was a pitcher as well as a hitter. On April 18 he struck out 17 against Williams

Henry Louis "Lou" Gehrig

College, a university record that stood for 45 years, but the feat was eclipsed by the other big New York baseball news of the day: the opening of Yankee Stadium. By September of that year, Gehrig would join the Yankees in the "House That Ruth Built" as a late-season call-up, and by 1925 he became a fixture in the lineup, beginning his streak of 2,130 consecutive games played on May 31.

The life and career of Lou Gehrig, though tragically short, can in no way be encapsulated fully in one book, much less one chapter. But I would be remiss not to point out some of the highlights of the extraordinary achievements of this extraordinary man. Gehrig spent much of his career in the larger-than-life shadow of Babe Ruth, but there is no eclipsing his still-standing records for American League RBI in a season (184 in 1931) and grand slams, a major-league-best 23 lifetime. At the time he was forced into retirement by the progression of amyotrophic lateral sclerosis—the disease more commonly known as Lou Gehrig's disease—Gehrig was second on the all-time home run list, behind Ruth. Lou was a model of consistency, not only for the streak (since surpassed by Baltimore Oriole Cal Ripken Jr.) but also for driving in 100 runs and scoring 100 runs every full season of his career, a streak of 13 years. Gehrig hit four home runs in a game (see chapter 9), something Ruth never did. And he hit for the cycle twice, another feat Ruth never accomplished even once.

The first time Gehrig connected for the cycle, he was having what may have been the best year of his career, 1934. He would finish the year as the winner of the Triple Crown (49 HR, 165 RBI, .363) and play in his 1,500th consecutive game, despite suffering a concussion from being beaned in an exhibition game in June and back spasms in July so severe he had to be helped from the field. Gehrig battled Philadelphia's Jimmie Foxx for the home run crown through September, eventually hitting a career-high 49 to win the title. And yet Mickey Cochrane won the American League MVP Award (2 [!] HR, 76 RBI, .320). Even a fellow Yankee, pitcher Lefty Gomez, finished ahead of Gehrig in the voting, Lou pulling in a mere fifth. Two years later, with Ruth retired, Gehrig was awarded the 1936 American League MVP on the strength of 49 home runs, 167 runs scored, 152 RBI, and a .354 batting average.

Although he put up very respectable numbers in 1938, including 29 homers, his batting average dipped below .300 for the first time since 1925, and after averaging more than 150 RBI per year for over a decade, he drove in only 114. Dan Daniels wrote in the *Sporting News* in July of that year that "Gehrig has been in a long and seemingly hopeless slump . . . he just can't keep going consistently once he does right himself. It is my conviction that Gehrig is a very tired man." ALS was beginning to take an early toll. As such, 1937 was Gehrig's last truly great season, and yet already he was being overshadowed by the Yankees' next great star, Joe DiMaggio.

On August 1 the Yankees were finishing up a series against St. Louis at the Stadium. "[The] Browns were the victims of Murderers' Row yesterday," lamented the *St. Louis Post-Dispatch*, recounting the 17-hit pounding. The bats hammered hard on Brownie pitcher Lou Koupal, who walked DiMaggio in the first, only to give up a two-run homer to Gehrig. Midway through the second inning Koupal, having given up six runs already, was replaced by Julio Bonetti.

Bonetti restored order for almost three frames before "he encountered one of those Yankee home run storms" (*Post-Dispatch*). Red Rolfe launched a two-run shot in the sixth, and then DiMaggio followed with his 31st of the year in the seventh, also for two. "A pitcher can't afford to make a mistake when Joe is at bat," Browns manager Jim Bottomley told the *Post-Dispatch*. "DiMaggio, Gehrig, and [Bill] Dickey comprise what is easily the best three-man run making combination to be found. The Yankee musclemen wear pitchers out." Bonetti was deemed sufficiently pummeled after the seventh, by which time he had given up six more runs and 10 hits. Bill Trotter took his place and gave up a two-run triple to Myril Hoag.

DiMaggio's homer was the talk of the New York papers the following day. "They said there would never be another Babe Ruth," is how Arthur Patterson opened his game story in the *Herald Tribune*. "But for the Babe's chief stock in trade, home runs . . . there is another Babe at the Yankee Stadium." What set off the fervor? DiMaggio's 31st put him ahead of Ruth's pace in his record-setting campaign of 60 in 1927. Five paragraphs later, Rolfe's homer is mentioned, Gehrig's not at all except for the subheadline.

The *New York Times* also opened with the DiMaggio homer. "A milestone in baseball was passed, or closely approached . . . at the Stadium yesterday," wrote James P. Dawson. "With this blow the sensational Italian either passed the intermediate mark Babe Ruth made . . . or approached within striking distance." At least the *Times* does give a nod to Gehrig, though. "There were two triples, three doubles, and nine singles in this devastating fire, Gehrig showing the way by hitting the cycle, a single, double, triple, and homer in five trips to the plate." Not only that, Dawson goes on to say: "On his fifth trip Lou narrowly missed a second homer in his favorite parking grounds."

The one place Lou Gehrig is not overshadowed is in our memory. Where he should have been fixed by his mere greatness, he became enshrined by an early death. Although he did not die until 1941, early in the 1939 season it became clear that the "enfeeblement" Gehrig was suffering had made him a danger to himself on the field and a liability to the team. On May 2 he benched himself, and never again took the field, as the disease robbed him of muscular control. In that same year, 1939, the National Baseball Hall of Fame in Cooperstown opened. Gehrig was inducted immediately, without the usual waiting period. The rush was spurred by his illness, but his greatness as a player is unquestionable. Hollywood immortalized him as well, in the 1942 film *The Pride of the Yankees*, which starred Gary Cooper in the Gehrig role (and Babe Ruth as himself) and garnered eleven Academy Award nominations. But Gehrig's lasting legacy was perhaps crystallized best by his own words, spoken on July 4, 1939, Lou Gehrig Day at Yankee Stadium:

Fans, for the past two weeks you have been reading about the bad break I got. Yet today I consider myself the luckiest man on the face of the earth. I have been in ballparks for 17 years and have never received anything but kindness and encouragement from you fans. Look at these grand men. Which of you wouldn't consider it the highlight of his career just to associate with them for even one day? Sure I'm lucky. Who wouldn't consider it an honor to have known Jacob Ruppert? Also, the builder of baseball's greatest empire, Ed Barrow? To have spent six years with that wonderful little fellow, Miller Huggins? Then to have spent the next nine years with the best manager in baseball today, Joe McCarthy? Sure I'm lucky. When the New York Giants, a team you would give your right arm to beat, and vice versa, sends you a gift—that's something. When everybody down to the groundskeepers and those boys in white coats remember you with trophies—that's something. When you have a wonderful mother-in-law who takes sides with you in squabbles with her own daughter—that's something. When you have a father and a mother who work all their lives so you can have an education and build your body—it's a blessing. When you have a wife who has been a tower of strength and shown more courage than you dreamed existed—that's the finest I know. So I close in saying that I may have had a tough break, but I have an awful lot to live for.

Extra Innings

- Gehrig was the first player in major-league history to have his number retired. Gehrig wore the number 4, and Ruth 3, to reflect their places in the batting order. The Yankees retired Gehrig's number in 1939.

- Only two players have ever hit more than 400 home runs and also stolen home 10 or more times. Lou Gehrig was one. Can you name the other? (Babe Ruth—Ruth stole home 10 times, Gehrig 15, both men usually benefiting from the double steal.)

- Lou Gehrig's first appearance in a major-league park came long before his debut with the Yankees. While playing for New York City's Commerce High School, Gehrig played in the national high school championship held at Wrigley Field (then called National League Park). In the game versus Lane Tech, Gehrig was the hero, hitting an eighth-inning grand slam completely out of the park for a 12–8 win.

Nine Little Indians

In which Monte Pearson notches a tenth consecutive win in style

On August 27, 1938, the Yankees were scheduled to play their fifth double-header in a row at the Stadium and were facing Ossie Vitt's Cleveland Indians. The Stadium crowd was wowed in the first game as Joe DiMaggio hit three successive triples, the final one the two-run game winner in the bottom of the ninth, as the Yankees won 8–7. But an even more rapturous performance awaited the 40,959 spectators in the "nightcap" (the second game was actually played in the late afternoon).

Monte Pearson took the hill for the Yankees with high confidence, the result of notching wins in his previous nine starts. The only potential worry was that with ten games scheduled in five days, a schedule today's baseball would never allow, Pearson was being forced to pitch on only two days rest. "Marse Joe" McCarthy, the Yankees' manager, had come under fire for trading Johnny Allen to Cleveland for Pearson in the off-season. Pearson, a California native, was known in Cleveland for sometimes being wild, and also for sometimes refusing to pitch if he didn't feel at his best. Yet here was Pearson facing his old club on short rest. If he didn't feel right, no one could tell.

Pearson set the Indians down in the first three innings "like reeds before a high gale," wrote John Drebinger in the *New York Times*, and "the crowd began to sit up and take notice." But then Pearson committed the cardinal sin of pitching: he walked the leadoff man, Lyn Lary, in the fourth. He compounded the situation by walking the next man, Bruce Campbell, as well. Thanks to a five-run rally in the first inning, and some other wallops, the Yankees already had a seven-run lead at that point, so the two free passes were not a huge cause for concern, except perhaps for Pearson's pride.

He responded to the jam by striking out Jeff Heath, retiring Earl Averill on a weak grounder, and then fanning Hal Trosky. Pearson had buckled down and did not let up for the remainder of the game. To start off the ninth Vitt inserted two pinch hitters to try to break up the no-hit bid, but Julius Solters struck out and Frankie Pytlak bounced out harmlessly.

The Indians' last hope then was Campbell. If any in the crowd held their breath waiting for the outcome of his at-bat, they would have passed out, as the game paused for a few minutes while Joe DiMaggio called for time and ran to retrieve his sunglasses. With the sun setting on the late game, DiMag had the glare right in his eyes. Could you imagine if he had let a ball fall in for a hit and ruined Pearson's work? Joe D. would never utter those bush-league words "I lost it in the sun."

Indeed, he did not have to, though Campbell came close to doing the job. He smashed a grounder down the first-base line that was called foul. Then he went the other way, hitting a sinking liner to left. But George Selkirk was able to make the play and send the crowd into ecstasy. Fifteen years had passed since Sad Sam Jones had accomplished the same feat, and Pearson, being the first pitcher to do it at Yankee Stadium, was quickly mobbed by the raucous home crowd.

Cut off from his teammates by the mob, Pearson found only Cal Hubbard, an umpire, there to help him as one member of the frenzy made off with the pitcher's hat. Two policemen eventually rescued him and dragged him off the field. In the clubhouse a celebration reigned as well, though one less likely to injure the guest of honor.

Extra Innings

- In Monte Pearson's no-hitter, only five balls made it out of the infield, all caught on the fly for outs. He also struck out seven.

- The final score stood 13–0, and the Indians, predicted to rival the Yanks before the season, lost five of the six in three days to fall well back in the pack, prompting the *Sporting News* to run the headline A.L. GROWING PANICKY OVER YANKEE DOMINATION.

13

July 19, 1940: Cleveland at New York

The Neatest Trick

In which everything goes right for Buddy Rosar

It was "Ladies' Day" at Yankee Stadium on July 19, 1940, and 18,919 spectators (reports specify 6,768 were ladies) gathered to see the Yankees take on the Cleveland Indians. At the time, Cleveland stood in second place in the standings; the Yankees, fourth. Although the 1940 Yankees were a solid team, they could not seem to sustain a winning streak and kept finding themselves behind the leaders. They had just taken four of six on their home stand before beating the Indians in the first two games of the three-game set.

For the finale, two lefthanders would face off, Lefty Gomez for the Yankees, Al Smith for the Tribe. Smith would not last long—drummed out of the game in the first inning as the Yankees pounded him for six runs. The drubbing began, as so many seem to, with a leadoff walk. Frank Crosetti drew a free pass and then Red Rolfe reached on third baseman Ken Keltner's error. Tommy Henrich brought them in right away with a two-run double. Joe DiMaggio tried to join the fun but flew out to center, bringing backup catcher Buddy Rosar to the plate.

Rosar was a New York native, born in Buffalo, playing his second year in the big leagues. Bill Dickey was the Yankees' front-line catcher but Rosar appeared in 73 games in 1940, batting .298. Rosar was the shortest guy on the team, a bit on the stocky side, but he legged out a triple to start his day. Joe Gordon then hit a dinger to bring him in, and Buster Mills tripled also in the expansive outfield of old Yankee Stadium.

That was it for Smith, who was replaced by Joe Dobson, who gave up a homer to Babe Dahlgren to make it 7–0 Yankees, before inducing Lefty Gomez to ground out, and catching Crosetti looking.

Dobson didn't get much chance to do more, though, as he was lifted for a pinch hitter in the next half inning. Jeff Heath had led off with a double, and after registering two outs, Gomez walked Rollie Hemsley. Perhaps manager Ossie Vitt felt that if they were going to get to Gomez, this would be the time? Odell Hale hit for Dobson—or failed to, striking out.

So the Yankees faced Johnny Humphries in the second inning. The inning started easily enough for him: Rolfe popped up in the infield. Henrich walked, but then DiMaggio popped up as well. If Humphries could get Rosar, he could stop the bleeding and perhaps the Indians could climb back in the game. But Buddy singled and advanced to second on the throw. Humphries walked Joe Gordon intentionally, but Buster Mills spoiled that strategy by doubling to left, scoring all three runners. Humphries hit Dahlgren with a pitch, but retired Gomez on a fly ball to left. Still, at 10–0 the hole was getting deeper.

The Indians were not about to let that deficit stand for long. They tallied three runs in the third as Gomez was a bit wild, walking a man, throwing a wild pitch, and allowing a three-run homer to Hal Trosky. Humphries responded by setting the Yankees down in order in the third, and in the fourth, the Tribe tacked on two more runs. With two outs, Ben Chapman singled to bring Roy Weatherly to the plate.

Weatherly hit a liner right back at Gomez, who took it off the wrist. It was an unlucky turn for Lefty, who had been nagged with injuries all year and had up to then recorded only two wins. He had to be helped from the field and to the hospital for X-rays (which were negative). Johnny Murphy came in from the bullpen to try to finish the job, but after a hurried warm-up, gave up a triple to Lou Boudreau before getting Trosky to pop up. The lead was cut in half, 10–5.

But now Humphries faced DiMaggio, who singled, to bring up Rosar again. Buddy hit a two-run shot the opposite way into the short porch in right field, to put the Yanks up, 12–5. Dahlgren added one for good measure, 13–5. And so the score stayed until the sixth, when Rosar led off the inning, facing Bill Zuber, fresh from the bullpen. Rosar had already tripled, singled, and homered. This time he completed the set, pulling the ball to left for a double. He moved to third on a ground out and scored on another grounder, his the only hit in the inning, and the only run. 14–5 Yanks.

In the eighth, to put a topper on his perfect day, Rosar drew a walk as part of a rally that produced yet another run. "Buddy Rosar turned the neatest trick of the season," wrote Harry Cross in the *New York Herald Tribune.* "The young catcher was the big noise in the . . . highest scoring jamboree they have had this season."

The Indians would come back and notch one more in the top of the ninth, but ultimately lose, 15–6. The game completed a three-game sweep of second-place Cleveland. But the next day the first-place Detroit Tigers came to town and treated the Yankees to some of their own medicine, taking three in a row. The Yankees would finish the season in third place, while Detroit would go on to the World Series (only to lose game seven to the Reds).

Buddy Rosar, meanwhile, would bloom into an All-Star in 1942, his final year with the Yankees. He would be traded to Cleveland, ironically, and then move on to the Philadelphia Athletics, where in 1946 he set the single-season record for errorless games by a catcher, making not a single error in 117 games. In 1947 the streak continued to 147 games, a record that would eventually be broken by the man who would replace Bill Dickey: Yogi Berra.

Extra Innings

- Rosar was behind the plate for two no-hitters while he played for the A's: Dick Fowler's (September 9, 1945, vs. St. Louis) and Bill McCahan's (September 3, 1947, vs. Washington).

- Rosar's single-season consecutive-game errorless streak stood until 1997, when Charles Johnson of the Florida Marlins played 124 games without an error (and only one passed ball).

14

September 8, 1940: New York at Boston

Bombed in Boston

In which Joe Gordon has a perfect day at the plate

When September 1940 rolled around, Cleveland, Detroit, and New York were all in the pennant race, with Boston just a few games behind the pack. The hitting stars of the day were the likes of Ted Williams, Joe DiMaggio, Luke Appling, and Hank Greenberg, but on September 8 a somewhat less likely star led the Yankees in knocking Boston back another notch in the standings.

Second baseman Joe Gordon was a one-man wrecking crew that day. In five trips at bat, Boston never retired him. Gordon was a product of the Yankees' farm system, a slick fielder and also quite a hitter. His onslaught started in the very first inning when the acrobatic All-Star smacked his twenty-fifth homer of the year over Fenway Park's Green Monster. The pitcher he faced, rookie Bill Fleming, was new to the Red Sox and the rivalry. "Fleming is newly imported from Hollywood," wrote Harry Cross in the *New York Herald Tribune.* "He pitched as if he had been doing slow-motion picture work." He walked George Selkirk and Joe DiMaggio, but although he gave up a few more long flies in the first, no more balls left the yard.

Bobby Doerr tied the score at one with a homer of his own off Spud Chandler in the bottom half of the inning, and the battle was on. Gordon singled in the second, though he did not score. The Yankees pecked away at Fleming in the third as DiMaggio drew a one-out walk. Charlie Keller lofted a ball deep into the left-field corner that evaded Ted Williams after a long run, but the relay throw caught DiMaggio at third base. Buddy Rosar then singled Keller to third, and advanced to second himself on a bad throw. Babe Dahlgren then singled them both home, and that was the end of Fleming's day. Player-manager Joe Cronin replaced him with Fritz Ostermueller, who stopped the bleeding at 3–1 Yanks.

The Bostons roared back. Chandler had been struggling in recent weeks and the Red Sox looked to take advantage when Doc Cramer's one-out single went off Gordon's glove. Jimmie Foxx doubled to left center, and Cramer scored on DiMaggio's wild throw to second. A single from Doerr then brought Foxx in before Chandler could bear down and escape the inning with the score tied.

Ostermueller presented no more of a challenge to the Yankees than Fleming had. Gordon now added a triple to his box score, then came in on a double by Red Rolfe. Rolfe moved to third on an infield single by Selkirk, and DiMaggio hit a ball hard on the infield. Rolfe scored on the resulting double play.

Gordon doubled in the fifth to complete the cycle with four hits in a mere five innings.

Chandler, meanwhile, determined not to give up the lead again, quieted the Boston bats for a few innings, but with two already out in the seventh, he walked the slugger Foxx. The consummate hitter, Williams, doubled off the center-field wall amid thunderous crowd noise. The Boston fans tried hard to rattle Chandler, sensing weakness. Joe Cronin came to the plate with the tying runs on. "Boss" Cronin fouled off four pitches and worked the count to 2–2, when Chandler threw him a bender. "Cronin fanned amid an astonishing wave of silence," wrote Harry Cross in the *Herald Tribune*.

Perhaps energized by their starter's gutsy escape, the Yankees went to work again in the eighth, knocking Ostermueller out of the game. Fritz walked Gordon to start the inning, and Rolfe singled hard. Cronin had seen enough and brought Earl Johnson in after a quick warm-up. Johnson promptly walked Selkirk to load the bases and faced Joe DiMaggio. He got two strikes on DiMag but then gave up an RBI single. Johnson got a ground out from Keller, which brought in another run. The Red Sox opted to walk Buddy Rosar to load the bases again and set up the double play, which they did not get. Johnson instead uncorked a wild pitch that scored Selkirk. Then Johnson threw two straight balls to Dahlgren, and Boss Joe yanked him midbatter and replaced him with Jim Bagby. Bagby completed the free pass and Frank Crosetti grounded out to bring in one more, totaling four runs on only two hits in the inning.

The Sox scratched one more run after that, but with the final score at 9–4, the *Boston Globe* concluded, "The Red Sox didn't have it." Boston would end the season eight games out of contention. The Yankees would hang in the race to the very end, ultimately pulling in behind both the Tigers and Indians by a mere two games and a game, respectively. In 1941 the Yankees would return to world champion form, winning the American League pennant over Boston by seventeen games. In the '41 World Series Joe Gordon would distinguish himself, batting .500 (7 for 14) and slugging .929, as well as neutralizing the Dodgers' attack with great glove work in the field.

◀ Extra Innings

- Joe Gordon tallied an even 1,000 hits in 1,000 games played for the Yankees.

- Gordon went on to win the American League's MVP Award in 1942.

- Gordon held the American League record for most home runs by a second baseman in a season (32) until 2001, when the record was broken by Bret Boone of the Seattle Mariners (35). The following year another Yankee, Alfonso Soriano, hit 39.

June 29, 1941: New York at Washington

Clipping the Sizzler

In which Joe DiMaggio reaches one milestone on his way to another

In 1941, when Joe DiMaggio set out to play his sixth season with the New York Yankees, he was already a legend, already firmly inscribed in the record books. In 1936 he had grabbed a share of the record for most home runs in an inning (two), and in 1938 tied the American League record for most triples in a game (three). In 1939 he was named the American League's Most Valuable Player and was named Player of the Year by the *Sporting News*. He was regularly described as the epitome of grace under pressure and in the field.

So in 1941, of course great things were expected of DiMaggio, regardless of the team's fortunes. The Yankees had racked up a modest 88–67 record in 1940, a letdown after their 106-win season and fourth consecutive world championship in 1939. Word of the war overseas packed the newspapers and jammed the radio waves, but diehard Yankees fans had another concern: could the team bounce back?

The team did not blaze hot out of the gate but played .500 ball for the first several weeks of the season. DiMaggio himself began the season in a slump. On May 15, when the team faced Chicago in the Bronx, the Bombers' record was 14–14, and DiMaggio's average had climbed to .306. He managed a single off Eddie Smith in that day's 13–1 loss.

The next day, DiMaggio's performance was a bit more inspiring. He got two hits off Thornton Lee—a triple and a homer—and the Yankees squeaked out a 6–5 win.

It was the beginning of what some consider the greatest feat in baseball history, but at the time no one knew it. Even ten days later, when DiMaggio went four for five in a game against the Senators, the hitting streak stood at a modest 12 games. But in a nation starved for something to brighten the war-darkened skies, DiMaggio's hot hitting was welcome news.

When DiMaggio stretched the streak to 16 with a fly ball that Boston out-fielder Pete Fox lost in the sun, it seemed Fate was beginning to smile on the Yankee Clipper. The American League record for hitting in consecutive games had been set by George Sisler in 1922 at 41, while in the National League, Wee Willie Keeler had gone to 44 back in 1897. Sisler's feat seemed out of reach, but the speculation gave newspaper columnists and radio commentators something to talk about. DiMaggio would later say the media attention at that point was what made him aware of the streak.

The hits kept on coming. The day Lou Gehrig died, June 2, DiMaggio got two knocks off Bob Feller in Cleveland, but the Yankees lost, 7–5. Three days later he was more than halfway to Sisler, at 21 games, after having faced Dizzy Trout and Hal Newhouser in Detroit. St. Louis, Chicago, Cleveland, Philadelphia—DiMaggio passed through all these places in June, recording a hit every day, in every game. In Philly he and his roomie, Lefty Gomez, made a hospital visit to 10-year-old Tony Morrell. Was DiMag trying to get his mind off baseball? "I never really gave the record much thought until I had hit in about 33 or 34 games," DiMaggio told the *New York Herald Tribune* before the next day's game. "The first time I think I really worried was yesterday in Philadelphia."

June 29 dawned hot and muggy in the nation's capital, the site of the Yankees' next contest. Even as the front page of the *New York Times* declared NAZIS SEE VICTORY and GERMANS REPORT THEY HAVE PASSED MINSK, Griffith Stadium was the focus of fervent attention. The Senators and Yankees were set to play a doubleheader. And what an auspicious time for a twin bill! A hit in the first game would tie Sisler; a hit in the second, surpass him. Joltin' Joe was mobbed by fans upon his arrival at the ballpark. With the crowds interfering with his batting practice, he accommodated them by signing autographs instead.

If Joe was as nervous as he told the press, the thirty-one thousand fans who turned out to see if he could do it began to feel nervous, too, as DiMaggio went hitless through five innings. The temperature at game time hit 98 degrees, but DiMaggio would have been sweating regardless. In his first at-bat he tagged the ball, but lined right to center fielder Doc Cramer. He came up again in the fourth and worked the count to 3–0. Expecting to get a good pitch to hit, he swung mightily but only managed a weak pop-up to third. "I was tense out there today," he admitted to reporters in a rare exhibition of weakness.

But tense or not, he came to the plate in the sixth inning with the Yankees up, 3–0. The Yankees' starter, Charley "Red" Ruffing, had cruised through the first five innings, allowing only one hit, and Joe Gordon, Phil Rizzuto, and

Ruffing himself had just hammered Emil "Dutch" Leonard the previous inning to put up three runs, so perhaps some of the pressure was off as the Yankees appeared to be cruising to a victory.

DiMag swung and missed at Leonard's first pitch in the sixth, then looked at a ball. On the next pitch, a low fastball, he sparked a rally with a double that rolled to the 422-foot sign. CROWD FORGETS HEAT ran a headline in the *Times*, as the mob dissolved into ecstasy, even as their hometown team went down by another three runs. DiMaggio would eventually score on a passed ball, greeted first at the plate by a handshake from Gordon, who was up at the time, and then by all his teammates on the dugout steps, clapping him on the back.

Maybe the excitement was too much for Ruffing, who suddenly melted down in the bottom of the frame and gave up four runs. But Johnny Murphy came out of the pen to set down the next 10 Senators in a row and ensure the 9–4 victory.

In the clubhouse between games, the beat writers asked Joe how he felt about matching Sisler. The Yankee Slugger was modest. "Sure, I'm tickled. Who wouldn't be?" He deflected some of the credit to Yankee manager Joe McCarthy, for letting him swing at 3–0 pitches. "It brought me many a good ball to swing at," he explained, before declaring Keeler's 44-game mark as his next goal. And after that? "I'll keep right on swinging and hitting as long as I can."

The nightcap had McCarthy's men facing Sid Hudson, a tall righthander who had dominated the Florida State League before debuting with the Senators in 1940. In his rookie year he racked up 17 wins for a weak Senators team, including two one-hitters, and in 1941 he looked just as sharp, making the All-Star team. But DiMaggio had tripled off him the last time they had met, just a few weeks before.

The Yankees jumped out to a two-run lead after Johnny Sturm tripled to lead off the game. But they were sloppy as they took the field. In the bottom of the inning, Gordon made two errors and Rizzuto one. Charley Stanceau somehow bore down and escaped the bases-loaded jam, giving up only one run. Gordon smacked a homer into the left-field bleachers in the top of the second, but in the bottom of the frame made another error, leading to two Senators' runs and a tie game.

In the fourth the Yankees again pulled ahead, and again the Senators tied it in their half of the inning. The Yankees then got a bit of their trademark luck, as Gordon—yes, him again—was bailing out on a pitch but hit an "excuse me" looper over the infield. Two walks then loaded the bases for pinch hitter George Selkirk. Selkirk, too, took only half a swing at a pitch, and ended up knocking in two runs.

But no such lucky hit for DiMaggio. He had come to the plate three times, only to go back to the bench empty-handed, leaving the crowd groaning each time. Perhaps Hudson had figured out how to pitch to him. But the tough Tennessean didn't last. In the seventh, Arnold "Red" Anderson took the mound. There were two outs and the crowd cheered their encouragement to the Yankee Clipper as DiMaggio faced his last chance to extend the streak.

Anderson's first pitch was inside, knocking Joe off the plate. The pitcher tried to come inside a second time, but this time DiMag was ready, and lined a hard shot into left. Keller then tripled, bringing him in to more thunderous applause. Sisler had been passed, and DiMaggio was officially the nation's new hero. To further sweeten the pot, the Yankees pulled out a win, 7–5, swept the doubleheader, and also pulled 1½ games up on their nearest rival, Cleveland. Although DiMaggio's streak would eventually end at 56 games, the Yankees would go on to capture both the American League pennant and the World Series.

Extra Innings

* *Streak stats:*

  Joltin' Joe went four for five four times during the streak.

  The 56 games included 22 multihit performances.

  DiMag seemed to get hotter as the streak went on. In the 16 days of May he had only four multihit performances, or about one every four days. In June he racked up 10, or about one every three days. In the first 16 days of July, he racked up eight, getting more than one hit every other game!

  After the streak was stopped by an oh-fer on July 17, Joe immediately reeled off a 16-game hitting streak.

* Between the games of the doubleheader, a fan stole the bat that DiMaggio had been using throughout the streak, a 36-inch, 36-ounce model that DiMaggio had sandpapered to make the handle slightly thinner. At the time it was not so unusual for fans to wander on the field when games were not in progress, and one fellow walked off with the bat. He was later spotted leaving the park with it. Despite exhortations from the Yankee bench to stop him, the bat thief got away. Fortunately, DiMaggio didn't depend on a "lucky bat" and continued hitting. Joe eventually recovered the bat as the exploits of the braggart were overheard by friends of Joe's in the Newark neighborhood where the thief lived, and they recovered it for him.

- Almost lost amid the hullabaloo over the streak was the fact that the Yankees set a new team record, hitting home runs in 25 consecutive games (40 dingers overall during the 25-game stretch).

- If Joe could have stretched the streak to 57 games, the H. J. Heinz Company was ready to sign him to a commercial endorsement deal reportedly worth $10,000. The ketchup and condiment giant Heinz featured the slogan "57 Varieties." In reality, they had many more than 57 products, but Henry Heinz had seized on 57 as a unique and marketable number back in 1906, and the company was always looking for promotional gimmicks based on the number. The deal never came to be, as the streak was stopped at 56 games.

October 5, 1941: New York at Brooklyn

Making Out Just Fine

In which Old Reliable figures out how to win a game after the final out

In 1941 the team returned to form. Between the Joe DiMaggio hitting streak and their domination of the Red Sox in midseason, the Yankees were beginning to look like champions again. They clinched the pennant on September 4, the earliest date ever for a 154-game season, and cruised into October to meet the Dodgers for the first time.

The Dodgers had not had it so easy. They'd clawed their way through the Cardinals in a pennant race that went down to the wire. The infield was stellar, with Cookie Lavagetto at third, a young Pee Wee Reese at short, and Billy Herman at second. Ultimately, the MVP season of Dolph Camilli, the hitting of Pete Reiser (.343), the bullpen magic of Hugh Casey, and a couple of 20-plus game winners in Whit Wyatt and Kirby Higbe were enough to prevail. It was their first pennant in 21 years, and it came at a heavy price. According to the *Sporting News*:

> The Dodgers went into the series tired physically and frazzled mentally. They had taken part in the longest two-club race in the history of the majors. They took the lead on April 28th, lost it in the middle of June. . . . In fact, the Dodgers took first place no fewer than ten times. At no stage of the race was either club more than four games in front.

The Dodgers were led by former Yankee Leo "the Lip" Durocher, who had been with the Yankees for the championship in 1928. A slick-fielding shortstop, Durocher was as known for his brash manner as for his glove. In his short time with the Yankees, Durocher clashed with Babe Ruth, who accused him of stealing from him. Durocher was ill-liked enough in the Bronx that they traded him in 1930 to the Reds for a marginal utility man who never even reported to the Yankees. By 1933 Durocher was with the "Gashouse Gang" Cardinals and found his niche among them as a tough-talking, gritty leader.

In 1939 he had come to the Dodgers, and in 1940 player-managed them into second place, finally reaching the top of the heap in 1941, where the Yankees were waiting for him.

The first three games of the Series were one-run affairs. The Yankees, with almost a full month to set up their pitching rotation, went with veteran Red Ruffing in the first game, while the Dodgers countered with 38-year-old journeyman Curt Davis. Davis threw a sidearm sinker and was fairly effective, allowing the Yankees only two runs over five innings. With the score 2–1 in their favor, the Yankees chased Davis in the sixth on a one-out walk and two singles, bringing bullpen ace Hugh Casey into the game. The Bombers were scoreless after that, and the Dodgers scratched a run in the seventh, but the Yankees held on to win, 3–2.

The next day the Dodgers turned the same trick, as Whit Wyatt pitched the complete game and won, 3–2, while Spud Chandler was chased in the sixth. And in the third game, with the Series moving to Ebbets Field, Marius Russo faced Freddie Fitzsimmons. Russo had won 14 games for the Yankees that year. A lefty who induced a lot of ground balls, he was a good choice to pitch in the hitter-friendly bandbox that was Ebbets Field.

Fitzsimmons for his part kept the Yankees baffled by a knuckleball, allowing only four scattered hits, but found himself knocked out of the game just the same, by Russo, of all people. With two out in the seventh and the game still scoreless, Russo hit a line drive that whacked Fitzsimmons in the left knee. The ball kangarooed and was caught for a pop out, but Freddie's kneecap was broken. His day, and his season, were over.

This time Casey could not hold them, and the Yankees scored two in the eighth. Brooklyn got one off Russo in the bottom of the inning, but ended the game 2–1 losers.

If this pattern kept up, game four would go to the Dodgers by one run, and that is almost what happened that sweltering October afternoon. Almost. "Though the meteorological records may still contend that this was the brightest, sunniest, warmest day in world series history, it was easily the darkest hour that Flatbush has ever known," wrote John Drebinger on the front page of the *New York Times*.

This time the Dodgers had their other 20-game-winner on the mound, Kirby Higbe. Higbe had won 14 games and led the league in strikeouts (137) for the last-place Philadelphia Phillies in 1940, and both the Dodgers and the Giants had wanted him. The Dodgers landed the hard thrower, who appeared in 48 games, 39 starts in Brooklyn's 1941 drive to the pennant. The Yankees countered with their number four, Atley Donald. Donald had come up to the Yankees in 1939 and won 12 games in a row as a rookie, racking up a 13–3 record. But he was never an ace for them.

Higbe took the hill and got Johnny Sturm out on a grounder to short. But Red Rolfe singled to left. Tommy Henrich flied out, but Rolfe advanced to second when Joe DiMaggio walked. Many people wonder why DiMaggio's greatest World Series was his first. One answer is that thereafter, managers in October often opted to pitch around him. The base on balls hurt as Charlie Keller cashed Rolfe in with a base hit to make it 1–0 Yankees.

The trouble for Higbe began in the fourth. Keller doubled to center and Bill Dickey drew a walk. Joe "Flash" Gordon dropped a single to left, loading the bases. Up came Phil Rizzuto, capping his outstanding rookie year with his first World Series. Unfortunately in this instance, he grounded into a force play, and Keller was out at home. Then Donald struck out on three pitches and it looked like Higbe might escape the jam, but Sturm lined a single to center, scoring Dickey and Gordon and moving Rizzuto to second. Higbe's day was done. Larry French replaced him on the mound and had one of the easiest relief outings in history. Both runners tried to advance on a passed ball. Catcher Mickey Owen was able to recover the ball in time to catch the Scooter, ending the inning with the Yankees up, 3–0.

Donald could not bear the charity of the three-run lead. With two out in the bottom of the inning he walked Mickey Owen and Pete Coscarart. French was lifted for pinch hitter Jimmy Wasdell, who smashed the ball down the left-field line. While Keller dug it out of the corner, both runners scored. Donald induced a grounder from Reese to end the inning, but Brooklyn had edged back to 3–2.

In the fifth, Johnny Allen took the mound for the Brooks. Rolfe flied out, but Henrich was hit by pitch. DiMaggio hit a liner to left that was caught. Keller then managed a single off the leg of Coscarart, and Bill Dickey walked to load the bases. Durocher went to Casey, who induced an easy fly ball from Joe Gordon to end the threat, giving Brooklyn a chance to grab the momentum.

They did. Dixie Walker doubled off Donald, and Pete "Hard to Beat" Reiser hit a two-run homer to end Donald's day. Marv Breuer came in, but the Dodgers had taken a 4–3 lead, which they held right up until there were two outs in the ninth inning and Tommy Henrich at the plate. Play-by-play announcer Mel Allen had nicknamed him "Old Reliable" for his clutch hitting, but in this case it was quick thinking that distinguished Henrich.

Casey was still on the mound for the Dodgers, and Henrich worked the count full. "Dodger fans were

Thomas David "Tommy" Henrich

poised on their chairs to give their joyous yell of victory," according to the *Sporting News*. "Then the pitcher broke off one of the strangest curves ever thrown. It fooled not only Henrich, but Owen as well." Some observers thought it might have been a spitball. "The curve broke very low and far on the inside and Henrich swung feet away from the ball. Had he taken it, he would have walked."

Henrich himself described it this way: "It was a bad pitch, that three-and-two pitch. It came up nice and it looked good and I went for it. But when I started to swing I saw it going to break badly away from me and down. But I was going through with my swing. I couldn't stop it." He swung, missed, but with the wicked break on the ball, it tipped off Owen's glove and rolled behind him, toward the first-base dugout. Henrich had turned his head to see the umpire's arm signal strike and saw the ball go free. Police were already storming the field. Henrich took off for first and made it easily while Owen scrambled for the ball. It was the crack in the door that Yankee teams throughout the ages always seem to exploit. Rud Rennie in the *New York Herald Tribune* called it "a tribute to the tenacity and skill of the Yankees when the chips are down. Once again . . . they demonstrated that they are all over an opponent, crushing him if he makes a mistake."

Next came Joe DiMaggio, the nation's hero of that summer for his 56-game hitting streak. Casey got two strikes on him as well, only to have the Yankee Clipper single to left. Even then the Brooks could have escaped, if only Casey had been able to close the door on Keller. He had him down 0–2, but then left one right in the middle of the plate, and Keller crushed it for a double off the right-field wall. The Yankees had taken the lead, but they were not done with the undone Casey. Bill Dickey walked, and Joe Gordon doubled for another two runs.

"It was the break of the game," McCarthy told the *Times*. "They get 'em and we get 'em. They may come in the first inning or the third. Or they may come as this one did, right at the finish."

So a game that the Dodgers had won, that should have been over already, went to another half inning. "In Brooklyn's half of the ninth, three stunned athletes went out meekly, in order," read the front-page story in the *Sporting News*. Two miracles in one day were not forthcoming. The Yankees had snatched the game, 7–4, and turned the Series around. Instead of a 2–2 tie, the lead was now in the Bombers' favor, up three games to one. Few people believed the Dodgers could win three straight after that. Tiny Bonham and his forkball allowed the Dodgers only four hits as they went down in game five, 3–1, and the Yankees brought home their ninth World Series trophy.

Extra Innings

* Hugh Casey, whose wild pitch may or may not have been a spitball, was a hard-drinking loner who became friends with Ernest Hemingway. Urban legend has it that Casey never got over the 1941 Series, and he committed suicide in 1951. (A more likely cause of his distress was the breakup of his marriage.)

October 3, 1947: New York at Brooklyn

Almost Immortal

In which Floyd "Bill" Bevens needs one more out

The 1947 World Series must be rated among the greatest of all the Fall Classics. The presence of Jackie Robinson in the Brooklyn lineup made it a historic occasion to begin with, but any World Series that goes to seven games provides ample twists of fate, moments of heroism, and nail-biting excitement for the fans. Some experts expected the Yankees to maul the Dodgers, and after the Bombers won the first two games, the predictions looked to be right. But in game three Brooklyn roared back. Rookie Yogi Berra pinch-hit a homer in the

Floyd Clifford "Bill" Bevens

game—an auspicious start to a lengthy career as a World Series hero—but the Dodgers squeaked out a rapturous 9–8 win.

Game four, though, stands out above even the final and deciding game for excitement and drama. "A demented Hollywood scenarist . . . wouldn't have dared produce a script as utterly fantastic as the stark drama which was unfolded before the eyes of the Flatbush faithful at Ebbets Field yesterday," wrote an incredulous Arthur Daley in the *New York Times*, reporting that another denizen of the press box had remarked to him, "Don't bother writing about it, because no one will believe you anyway."

In 1947 the Yankees had not made a World Series appearance in four years, and Bucky Harris, managing the team for the first time, found himself relying on a pitching staff significantly different from the 1943 champions. Allie Reynolds and Frank "Spec" Shea were the mainstays of the rotation, with Vic Raschi, Spud Chandler, and former Dodger Bobo Newsom filling in most of the other starts. And then there was Floyd Clifford "Bill" Bevens.

Bevens matched Shea with 23 games started that year, second only to Reynolds, who had 30. But of the 17 men who pitched for the Yankees in 1947, Bevens was the only one with a losing record. He was 7–13 with a 3.82 ERA. The native of Hubbard, Oregon, had bumped around the minors for years before making the Yankees at age 27 in 1944, when the talent pool was thinned by the war. In '47 he had eaten up innings after Chandler had gotten injured, and found himself on the World Series roster.

And starting in game four. Bevens was a husky righthander who was known for control problems. On this day, he was so wild that the Dodgers were kept off-balance. In this way, the wildness contributed to two World Series records Bevens set that day: one was for most walks issued by a pitcher in a World Series game (10), and one for most consecutive innings pitched without a hit. Previously, Charley "Red" Ruffing held the mark of 7⅔ hitless frames. Bevens would top that, but when he took the hill the Yankees figured their strategy should be to jump on the Dodgers early and hope to get the ball to bullpen ace

Joe Page deep in the game. Page had pitched three innings the day before, and Harris hoped if he was needed, it would be for just a few outs.

The Dodgers' number four starter was another journeyman, Harry Taylor, and the Yankees felt they could hit him at will. Snuffy Stirnweiss started the game off with a hit off Taylor, followed by one from Tommy Henrich. Taylor induced a grounder off the bat of Berra then, right to first baseman Robinson for what could have been a 3-6-3 double play. But Pee Wee Reese bobbled it on the pivot, loading the bases without recording an out. Taylor, never a control pitcher at the best of times, then forced in a run when DiMaggio drew a walk. That was enough for Burt Shotton, who was serving as interim manager of the Dodgers for a year while Leo Durocher was suspended for "conduct detrimental to baseball." (In addition to scandals involving suspicion of gambling, inappropriate relations with a divorcee, and other unsavory topics, Durocher's most damning crime may have been attacking the Yankees in the newspapers that spring after one of his coaches had been lured away.) Shotton pulled Taylor and called on Hal Gregg, who induced a pop-up and a 6-4-3 double play to get out of the inning.

Bevens, meanwhile, was wild, issuing walks to Eddie Stanky, Dixie Walker, and Spider Jorgensen in the first two innings, but he managed to escape without trouble. Bevens "held the bats of Brooklyn's Bums even more silent than a tomb," wrote John Drebinger in the *Times*. The Yankees pressured Gregg in the third but failed to capitalize on the scoring opportunity. DiMaggio had walked, and then George McQuinn hit a dribbler that didn't even reach the mound. He advanced all the way to second as Bruce Edwards jumped out from behind the plate and threw wildly. Yankee third-base coach Charlie Dressen waved DiMaggio home, but right fielder Walker had recovered the ball and DiMag was out by 15 feet. In the fourth Billy Johnson tripled and Johnny Lindell followed with an RBI double, but that would be all the Yankees would get off Gregg.

Up 2–0, Bevens's control did not improve. In the fifth he walked Jorgensen, and then even issued a free pass to the opposing pitcher. Stanky sacrificed the men over, and Jorgensen came in to score on a ground out. The Dodgers were on the board without the benefit of a hit.

The score still stood at 2–1 when Bevens sat the Dodgers down one-two-three in the eighth, surpassing Ruffing's old record for hitless ball in a World Series game. In the top of the ninth, the Yankees looked to pad their lead. Lindell singled, then was forced at second as Phil Rizzuto reached. Bevens came to the plate and laid down a bunt. Edwards tried to nip the Scooter but was not in time, and both men were safe. Stirnweiss then served a hit into center, loading the bases. Shotton went to a face the Yankees knew well, Hugh Casey, the man who had thrown strike three to Tommy Henrich in 1941 only to lose the game when the ball squirted away from catcher Mickey Owen. And who would be at the plate waiting for Casey? Henrich, of course.

This time Casey had his revenge. On his first pitch, he threw a low curve that Henrich smashed right back at him on the ground. Casey snared the ball, tossed to Edwards for the force at home, who threw to Robinson at first to complete the double play. The Yankees' fate was in Bill Bevens's big hands.

Edwards stepped in to lead off the ninth and walloped a long fly off Bevens. The ball carried deep into left field, but Lindell caught it against the wall. Bevens then walked Carl Furillo, his ninth walk of the game. Jorgensen popped a ball foul to first, and Bevens found himself one out away from pitching the first no-hitter in a World Series. Shotton sent Al Gionfriddo to pinch-run for Furillo. With the pitcher's spot coming up next, Shotton replaced Casey with slugger Pete Reiser.

Reiser had bloomed with the Dodgers in 1941, hitting .343 and becoming the youngest man to wear the National League batting crown. But he played the outfield recklessly, crashing into then-unpadded walls and landing, more often than not, on the disabled list. In 1947 he had such a violent collision with the center-field wall at Ebbets Field that he was given last rites. Now here he was in October, his ankle still too swollen to run on, but ready to mash.

Reiser had a 2–1 count when Gionfriddo broke for second, spinning his wheels for a moment before he got solid footing. Berra whipped a waist-high throw to Rizzuto, who slapped the tag onto Gionfriddo's head-first slide. Umpire Bill McGowan called him safe. Bevens faced Reiser now with a man in scoring position and the count 3–1. With first base open, Harris bucked baseball wisdom and decided to put the winning run on, signaling Bevens to walk Reiser.

Who knows? Maybe with Bevens as wild as he was, a walk would have been the outcome anyway. Or if Bevens had put one right down Broadway, maybe Reiser would have smashed a game-winning two-run shot. We'll never know. Reiser limped to first and was replaced with another pinch runner, Eddie Miksis.

Bevens still needed only one more out for the win and immortality. Stanky was due next. But Shotton was emptying his gun, and he called Stanky back in favor of Harry "Cookie" Lavagetto. Lavagetto was no obvious advantage over Stanky, both right-handed veterans and both pull hitters. He swung and missed Bevens's first offering, his 136th pitch, on the inside part of the plate. Bevens then went away with the next pitch, high and away. Lavagetto swung late and inside-outed the ball to right field where Henrich, playing him to pull, was shaded toward center. The race was on, as "the two most obscure pinch-runners ever to make world series history" (*New York Times*) were off with the crack of the bat. "Old Reliable" ran back to the wall where just the previous inning he had snared a smash similar to this one off the bat of Gene Hermanski. If he could catch this one, the Yankees would win the game and the no-hitter would be preserved. If he played the carom off the wall, it would be a hit, but . . . Henrich leaped, trying to snare the ball flying over his head, but could not make the grab. The ball bounced off the wall, then off Henrich's chest, and by the time he could gather it up, Gionfriddo and Miksis had crossed the plate.

The Dodgers had won the game, 3–2, on that solitary hit. LAVAGETTO'S CLIMAX LEAVES 33,443 LIMP IN MOST DRAMATIC WORLD SERIES GAME read the headline in the *New York Herald Tribune*. "Cold print cannot do justice to what went on," wrote Al Laney in the accompanying story. "It will be preserved in the memories of all who were there . . . they will be telling others less fortunate about it as long as they live."

"You know," Pee Wee Reese remarked about Bevens after the game, "I feel sorry for that guy."

"I wasn't even thinking of the no-hitter," Bevens told reporters after they were finally allowed into the clubhouse after a twenty-minute lockout. "I knew it was riding but never mind about that. I'm trying to win. Those bases on balls sure kill you."

The Yankees eventually prevailed in seven games. Bill Bevens never started another major-league game. The following year he hurt his shoulder during spring training and never recovered enough to make the roster. After several months of rehab and an unsuccessful stint with the Yankees' AAA farm team the Newark Bears, Bevens tried his hand with the Pacific Coast League and the Texas League, but the shoulder would not respond. He eventually settled back near his hometown in Salem, Oregon, went to work for Sears, Roebuck, and was last seen playing first base with the City League softball team the Campbell Rock Woolers.

Extra Innings

- In 1947 Bruce "Bull" Edwards had led all National League catchers in putouts and double plays. He also was involved in one of the most curious defensive plays of the year, when on July 20 Ron Northey of the Cardinals hit a long fly ball that bounced off a railing and back onto the field of play. Umpire Beans Reardon ruled it a home run, but when Northey arrived at home plate, he found Edwards there with the ball, and home plate ump Jocko Conlon called Northey out. The Cardinals, who ended up losing, 3–2, protested the game. National League President Ford Frick ruled that the game should be replayed. The Dodgers won the replay as well.

- Two other pitchers had thrown one-hitters in the World Series before Bevens's defeat. Ed Reulbach of the Cubs did it in 1906, and Claude Passeau, also for the Cubs, in 1945. They were both victories.

- Red Smith produced this humorous end to his column in the *New York Herald Tribune* after the game. "The unhappiest man in Brooklyn is sitting up here now in the far end of the press box. The 'V' on his typewriter is broken. He can't write either Lavagetto or Bevens."

May 20, 1948: New York at Chicago

Jolt from the Blue

In which, 11 years later, Joe D. repeats a feat

By 1948, Joe DiMaggio had accomplished many hitting feats worthy of the record books in his career. In 1936, when DiMaggio was just a rookie, he became the fifth major-league player to hit two home runs in one inning. In 1937, he hit for the cycle against the Washington Senators. In 1938, he became the third Yankee to hit three triples in one game. And in 1941, he accomplished one of the most memorable and lauded feats of all, hitting in 56 consecutive games. But he lost three years of playing time to military service beginning in 1943. Any questions about whether he could still play at the highest level after his time off were assuaged in 1947, the year he won his third MVP award, edging Ted Williams by one point. And then in 1948, the Yankee Clipper added another line to his Hall of Fame résumé.

On May 20, 5,001 dispirited White Sox fans paid two dollars each or less to come to old Comiskey Park and watch the last-place Sox lose. Chicago had lost every game they had played at Comiskey in the young season and were 4–18. Manager Ted Lyons tapped pitcher Orval Grove to take the mound against the Bronx Bombers. Grove had showed promise early in his career—he was one of the earliest products of the White Sox farm system and won his first nine decisions as a rookie in 1943. On July 8 of that year he had faced the Yankees and carried a no-hitter into the ninth inning, only to have it broken up by Joe Gordon. But by 1948, Grove was not at the top of his form. The previous year, his ERA had ballooned to 4.44, but when he beat the Browns in a complete-game start on April 25—the only White Sox pitcher to go the complete nine thus far in the season—Lyons hoped the righthander might be putting together a good season.

A vain hope. The Yankees came to the park that afternoon ready to mash. They had Vic Raschi, the Springfield Rifle, on the hill, but before Raschi could even take the mound, it looked like the Sox might be in for a long day. Grove started the game by walking Bobby Brown. Charlie Keller came up and hit a roller that should have been a 1-4-3 double play. Grove threw the ball away, and DiMaggio made him pay with a three-run home run.

In the second it was not much better. Raschi, Brown, and Keller hit consecutive singles for another run, giving them a 4–0 lead. In the top of the fourth, Keller walloped a ball to deep center, but Dave Philley snared it in one hand just before the flagpole—a loud out but indicative of things to come. DiMaggio singled in the third but was stranded.

Apparently Raschi didn't know what to do with his easy lead, and in the fourth inning suffered a strange bout of wildness, walking four men in the inning, the final one forcing a man home. But Johnny Lindell made a shoestring catch off of Taffy Wright, and Billy Johnson started a double play with Cass Michael's grounder to get Raschi out of the inning.

DiMaggio faced Grove in the fifth with the bases empty and sent another ball soaring into the upper stands in left field for a 5–1 Yankee lead. Lyons let Grove finish the inning, but having given up five runs and nine hits, he sent him to the showers.

Fred Bradley came on to pitch the sixth, but Raschi and Lindell singled and Keller walked. DiMaggio tripled to bring all three men in, his fourth hit of the day. Earl Harrist came on for Bradley but gave up a double to Yogi Berra, scoring DiMaggio with the fourth and final run of the inning before escaping further trouble.

In the ninth the Yankees were at it again, this time against pitcher Earl Caldwell. Bobby Brown singled, Cliff Mapes doubled, and Lindell knocked a two-run homer. DiMaggio collected the final piece of his day's hitting collection, a double, and crossed the plate himself for the fourth time when Johnson did the same. Four more runs had crossed the plate before Ike Pearson, the only White Sox pitcher not to be touched by the Bombers, put a merciful end to the slaughter, 13–2. Rud Rennie summed it up in the *New York Herald Tribune* with "Joe had his best day of the year with that big bat of his."

When all was said and done, not only had Joe hit for the cycle for the second time in his career, but also the Yankees had banged out 22 hits for a total of 38 bases. James P. Dawson of the *New York Times* called it "the greatest batting day Joe DiMaggio has enjoyed since pre-war times." And to think Joltin' Joe would have gone 6-for-6 if in the eighth inning Ralph Hodgin had not been able to pull in a ball with his back against the outfield fence.

The next day the Yankees were shut out by the White Sox' Bill Wight, 3–0, but DiMaggio's hot streak carried over into Cleveland, where on May 23 he hit three home runs in three successive trips to the plate, giving him six homers in four days. Joe had hit three homers in a game once before, in 1937. "To turn a trick like that after an interval of eleven seasons, three lost from baseball in the Army, was a monumental achievement," wrote Dan Daniel in the *Sporting News*. "But then, Joseph Paul DiMaggio is a monumental ball player."

Extra Innings

- It was an unlucky day for pitchers throughout the majors. Not only did the Yankees win by a score of 13–2, but also the Indians beat the Red Sox, 13–4, the Cardinals overcame the Dodgers, 13–4, and the Pirates downed the Braves, 13–0.

- The only Yankee who did not record a hit in the 22-hit attack was George Stirnweiss.

- DiMaggio became the third Yankee to hit three triples in a game on August 27, 1938. The other two were Hal Chase (August 30, 1906) and Earle Combs (September 22, 1927).

19

October 2, 1949: Boston at New York

To the Wire

In which Boston needs to win only one of two for a pennant

On Saturday, October 1, 1949, the *Boston Herald's* front-page headline read SOX SEND PARNELL TO CLINCH FLAG TODAY. This bold proclamation superseded the news of a strike of more than half a million steelworkers, but the fate of the

Joseph Paul DiMaggio

Red Sox has ever been of prime concern in Beantown. SERIES TICKETS ON SALE TOMORROW IF SOX WIN said a small story on the same front page. These were the Red Sox of Ted Williams, Dom DiMaggio, Johnny Pesky, and Bobby Doerr in their prime. In 1949 Teddy Ballgame led the league in most offensive categories: walks (162), home runs (43), runs scored (150), on-base percentage (.490), and doubles (39). George Kell of the Detroit Tigers edged him by mere percentage points for the batting title (.34291 for Kell, .34276 for Williams), preventing the greatest hitter who ever lived from winning his third Triple Crown. What might have been different if Williams had mustered one more hit on the final day of the 1949 season?

To truly appreciate the drama of the finale of 1949, let us turn the clock back to the close of 1948. Pennant fever had run hot in Cleveland, New York, and Boston, with all three clubs in striking distance entering the final week. With two games left to play, Boston triumphed over New York, knocking the Yankees from the race. On the final day, if Cleveland lost and Boston won, the Sox and Indians would meet in a one-game playoff. That morning, brothers Dominic and Joseph DiMaggio arrived at Fenway together from Dom's Boston-area home. Elder brother Joe reportedly told Dom that he personally would ensure that the Red Sox did not get the chance.

Joltin' Joe almost made good on his promise, but the real battle was not between brothers but between Joe and Teddy, the two brightest stars in their respective constellations. On that day DiMaggio went 4-for-5, but the score stood 10–5 in the Red Sox favor in the ninth, thanks in large part to Williams, who reached base in eight of his final 10 plate appearances.

But in the one-game playoff against Cleveland, onetime Yankee manager Joe McCarthy, now leading the Red Sox, chose Denny Galehouse as his starter, a decision that baffled both teams. Galehouse had been kept warm in the bullpen the day before, thanks to DiMaggio and the constant Yankee offensive threat, and was gassed. Four innings and two home runs over the Green Monster later, with the score 4–0, Galehouse left the game. The Sox were unable to rally much, losing, 8–3. So close . . .

And yet they had beaten the Yankees in the standings. The loss precipitated changes in New York, the acquisition of a new manager, Casey Stengel, being the prime one. Many baseball observers considered Stengel, previously the manager of two weak National League teams, a buffoon, and the Boston papers crowed that his hiring was surely the nail in the Yankees' coffin. "He was a little tense to start with," recalled Tommy Byrne, a lefthander Stengel would later come to rely on in his tenure. "There was pressure for him, and the fact that he wanted to get in the act and get the Yankees going again."

The spring of the 1949 season began chilly, at least concerning the relationship between Stengel and his biggest star. DiMag had just signed baseball's first ever six-figure contract, $100,000 for the year, and was confident that the bone spur in his heel was fine. He was wrong. Joe had to miss spring training and several months of the regular season. The front office had not done much else to shore up the club in the winter. The season opened with the dedication of a monument to Babe Ruth in center field, joining those of Lou Gehrig and Miller Huggins. With DiMaggio out and the aforementioned heroes long passed, Casey quickly realized that he would have to judiciously shuffle the fading stars, rookies, and fill-ins on his bench to create winning situations.

Platooning worked. That and a strong starting rotation of Vic Raschi, Allie Reynolds, Tommy Byrne, and Eddie Lopat helped the team jump out of the gate to a 10–2 start. Two months into the season they were 25–12, but as the weather heats up, so—tradition has it—do the Red Sox. The Sox surged in June, only five games back when the Yankees visited Fenway at the end of the month.

Joe DiMaggio returned to the lineup just in time to face Ted, Dom, and companions. The recovery time had done him good. He was a wrecking crew against Boston, knocking in the crucial runs in the first game, notching a pair of home runs in a 9–7 comeback victory (after the Yankees had trailed 7–1), and another the next day to seal the three-game sweep.

Boston was on the ropes but bounced back. They crept up on the injury-ridden Yankees in July and August, and both teams entered September with 77 wins, the Sox behind by two as the Yankees had played and lost four fewer games. The Yankees might have run away with it, but a late-season acquisition, the power-hitting "Big Cat" Johnny Mize, hurt his shoulder, and DiMaggio contracted pneumonia. The Red Sox pounced while DiMag was on bed rest, sweeping three games from the Yankees at the end of the month and grabbing a one-game lead with only five games left to play. "Rudely jarred out of first place . . . a post they had held tenaciously in spite of heart-breaking adversity since Opening Day, the Bronx Bombers apparently had shot their bolt," wrote Arthur Daley in the *New York Times*.

The Sox held a piece of first place through September 30, squeaking out a win from the Washington Senators, 11–9, by escaping a bases-loaded situation in the ninth with a game-ending double play. The Yankees had already lost to the A's earlier in the day in a game where DiMaggio had been too weak to play. The Associated Press reported the Yankee clubhouse was a gloomy place after the loss. Only Stengel reserved some optimism. "[The loss] gave me a chance to save Joe Page in case we need him," Stengel said of his bullpen ace, adding, "I feel that now we're going to go out and beat the tar out of the Red Sox tomorrow and Sunday." Whitney Martin, a skeptical Associated Press reporter, observed that "[Casey's] face didn't quite reflect the optimistic words."

And so it was that the *Herald* felt confident that the Sox would take a game from the ailing Yankees and clinch on the first of October. With two games remaining, both at Yankee Stadium, the Olde Towne Team would have to win only one to bring the pennant to Boston. Imagine the glee in every Boston rooter's heart when during the "Joe DiMaggio Day" celebration that took place prior to the game, brother Dom had to help Joe stay upright through the cercmony. The Yankees had planned the promotion months before, when they thought the pennant race would be over and they would need something special to bring the fans to a "meaningless" game. Joe gave a speech that ended with a quote that today hangs on a sign in the runway from the Yankee clubhouse to the field: "I'd like to thank the Good Lord for making me a Yankee." Then, weak but indomitable, Joe took his place in center.

The American League, realizing the importance of the game, tapped six umpires for the day. McCarthy put Mel Parnell on the hill for the Sox, with Ellis Kinder slated to pitch the following day. Some would say either of those two pitchers should have had the start the previous year, in the 1948 one-game playoff against the Indians. The question of how each would fare in 1949 against the Yankees, though, was a different matter.

Stengel for his part tapped "Superchief" Allie Reynolds, who had come to the Yankees after the 1946 season ended, when DiMaggio had urged the front office to get him instead of Red Embree. With Parnell the 25-game winner, and Reynolds the hard-throwing one of four "aces," one might anticipate a pitchers' duel.

Reynolds could not meet that expectation; his control was absent from the start. In the first inning, Dominic DiMaggio (perhaps thinking about his brother's comments of the year before) got the action started with a single. He was forced at second as Pesky hit a comebacker, but broke up the double play with a hard slide into Phil Rizzuto. Ted Williams's base knock moved Pesky to second. The hit might have been a double and scored Pesky, but Tommy Henrich at first grazed it with his glove, deflecting the ball just enough so it hit umpire Cal Hubbard in the leg. Reynolds himself moved them up with a wild pitch, and Pesky came in to score on a sacrifice fly by Vern Stephens. Reynolds was wild again, moving Williams to third, but caught Bobby Doerr looking at strike three. 1–0 Sox.

The Yankees tried to answer in their half of the inning. Phil Rizzuto led off with a walk, and stood on third after Tommy Henrich and Yogi Berra grounded out. Joe DiMaggio came to the plate. And struck out.

In the second Reynolds seemed to right himself partly, though he issued a walk to Birdie Tebbetts. He faced pitcher Parnell with two outs and struck him out. Parnell answered with three quick outs, allowing only a base hit to Johnny Lindell.

Superchief went haywire thereafter. Though Dominic flied out to open the third, Reynolds walked Pesky, Williams, and Stephens in succession. Doerr dropped a single into right field, scoring Pesky and keeping the bags full. Stengel had seen enough and his words uttered in Philadelphia after the loss there proved prophetic. Down 2–0, Reynolds gave way to Joe Page.

"Lefty Joe" had been with the Yankees since 1944 and was another Yankee who had history with Joe McCarthy. McCarthy, who had led New York to seven pennants, is the manager credited with creating the dynastic Yankee image we know so well today. The freewheeling Murderers' Row teams of Ruth in the late 1920s were transformed into the professional, businesslike champions of 1936–1939 under McCarthy's leadership. When he had arrived in 1931, "Marse Joe" took the reins at a time when Ruth himself had openly campaigned for the managerial post. He expected his players to practice; work hard, and the wins would follow. This approach did not sit well with the veterans at first, but as the men of Ruth's era moved on, McCarthy was able to put his stamp on the team. He also preached that a team should score more runs in the ninth inning than any other inning, an attitude that made late-inning lightning seem like an act of will. But by 1945 new general manager Larry MacPhail felt Marse Joe had overstayed his welcome. After McCarthy got into a shouting match with Joe Page on a team flight, MacPhail fired the manager, who landed at the helm of the Red Sox.

Page was a relief specialist whose success helped convince other managers that having a bullpen ace or two was the wave of the future. He won 14 games in relief in 1947 (an American League record until 1961, when Yankee Luis Arroyo broke it), and in 1949 recorded 27 saves. (At the time the "save" was not a recorded statistic, but if the numbers had been kept in 1949, Page's 27 would have been the American League record until 1961 as well. The save became an official statistic in 1969.) For Stengel, who had no qualms about platooning or pulling a starter, Page was money in the bank. Down by two runs, if Page could hold them, if he could escape bases loaded, the Yankees had a chance.

To the exasperation of the Bronx faithful, Page walked the first man he faced, Al Zarilla, forcing in a run. It got worse. Page walked Billy Goodman for one more. The Red Sox were up four runs and there was still only one out in the third, sacks full. The Red Sox wives, who had been waiting for the word in Boston, boarded a train bound for the victory celebration in New York.

But then the wind of fate stopped blowing the ball wide of the strike zone. Page struck out Birdie Tebbetts and got Parnell looking. Then he led off the bottom of the inning with a single and Rizzuto, one of the best bunters in the modern era, sacrificed him to second. Tommy Henrich walked and the Yankees might have had something cooking if Yogi Berra had not ground into a double play.

Page set DiMaggio, Pesky, and Williams down in order in the fourth, bringing the pneumonic Joe D. to the plate. He popped a fly to right that hit just fair and bounced over the wall for a ground-rule double. The providential hit was enough to begin a rally. Two batters later DiMag came in to score on a Hank Bauer single. Then Johnny Lindell got his second hit of the day off Parnell, moving Bauer to third. Second baseman Jerry Coleman contributed a sac fly for the second run of the inning. Page was called out on strikes to end the rally, but the Sox lead had been halved.

Vern Stephens led off the fifth with the Red Sox' sixth walk of the game, but was quickly erased on a double play turned by Rizzuto and Coleman. It had been Stengel's idea to turn Coleman into a second baseman, and he was rewarded with one of the great double-play combinations of the era. Page then hit Zarilla with a pitch, but with two outs Goodman tried to bunt for a hit and was thrown out.

The Yankees got back to work. Rizzuto and Henrich started off with back-to-back singles, putting men on the corners. Then Berra followed suit with a single through the box, bringing home the Scooter and moving Henrich to second. McCarthy had seen enough of Parnell. Joe Dobson came out of the bullpen to face DiMaggio.

By now the astute reader will have come to expect something great of Joltin' Joe. What you get is the next best thing, a hopper in front of the mound that bounced off Dobson's glove and went for a hit, loading the bases with no one out. Billy Johnson, whose rough day at the plate (two previous strikeouts) then worsened, grounded into a double play, but brought in the tying run. Hank Bauer flew out, stranding Berra with the score 4–4 and three innings to play.

Page had hit his stride, and sat the Red Sox down in order in the sixth and seventh. A leadoff single from Bobby Doerr in the eighth went for naught as Zarilla popped up a bunt that Yogi caught, and Goodman hit into a 6-6-3 double play.

The Yankees for their part couldn't break through against Dobson, either. In the eighth, Stengel sent Bobby Brown to bat for Johnson, whose double-play ball had brought in the tying run. Brown wasn't much better, flying out. Stengel sent Cliff Mapes in to bat for Bauer and he grounded out. So up came Johnny Lindell.

Lindell had started out as a pitcher when he had come to the Yankees in 1942, a knuckleballer with a substandard fastball. Joe McCarthy had converted him to the outfield during his managerial stint with the Yankees and by 1944 Lindell was hitting .300 with 18 home runs. In 1948 he had hit .317 with 13 home runs, but in 1949 his offensive production had dropped off. His average was below .250 and he'd hit only five dingers. The last one had been two months before.

Dobson served him a high fastball. "It wasn't a bad pitch," wrote Arthur Sampson in the *Herald*. "Dobson put the ball just where he wanted to, and has frequently retired Lindell on a similar pitch." This time Lindell pulled it, and buried it deep in the left-field seats beyond the foul pole. 5–4 Yankees. It was all they would get as Coleman singled but Casey elected to let Page bat for himself. Page struck out, but the Red Sox had the eight, nine, and one hitters coming up. To that point Page had pitched nearly six innings of scoreless relief, and Casey left him to finish the job. Page did not fool around. He caught Birdie Tebbetts looking. Matt Batts, whose name must have destined him to be a ballplayer, then pinch-hit for Dobson, only to ground to Rizzuto. Then came Dom DiMaggio, who suffered the same fate. The Yankees had spoiled the Red Sox plans for one more day, and opened the door for themselves.

Lindell, who ended the day with three hits, including the game-winner, told reporters, "The whole thing is Joe McCarthy's fault anyway," referring to his conversion to the outfield. "Today the shift paid off." Eddie Lopat kidded him mercilessly. "That home run you hit would have been caught in Boston."

"Yeah, in the street," Lindell replied.

Meanwhile, Joe DiMaggio had gone 2-for-4 on lucky hits that made the difference in the game. Ted Williams, on the other hand, had the other end of the stick—his line shot that struck an umpire was his only hit of the day.

And so the clubs faced each other again on October 2, tied for the lead. "Unless they . . . deliver a few long timely clouts, [the Red Sox may] have the dubious distinction of being the first major league club in history to lose two successive pennants on the final game of the season," Sampson reported morosely in the *Herald*.

He was prophetic. Two twenty-plus-game winners, Vic Raschi and Ellis Kinder, faced off. The 35-year-old Kinder had bounced up and down the major and minor leagues for years, but had finally bloomed under McCarthy. "Suddenly, this season, in the twilight of a dim career, he has become one of baseball's best," wrote Grantland Rice prior to the two-game set. Harold Kaese praised Kinder in the *Boston Sunday Globe*, saying "the one Red Sox player with the best chance to [sink the Yankees], is the season's most astonishing performer—Ellis Kinder." Kinder had won 23 games and lost 6 that season, with 6 shutouts.

But New Yorkers had just as much confidence in Vic Raschi. "For blocks around Yankee Stadium . . . before the game started there was a very special sort of carnival hum in the air," wrote Rice. Raschi, a native of Springfield, Massachusetts, was called the "Springfield Rifle" for his gun of an arm, which he flung with a sidearm motion. And Stengel knew he could call on Lopat as insurance as well.

Kinder was good on this day. In the first he went to a full count on Phil Rizzuto, and perhaps not wanting to walk the leadoff man, instead gave up a triple. The Scooter scored on a ground out by Tommy Henrich, the next batter. Otherwise Kinder held the Yankees down through seven innings. Raschi was better, holding the Red Sox scoreless and Ted Williams hitless through eight innings.

In the top of the eighth, with the Red Sox down 1–0, McCarthy lifted Kinder for a pinch hitter, to no avail. Still down by one, now he would have to hope for his offense to come to life in the ninth and turn to his bullpen for six more outs. Some would say this was the biggest difference between McCarthy and Stengel. McCarthy always depended on a core of stars for success, while

Stengel had mixed and matched, platooning and working every arm in the bullpen at times. McCarthy did not have a relief ace to depend on. Instead, he tapped Mel Parnell, the previous day's loser.

Parnell's arm was in the condition of a lasagne noodle in Mama DiMaggio's pot: cooked. Tommy Henrich homered on the second pitch he saw. Berra followed with a single, and Parnell was yanked. In came Tex Hughson, who induced DiMaggio to hit into a double play, but ultimately he did not fare much better. Lindell and Johnson singled, and Cliff Mapes walked.

With two out, the runners were off with the crack of the bat. Jerry Coleman hit a pop fly that Al Zarilla dove for in short center. The ball just eluded Zarilla, who was shaken up on the play and had to be helped back to the dugout. No one had to help the base runners to cross the plate, however, as all three came in to score. Coleman recalled the words of long-past Yankee Wee Willie Keeler to sum up his achievement: "I just hit the ball 'where they ain't.'"

Up 5–0, Raschi was three outs from the pennant. Pesky fouled out, but the Sox did not go quietly. Ted Williams, still hitless, took a walk. Stephens singled, and both men came in as Bobby Doerr tripled beyond the reach of an exhausted Joe DiMaggio. "I should have removed myself [earlier]," DiMaggio would later say, but missing Doerr's catchable fly was the last straw. The Yankee Clipper had had enough, and he benched himself, giving way to Cliff Mapes. Zarilla, his wind and wits restored after the previous inning's diving play, then batted, hitting a fly to center. Mapes made a rifle throw after the catch that held Doerr at third.

But Doerr came in on Billy Goodman's single, and the Yankee lead was cut to 5–3 with one out remaining. The tying run came to the plate. Birdie Tebbetts hit a twisty pop foul that Tommy Henrich was just able to rein in at the fence, and the game was over. The Yankees had won the pennant. Bill Dickey, by then a coach with the club, jumped up from the bench as the final out was made and whacked his head on the dugout's cement roof, the final injury in an ailment-heavy year for the Yankees.

The pennant was Stengel's first, and perhaps sweetest. "I want to thank all these players for giving me the greatest thrill of my life," he said during the raucous clubhouse celebration. Little did he know that a World Series victory would soon follow, and many more after that. Stengel was named 1949 Manager of the Year. The following year, he was New York's golden boy, while Joe McCarthy's days in Boston were numbered. He was let go midway through 1950 after missing the Father's Day game drunk. Stengel went on to lead the Yankees to five straight world titles, seven overall, with 10 pennants in his 13-year tenure.

Extra Innings

- In 1949 the Red Sox were 61–16 at home and 35–42–1 on the road.

- In 1949 the Yankees logged 71 players as ill or injured, the most in the majors that year.

- In a wild coincidence, the Dodgers also won their pennant on the final day, and the first- and second-place finishers in both leagues sported identical records: 97–57 for New York and Brooklyn, 96–58 for Boston and St. Louis.

- "Joe DiMaggio Day" turned out to be quite a family reunion. In addition to Joe and Dom who played, their mother, Rosalie, brother Tom, and Joe's son Joe Jr. were all in attendance. DiMaggio received gifts ranging from a speed-boat and a sports car to three hundred gallons of ice cream and a bicycle for his son. Seven hundred baseball fans also filled a nine-car passenger train, the "Joe DiMaggio Special," from New Haven, Connecticut, to attend the game. Ethel Merman sang in his honor. DiMaggio donated the ice cream to a children's institution and the gifts of cash he received to the New York Heart Fund and the Damon Runyon Memorial Cancer Fund.

20

July 12, 1951: New York at Cleveland

Hail to the Chief

In which Allie Reynolds twirls a gem

The Yankees spent the 1951 All-Star break with a bad taste in their mouths. They had lost five of six games going into the break, including a three-game sweep by Boston, putting them in third place behind the White Sox and Red Sox, and only two games ahead of Cleveland. Not only that, but the American League All-Stars, managed by Casey Stengel, dropped their second midsummer classic in a row, in part because of a disastrous outing by Yankee Eddie Lopat. Stengel's challenge was "revitalizing his world champion Yankees for the second half," according to John Drebinger in the *New York Times*. "To rehabilitate his pitching staff is Casey's immediate problem," Drebinger wrote. "He plans to start Allie Reynolds tomorrow night, and follow with Vic Raschi and Eddie Lopat in the next two games. Up until a few weeks ago, those three names would have sufficed to quiet any disturbing apprehension. The Big Three was functioning as about the best in the league. But that was before all three were shot down, one after the other, by the onrushing Bosox."

The first three games following the break were in Cleveland, where Reynolds would face Bob Feller. Feller had earned the nickname "Rapid Robert" for the blazing fastball he threw early in his career. Feller missed four years midcareer to a stint in the Navy, but came back strong. In 1946 he struck out 348 men, breaking Rube Waddell's record (though Waddell's total was later revised to 349), and won 26 games, one of them a no-hitter against the Yankees. As the decade drew to a close, he had some mediocre years, but in 1951 he was back on top of his game and very difficult to hit. "Feller had lost a lot of the zip in his fastballs," said Jerry Coleman, the Yankee second baseman. "He was into sliders and curveballs—he had pinpoint control. Feller was not my favorite guy to hit. I could never touch [him]." Feller had just pitched a no-hitter, the third of his career, eleven days before when the Tigers had been in town.

Allie Reynolds was not daunted by Feller, who had been his teammate on the Indians early in Reynolds's career, and whose equal he was on the mound (his fastball was sometimes estimated to reach 100 miles per hour) if not in accolades. In 1947, Reynolds's first season in New York, he led the league in winning percentage. In 1949 the hard thrower had thrown a two-hitter in the World Series to beat the Dodgers, 1–0. Stengel often used him out of the bullpen as well, allowing Reynolds to record not only 182 wins, but also 49 saves in his career. Nicknamed "Superchief" by his teammates and called "Wahoo" in the press because he was one-quarter Creek Indian, Reynolds was a mainstay in the Yankee rotation, and he took the hill on July 12 with the intention of righting the ship. "Reynolds is [a] merry pitcher," wrote Dan Daniel in the *Sporting News*. "Nothing ever really gets him down." Not the bone chips in his elbow that had curtailed his spring training, nor a nerve-wracking pitchers' duel in Cleveland.

The first five innings are easy to summarize. Nobody hit anything. Bobby Avila reached base in the first inning on what was ruled an error on shortstop Phil Rizzuto, but was erased on a double play. In the second inning, Reynolds walked two men in between outs but did not seem to struggle. Nor was he overpowering, striking out Al Rosen in the fourth (part of a strike-'em-out, throw-'em-out double play) but otherwise allowing the Indians to make contact.

Both pitchers were working on no-hitters into the sixth, with Indians fans wondering if Feller might do the unthinkable—pitch two no-hitters in one season and become the first major-league hurler to throw four no-hitters in his career. But with one out in the top of the inning, Mickey Mantle connected with a Feller pitch for a double, while Reynolds continued to cruise.

As he sat on the bench in the top of the seventh inning, Reynolds tempted fate. He turned to fellow starter Eddie Lopat on the bench and said, "Think I can pitch a no-hitter, Eddie?" Lopat did not reply, too stricken by the common superstition that mentioning the no-hitter in progress could jinx the game. Instead, luck was on the increase. Gene Woodling, usually part of Stengel's left-field platoon with Hank Bauer but playing center for an ailing Joe DiMaggio, came up with one out in the seventh. Yogi Berra had just hit a fly into right field. Woodling did him one better, sending the ball over the 365-foot marker on the wall.

Reynolds almost gave the run right back in the bottom of the seventh. Sam Chapman sent a ball into deep left field. "The ball went over the wall and a strong wind blowing in off the lake blew it right back," said Jerry Coleman. "[He] was standing at the fence and literally the wind pushed it back. We saw that ball going and thought, oh, there goes the no-hitter, but [Bauer] was standing there waiting for it." Hank Bauer, "The Man of the Hour," caught the ball with his back to the wall. Luke Easter and Rosen followed with more conventional flies, leaving Reynolds with only six outs to go. In the beginning of the game he had relied on his curve, then switched to his slider but struggled with both, using them less as the game went on. As he went out for the eighth, he told catcher Berra that he was going to stick with fastballs, but not on the first pitch "since I had a no-hitter going and wanted to be careful." Reynolds cruised through the eighth, despite his teammates' certainty that he had jinxed himself. "They were scandalized," he told Dan Daniel of the *Sporting News*. "[But] it would have been silly for me to have made believe I did not know I was pitching a no-hitter."

In the ninth, he would have faced Feller to lead off the inning, but manager Al Lopez inserted pitcher Bob Lemon as a pinch hitter. Lemon was a respectable hitter, having posted averages of .321, .286, .269, and .272 in the previous four years, who threw right-handed but batted left-handed. Reynolds struck him out, only his second K of the day. Up next was Dale Mitchell, who grounded to second. And then came Avila, the man who very nearly had a hit in the first inning, but which had been ruled an error on Rizzuto. The count went to 1–2. Reynolds threw his hardest and ended up falling flat on the mound, laughing. Apparently in his zeal to strike out Avila, he overstrode right into the hole that Feller had dug. "[Bob] takes longer steps than I do, and I was sliding in a hole his spikes made in the mud," he told the Associated Press to explain the pratfall. With the count 2–2, Reynolds followed with another ball. With the count full, Avila fouled off the next pitch, and the next, but his hacks were numbered. On the next he swung and missed, and so Reynolds wrapped up the no-hitter and the victory.

Reynolds faced only twenty-nine men in the game, which took two hours, twelve minutes to play. Feller gave up a mere four hits on the day, but Woodling's homer sunk him. "He was snakebit," said Yogi Berra. "Oh, I've seen that [happen to a pitcher]."

The next night was Friday the thirteenth, and Vic Raschi was due to pitch. Raschi borrowed the undershirt Reynolds had worn but it did little to lift the jinx, as he was rocked for five runs in the fourth, and departed in the midst of a four-run rally the following inning. Reynolds's luck held out, though, as the Yankees stayed in the thick of the pennant race, setting up an encore performance for the Superchief at the end of September.

Extra Innings

- Earlier in the year Casey Stengel had angered the Indians by joking that the reason Yankee relievers wouldn't ride the jeep from the bullpen in Cleveland's Municipal Stadium was that they preferred Cadillacs. The night of July 12, Indians vice president George Medinger parked his Cadillac convertible at the bullpen to poke fun at the city slickers during their rides to the mound. But there were no rides to the mound!

- Gene Woodling must have had it in for Cleveland. In three straight games against the Tribe he had the game-winning homer. June 23 off Bob Lemon (7–6), June 24 off Early Wynn (5–3, a two-run shot), and July 12 off Bob Feller (1–0).

21

September 28, 1951, Game One: Boston at New York

Reynolds Wrap

In which the Superchief does it again

How could Allie Reynolds possibly top his no-hit performance against the Cleveland Indians, outdueling Rapid Robert Feller, 1–0? Well, what if the foe were the Red Sox? And the game came at the end of the pennant race? And he became the first American Leaguer to pitch two no-nos in one season?

Going into September, the pennant race was closely contested among the Yankees, Red Sox, and Indians, who all suffered setbacks. As some reporters

Allie Pierce Reynolds

joked to Stengel about it, "three third-place clubs" were fighting for first. In the Yankees' case, nagging injuries, the aging of DiMaggio, and the need for platoons in left and at first base kept them from running away with it. Jimmy Dykes, manager of the Athletics, told the Philadelphia newspapers that "old-time Yankee heroes must shudder watching the 1951 edition." But the Sox went on a losing streak toward the end of the month, and Cleveland suddenly fell flat against Detroit.

On Friday, September 28, the Yankees were in first place, needing only two wins to clinch the pennant. That day they opened a three-day, five-game series against the Red Sox at Yankee Stadium, which began with the first of two doubleheaders. September 28 also was American Indian Day, according to the *Farmer's Almanac*, and the Superchief took the hill.

It didn't start off like a stellar pitching day should; Reynolds walked Dom DiMaggio to open the game. As Yogi Berra, who was his battery mate that day put it, "He could be a little wild." But Johnny Pesky hit a soft liner that Phil Rizzuto trapped in his glove. The Scooter stepped on second for the force-out and made a quick throw to Joe Collins at first for the double play. Reynolds then struck out Ted Williams to begin a streak of nine outs in a row. When Williams came up in the fourth with two men out, he walked. But Clyde Vollmer flied to Hank Bauer to begin another streak of nine men retired.

Meanwhile, there were two marked contrasts to the day's performance versus that July night in Cleveland. First, Reynolds was recording many more strikeouts: Ted in the first, both Vollmer and Billy Goodman in the second, Mel Parnell in the third. Second, the Yankees scored early and often. In the first inning, Rizzuto, Coleman, and Bauer led off the game with three successive singles off Parnell, scoring the Scooter and putting men on the corners for Joe DiMaggio. The Yankee Clipper lifted a fly into right field, where Williams hauled it in, but Bauer advanced to second. Gil McDougald walked to load the bases. Yogi grounded a ball that Parnell fielded and threw to first for the out, allowing Coleman to score.

Those two runs were already double the margin mustered for Wahoo's previous gem, but the Yankees tacked on two more in the third. Jerry Coleman walked to open the inning and stole second. Parnell struck out Bauer and induced DiMaggio to pop weakly to Pesky, but Gil McDougald singled to center, scoring Coleman. Berra followed with a similar stroke, which Dom DiMaggio boxed around for an error and an unearned run as McDougald scampered across the plate.

It didn't end there. In the fifth, Ray Scarborough replaced Parnell, only to give up a leadoff double to Collins. Reynolds bunted him to third, and Coleman brought him in with a fly. 5–0 Yanks. Reynolds continued to pile up the outs, striking out Goodman and Fred Hatfield in the fifth, Scarborough and DiMaggio in the sixth. "His fastball was hopping," reported the *New York Herald Tribune.* Collins hit a two-run homer in the seventh to make it 7–0 Yankees.

The closest Reynolds came to giving up a hit was in the eighth, when Boston hit a series of long flies, eliciting gasps from the tension-wracked crowd. Lou Boudreau, Fred Hatfield, and Aaron Robinson all sent balls deep into right field, Robinson's going the farthest of all. "I never turned around to watch the ball because I was sure it had gone into the right-field stand," Reynolds told Dan Daniel. But Hank Bauer was able to chase each of them down. Hatfield's sailed 365 feet but into the power alley in right center, and Robinson's he snared with his back to the wall.

The Yankees tacked on one more run in the bottom of the eighth, a solo homer by Gene Woodling, whose clout in Cleveland had been the only run, this time just a sweetener before the pièce de résistance. Reynolds came out for the ninth inning feeling good. "I threw mostly fastballs," Reynolds later said of the strategy he employed that day. "I had a good curve, too—just waited for the right time to throw it." The first batter he faced was Charley Maxwell, pinch hitting for Harry Taylor. He got two strikes on Maxwell, who grounded the next pitch to Coleman for the out. The next four pitches, though, were out of the strike zone, and Dom DiMaggio took first. With two strikes on Johnny Pesky, Reynolds went to the curve and nicked the corner for strike three.

That left only the great Ted Williams between Reynolds and a new height of immortality.

Berra took the opportunity to visit the mound. This time Reynolds did not joke with his teammates about the no-hit bid. "I got a lot of letters from fans giving me hell for violating a tradition of the game," Reynolds told reporters about how he had flown in the face of superstition and talked about the situation in Cleveland during the game. "So against the Red Sox it was all serious business. No quips." Yogi asked him what he wanted to throw to Williams, and Reynolds replied "anything."

While the battery mates strategized, the Yankee infielders put on a defensive shift for Williams's lefty stroke, Rizzuto taking a position to the right of second base, where he could chat with the second-base umpire, Charley Berry. Rizzuto suggested to Berry that they ought to walk Williams to get to Vollmer, but the ump would have none of it, opining that Reynolds ought to blow it by Ted. "Charley's cool," Rizzuto later told Red Smith. "He's got it all figured out—and I'm fainting."

Turns out Yogi and the Chief were thinking the same thing as Berry. They fed Williams nothing but fastballs. The first one Teddy looked at for a called strike. The second one he wasn't going to let get past and he swung. A towering pop went straight up from the plate. Both Berra and Reynolds rushed after it. The ball drifted back, then behind Yogi, who lunged backward for it, left his feet, and landed face down entangled with Reynolds's legs, the ball on the ground. Yogi didn't want to get up again he felt so bad about dropping what could have been the final out, but Reynolds was more concerned that he had spiked the catcher accidentally when they collided. After finding out that Yogi was merely nicked, Reynolds told him, "Don't let it bother you, let's get that guy now."

Yogi figured if it worked once, it might work again. "I called for the same pitch the same place, and he popped it the same way." This time Yogi hauled it in right in front of the Yankee dugout. Reynolds leaped on him, and the rest of the team leaped on them both in celebration. When asked if he thought he would live it down if Teddy Ballgame had gotten a hit, Yogi replied, "I think I would. Because we cinched the pennant that day. [Reynolds] probably would have kicked the hell out of me, though."

Jerry Coleman remembers saying to Phil Rizzuto, " 'If that were you or me, the next one would be over the right-field wall.' Only Berra could survive something like that. He was lucky. Listen, if you wanted to invest in something, you found out what Yogi was investing in. He was that lucky."

The Yankees had assured themselves of a tie for first with the win, and in the second half of the doubleheader they sealed the pennant as they pummeled the "staggered and apathetic Bosox" (*Boston Globe*) 11–3. Reynolds finished the year with seven shutouts, the most in the league (Feller, Lopat, and Raschi each had four) and the Yankee staff as a whole set a new season franchise record for shutouts with 24. They went on to win the final three games from Boston as well, and then to clobber Bobby Thomson's Giants in the World Series.

Extra Innings

- *No-hit numbers:* Reynolds threw 119 pitches, faced 30 batters, walked 4, and struck out 9.

- Between games of the doubleheader, the Yankee players celebrated the no-hitter and their guaranteed tie for first place by eating ice cream.

- The Hotel Edison, where Reynolds and several other players lived, changed his room number from 2019 to 0002 in honor of the two no-hitters.

- Before Reynolds, Johnny Vander Meer was the only other pitcher in the major leagues to have notched two no-no's in one season. In 1938 he beat both the Braves and the Dodgers in back-to-back starts, a feat that has yet to be equaled. In 1952 Virgil Trucks had two in a season, and Nolan Ryan pitched two of his seven no-hitters in 1973.

- Del Webb, co-owner of the Yankees in 1951, pitched a no-hitter himself in the California State League. He was in Cleveland to see Reynolds's first no-hitter and then did not see the Yankees play another game until he attended Reynolds's second one!

22

October 7, 1952: New York at Brooklyn

Top of the Pops

In which Billy the Kid snatches victory out of the air

In 1952, Brooklyn made their sixth World Series appearance. The Yankees made their 19th. The two clubs had faced off in October three times in the previous decade and the Dodgers had yet to win one, although they had pushed the Yankees to seven games in 1947. Five years later, both teams retained some familiar faces for the rematch: Allie Reynolds, Phil Rizzuto, and Yogi Berra for the Yankees, Jackie Robinson, Pee Wee Reese, and Carl Furillo for the Dodgers.

But gone was Joe DiMaggio, replaced by an Oklahoma miner's son named Mickey Mantle. Gone was "Old Reliable" Tommy Henrich. The Yankees had developed a starting rotation that featured Vic Raschi and Eddie Lopat alongside Reynolds. The Dodgers had added pitcher Preacher Roe and catcher Roy Campanella, while Duke Snider had blossomed into the most potent bat in their lineup.

Although the Yankees were favored to win, the Brooks took the first game, 4–2, behind the pitching of Joe Black and three home runs from Robinson, Snider, and Reese. The following day's *Brooklyn Eagle* headline read, "Experts: Drop Dead." In game two, the Yankees returned to form, winning 7–1 while Raschi held the Dodgers to three hits. Game three swung back in the Dodgers' favor as their heavily right-handed lineup touched lefty Eddie Lopat for ten hits. Preacher Roe threw 156 pitches and gave up homers to Berra and the "Big Cat" Johnny Mize, but won 5–3. For game four, both game one starters returned, but this time Allie Reynolds was the victor, 2–0, over Black, allowing

Philip Francis "Phil" Rizzuto and Alfred Manuel "Billy" Martin

only four hits and striking out 10 (Jackie Robinson three times, all looking). The seesawing did not end there, and game five was a seesaw affair, the Dodgers jumping out to an early 4–0 lead, the Yankees storming back 5–4, but Snider putting the cap on the score at 6–5, driving in both the tying run in the seventh and the winning run in the 11th. If the Dodgers could win another one, they would be champions, but in game six at Ebbets Field a battle of homers (two by Snider, one each by Berra and Mantle) was ultimately decided by an RBI single by pitcher Vic Raschi.

So it came down to winner-take-all, game seven, a game described by Arthur Daley in the *New York Times* as "another of those taut . . . thrillers that had emotions twanging like guitar strings." Charlie Dressen tapped Joe Black again to be his starter. The native of Plainfield, New Jersey, had played in the Negro Leagues before signing on with the Dodgers. Dressen had used him as a reliever throughout the year, but by September, realizing the talent the 28-year-old had, gave him two starts as preparation for the Series. Dressen's faith had been rewarded. In games one and four, Black had given up three runs total, nine hits, with eight strikeouts in 16 innings pitched. Although he had walked seven men in the same span, with a late-breaking curve and a hard fastball, Black had emerged as the most effective mound weapon the Dodgers had.

Stengel countered with Lopat, whose junkball style normally stifled power-hitting teams, even if he had been fairly well pummeled back in game three. Casey was not one to forget that Lopat had notched two wins in the '51 Series versus the Giants, 3–1 and 13–1. In 1952 Lopat had reached his then career-low ERA of 2.53.

The first three innings were quick and uneventful, neither team putting more than one runner on per inning. Black retired the Yankees on only 11 pitches in the first, and the entire three innings took fewer than 30 minutes to play. But in the fourth, the Yankees chipped away at Black. Rizzuto started things off with a double, advancing to third when Mickey Mantle grounded out to the right side. He scooted home on a Johnny Mize single, but the rally was squelched when the next batter, Yogi Berra, grounded into a double play.

Brooklyn answered immediately in their half of the inning. Snider singled, but the Brooks did not swing hard against Lopat this time. Robinson dropped a bunt down the third-base line and beat the throw, putting two men on. Campanella followed suit, dropping a bunt to load the bases. Casey had seen enough. Lopat gave way to Reynolds, who had racked up six saves in six chances during the season (in addition to winning 20 games of the 29 he started, 24 of them complete games). But the Chief had pitched the complete game four and recorded a save in game six as well, and with no off days between Series games for travel, he was tired. The first batter he faced, Gil Hodges, lined the ball into left. Gene Woodling ran it down, but Snider tagged up and scored, and Robinson took third on the throw to the plate. Reynolds bore down, struck out George Shuba, and got Furillo to ground to third.

The tie did not last long. Gene Woodling blasted a homer off Black to lead off the fifth. "My curve spun but it didn't move," Black would later say. With less break on the curve, the ball stayed out over the plate, eminently hittable, and Woodling did not miss. But Joe's mates tied the score again as soon as they came up to bat. Black himself took a called third strike, but Billy Cox doubled on a long drive that bounced off the wall in right center. Reese followed with an RBI single, but Allie retired Snider and Robinson to hold the score at 2-all.

In the sixth, with one out, Mickey Mantle added another slat to the picket fence the Yankees were building, launching a solo home run off another curve that lacked bite from Black. Mize followed that with a single, and Dressen pulled Black, inserting Preacher Roe. Roe struck out Berra, but Woodling singled, moving Mize to second. Stengel inserted Hank Bauer as a pinch hitter for Irv Noren. Bauer pulled the ball to Cox at third base, who juggled it, loading the bases. Up came Billy Martin.

"Billy the Kid" had played for Stengel when Casey had managed the Oakland Oaks in the Pacific Coast League. A native of Berkeley, California, Martin played hard and smart, and Stengel made sure the Yankees acquired him in 1950. Martin got his chance to start when Jerry Coleman was called for a stint in the marines. "He would do anything to beat you," Yogi Berra said of the hard-nosed Martin, who would go on to manage the Yankees in the 1970s. Martin got hold of a ball from Roe but Snider caught it in center to end the inning. Still, the Yankees had gone ahead again, thanks to the Mantle homer. This time could they hold the one-run lead?

The Dodgers wouldn't make it easy. Campy singled right off, but Reynolds came back to get a double play ball off the bat of Gil Hodges. Rizzuto to Martin to Mize cleared the bases, and Shuba grounded out for a relatively easy inning.

To start the seventh, Casey sent Ralph Houk to pinch-hit for Reynolds, who was out of gas. Houk grounded out, but Gil McDougald reached on a single. Rizzuto sacrificed him to second, putting him in scoring position for Mickey Mantle.

To this point in the series, Mantle was batting .333 with three walks and nine hits, including a double, a triple, and two homers. Not bad for a 20-year-old kid who almost packed it in after struggling during a rookie call-up the year before and being demoted to the AAA Kansas City Blues. He promptly brought McDougald in with an RBI single. Mize fouled out to end the inning and Casey brought in Vic Raschi to pitch with the two-run lead.

Raschi had not been used in relief all year, and had only one relief appearance in each of the previous three years. Unlike Reynolds, he said he had no knack for it. Indeed, put himself in hot water right away, walking Carl Furillo on five pitches. If Mantle had not tallied the insurance run, Roe might have sacrificed him to second. Instead, Dressen brought in a pinch hitter to swing away—Rocky Nelson. He popped up. The struggling Raschi then threw three balls to Cox, who eventually singled and moved Furillo to second. Raschi then walked Pee Wee Reese to load the bases. With Snider and Robinson coming up, Casey saw the writing on the wall, pulled Raschi, and sent in big, blond Bob Kuzava.

Kuzava was a lefty who played for eight teams in his major-league career, coming to the Yankees in 1951 when he was 28 years old. For Stengel he employed his live fastball and good control as a reliever and spot starter. In 1951 Kuzava had recorded the save in the final game of the World Series against the Giants, and perhaps Casey thought he could do it again, despite the fact that "the Brooks are certain death to left-handed pitchers. That's what the book says," according to Arthur Daley in the *New York Times*. "The records verify it. [Yet] the shrewd Ol' Perfessor [Stengel] comes through in the clutch with [a] lefthander."

Kuzava might have needed a little luck to get through the inning, but that is exactly what he got. With a full count on the Duke of Flatbush, he threw a fastball with a little hop on it over the plate. "The pitch was right down the middle," he told reporters later. "The type that Snider could powder a mile." But Snider's mighty cut was off just a hair, and he popped to McDougald.

Then came Jackie Robinson. Kuzava did not want to make the same mistake. With two out, the runners would be going on contact, and even a cheap hit might score two. He went to his curveball. "Nobody told me he could break it off that good," said Robinson later of the bender that he also popped up. The crack of the bat started the merry-go-round. The wind played with the ball a little and the infielders froze as it towered, first baseman Joe Collins and Kuzava craning their necks upward. "It was the Yankee first baseman's catch," wrote Red Smith in the *Herald Tribune*, "but with the sun slanting into his face across the grandstand roof, he couldn't see where it was. He stood gazing curiously aloft, wondering about life. Billy Martin stood gazing curiously at Collins, wondering about him." Two runners had already crossed the plate by the time the ball came down, and if it had touched the infield grass, Brooklyn would have tied the game.

But it did not touch the grass. Billy Martin, suddenly realizing that no one else could or would grab it, "ran out from under his hat and almost ran out of his shoes in a breakneck lunge" (Daley, *Times*) and snared the ball in the tip of his glove a few inches from the ground. "Just as the ball started to come down I could see nobody was going for it," Martin told the *Sporting News*. He plucked the ball off his shoetop and nearly fell into foul territory, his sprint for the ball had given him so much momentum.

The Dodgers' momentum, meanwhile, was stilled. "The [Brooklyn] crowd, which had been shouting with every pitch, was silent," wrote Roger Kahn in the *Herald Tribune*. "After that, no one doubted that the Yankees would win again." Kuzava was able to neatly finish up the final six outs, allowing only one base runner, and that on a fielding error, earning him the praise of columnist Red Smith, who called him "the specialist whom Casey Stengel keeps around exclusively for pitching in the final games of World Series." Pee Wee Reese made the final out, a fly ball to Woodling in left. Woodling ran in to join the celebration, "flinging his arms about and leaping like a man with a hernia" (Smith, *Herald Tribune*) while his teammates leaped on Kuzava, pounding him with joy.

The Yankees had not had to fight tooth and nail for a World Series in quite a while. "Never before has a Yankee team managed by Stengel been forced to scramble so hard to win," wrote Kahn. The victory depended on outstanding contributions from every team member. "How about the Kid's catch?" Stengel asked reporters in the raucous clubhouse after the game. "If he isn't awake they've got two runs across the plate."

"Mantle was the difference," was Jackie Robinson's opinion. "They didn't [even] miss Joe DiMaggio."

Ultimately, it was not one man who beat the Dodgers—in baseball it rarely is—but the Yankee spirit that edged them out. "The Yanks had to do more than stroll to win this series from the magnificent Brooks—they had to struggle and strain and fight their hearts out in seven incredible games. Yesterday they took the big one, the one they had to take. That is their tradition. Perhaps when the chips are down one pitches not to Mantle and Berra but really to Ruth and Gehrig," opined one *New York Times* editorial. The *Washington Post* shared this view. "For cold chills, sudden swoons, and assorted cardiovascular sensations, it was probably the most tremendous World Series in history . . . The contemporary New York Yankees may have seemed a bit seedy and down at heel in comparison to some of their illustrious predecessors, they still have whatever it is that it takes to win the games that must be won when the family honor, so to speak, is at stake."

"If there have been better Yankee teams, there have been none with greater resolution," wrote Joe Williams in the *New York World-Telegram & Sun*. Al Abrams of the *Pittsburgh Post-Gazette* wrote, "Yankee luck? No. They're champions, a team that doesn't know how to lose." The *Sporting News* editorial of October 15 summed up "those qualities in [the] players that have become known as the 'Yankee tradition.' Even among the partisans . . . who clamored for an end to the Yankee domination, there was grudging but nonetheless real respect for the continued ability of the Bombers to win the 'big ones,' to rise to the occasion when needed, even when they seemed on the verge of a knockout."

With the win, Casey's Yankees capped four World Championships in a row, equaling a record previously set by Marse Joe McCarthy with the Yankees from 1936 to 1939. They would win again in 1953 to make five in a row, and a rematch with the Dodgers was awaiting them two years after that.

Extra Innings

- Joe Black's game one victory was the first World Series win for an African American pitcher in baseball history. (The next would be Mudcat Grant in 1965.)

- The Yankees' team bus was escorted by police from Yankee Stadium to Ebbets Field. Partway there, a candy red sports car joined the caravan. A motorcycle cop in the escort dropped back to tell the interloper to buzz off, only to find it was Phil Rizzuto, who had decided to drive himself from his New Jersey home.

23

October 4, 1955: Brooklyn at New York

Dem Bums

In which the Wild Man tames the Dodgers, but the Yankees fail to score

The Yankees' opponents for the 1955 World Series would be the good ol' Brooklyn Dodgers again. The Dodgers contrived to drop the first two games in the Series, but came back to win three of the next four to once again go to a winner-take-all game against their pinstriped neighbors and rivals.

The Yankees called on Tommy Byrne, the pitcher nicknamed the "Wild Man," to turn back the Dodgers that day. Byrne was a bonus baby from Wake Forest University (he had studied math) who shared a bit of lineage with Babe Ruth. Like the Bambino, he had grown up in Baltimore, left-handed, and sometimes in the care of the state, and even met him once when Ruth visited the orphanage where young Tommy was staying. "As a kid, if you were left-handed and you came from Baltimore, you wanted to grow up to be Babe Ruth," Byrne said.

Thomas Joseph "Tommy" Byrne

But Byrne was one of the few who did. After being signed by the Yankees, he spent some time with their Newark farm club, but shortly after being called up for a look-see in 1943, he went into the military where he served as gunnery officer on a destroyer. In 1946 he joined the club in spring training. "They looked at me and I looked at them, and I didn't pitch. I just assumed they thought I was wild, or not in shape because I was in the service, but they didn't sell me and I figured they would use me sometime," Byrne remembered.

He had late-season call-ups in 1946 and 1947, and it wasn't until 1948 that he got a chance to show what he could do. "Midway through the season we had some games piling up, and they said, 'let's see if Byrne can do any good against Detroit . . .' and we shut 'em out and they said, 'hey, he's okay.'" Byrne thought maybe the front office had told Bucky Harris to keep him on the bench, but he fought his way into the rotation. But he had earned the "Wild Man" nickname by hitting a lot of batters and walking even more. "He had good stuff but he might strike out eight and he would also walk eight," according to Whitey Ford. In 1949 he had a breakout year, going 15–7 with a 3.72 ERA, breaking the top 10 in games started, shutouts (eighth), strikeouts (fifth) and winning percentage (sixth), but also leading the league in walks. His 1949 accomplishments and a good start to 1950 resulted in an All-Star game selection. But as the year went on, Byrne lost his momentum. "I probably just ran out of gas. I don't know why particularly," he said.

"The year before, despite the bases on balls, nobody hit me very well. Once they started pitching me in 1948, I thought I was on cloud nine, but the latter part of 1950, it seemed like . . . damn, nothing was working out for me. I lost a game up there in Boston where Billy Goodman, a little left-handed hitter, broke two bats and got two hits and drove in two or three runs. You feel like you made a pretty good pitch when you see the bat lying there in half." Byrne did not pitch in the 1950 World Series against the Phillies. The four-game sweep was accomplished by Vic Raschi, Allie Reynolds, Eddie Lopat, and Whitey Ford.

And by 1951, the Yankees had traded Byrne to Bill Veeck's St. Louis Browns. One rumored reason for his departure was that owner Dan Topping was impatient. "Topping had made the remark that 'it takes you too long to finish a game,' so consequently that was a problem. It took too long to play the game." Byrne found himself bounced around—Chicago, Washington, and even the minor leagues, where he learned what he had been missing in the majors.

"I changed my style of pitching. What I did when I had played for the Yankees was always try to throw so damn hard. When Lopat was out there, it would be 95 to 100 degrees, and he'd come in the dugout and he would put my hand on his arm and show me he wasn't sweating. And I was sweating like crazy." Byrne finally learned that less was more. "I took something off. I'd get them with the soft stuff, and then I could run it by them. I did it in Venezuela and pitched in the league down there 13–2, and on the West Coast." It wasn't long before major league teams came knocking again. "The Cardinals were interested in me, and I told the manager I didn't want to go to St. Louis because it was so hot there." But then the Yankees called. "I was somewhat surprised that the Yankees would take me back, because in those days once they turned somebody loose, the honeymoon was over. But Casey told me, you did a hell of a job for me here. When I came to Yankee Stadium from Baltimore the first guy I saw was Dan Topping, and he greeted me back like, 'well, I was sorry you had to leave.' That was nice. He was always real nice to me even though I didn't really speed up, I just didn't throw as many pitches."

So at 35 years old Byrne enjoyed a renaissance with the Yankees in 1955, going 16–5 with a 3.15 ERA, his best year ever, and earning the start in game two of the World Series. "I felt like I was supposed to be there all the time but nobody knew it but me," Byrne said. He won the game, 4–2, and allowed only five hits, and the good-hitting pitcher also drove in two of the four runs. "It was good for me at my age, I had waited a long time to win a game in a World Series!" The Yankees would need another performance like that from Byrne if they were going to sink Brooklyn and win their 17th world championship, and indeed, that's the kind of performance they got.

Tommy's opponent on the hill for the deciding game seven was Johnny Podres, who also had pitched well earlier in the Series. They were a study in contrasts: Byrne, the dark-haired veteran who had fought his way onto the mound again, and Podres, blond and brimming with the exuberance of the young player. "Podres threw a little bit harder. He had a good change and a good curveball. But Tommy had learned to throw a slider and he did a good job," said Yogi Berra when comparing the two pitchers. "Tommy Byrne used to be the hardest guy to catch. Then he got control. He was a tough man. He had good stuff, but at the beginning [of his career] he just didn't know where he was going. We thought he'd never get there because of his control, but he came a long way."

For the first few innings, neither pitcher budged an inch. Only two Dodgers reached base, both of them by walks, but neither of them got farther. The Yankees, meanwhile, began their customary assault with two out in the bottom of the third. Phil Rizzuto walked on four pitches, just the kind of crack in a pitcher's armor that the Bombers habitually capitalize on. Billy Martin followed with a single, bringing Gil McDougald to the plate, with Yogi Berra on deck.

McDougald was not as much of a "star" as Mickey Mantle, but in 1951, when both men had debuted, it was McDougald who captured the Rookie of the Year award. Although he had moved around the infield as various other Yankees retired or arrived (Rizzuto, Martin), he excelled no matter where they put him. McDougald battled Podres to a full count. Podres dealt and McDougald had a rough swing at it, just squibbing a roller up the third-base line. With third baseman Don Hoak playing back, there seemed to be no chance for him to get to the ball in time to make a putout. Indeed there wasn't, but the Scooter, scrambling over from second, slid into third and the still-rolling ball bounced off his outstretched leg. The batted ball had hit the runner and Rizzuto was out, ending the inning and the threat. "That's the way those things go. A lot of things happen on the way to the ballpark, to and from the bullpen," philosophized Byrne about losing the scoring chance.

The Dodgers seized the moment to chip away at Byrne. Snider struck out, but Roy Campanella doubled, and moved to third on a ground out. Gil Hodges would not go down so easily. With two out and the runner at third, and down by two strikes, Hodges served a single into left, and Campy scored. Podres, meanwhile, saved by providential luck the inning before, did not want to give the Yankees another chance. Berra doubled to lead off the inning, but could not advance on Bauer's fly ball to right. Skowron grounded to second and Yogi moved to third. But Podres got Bob Cerv to pop the ball up, and Reese caught it in short left.

In the sixth, the Dodgers added another run. Pee Wee Reese singled, and Duke Snider tried to sacrifice him to second. Instead he, too, reached base as he knocked the ball from Moose Skowron's glove as he passed the bag. Campanella was able to sacrifice both runners over, and Byrne was signaled to intentionally walk Carl Furillo. With Hodges coming up, Stengel lifted Byrne in favor of Bob Grim. "Casey might have forgotten that I struck out Hodges in the previous game. But he manages, you pitch, that's it," Byrne recalled. "I wasn't walking guys that much then, I wasn't tired or anything. But it was a percentage move on his part. Maybe Grim gets a ball down and hits a grounder to somebody."

Grim did not get a grounder. Hodges hit a sacrifice fly, scoring Reese. Grim then walked Hoak, reloading the bases, and Walter Alston, hungry for more runs, lifted Don Zimmer for pinch hitter George Shuba. But Grim stopped Shuba with a ground ball. The bleeding was stanched, but the Dodgers had doubled their score, adding what Robert Creamer described in *Sports Illustrated* as "what is aptly called the insurance run. This is the one extra run that limits the enemy's maneuvering, alters his strategy and generally provides the team that has it with a pleasant added measure of comfort and confidence in times of stress like, say, the last three innings of the final game of the seven-game World Series." Even still, "I figured two runs wasn't going to beat us," Byrne said.

With Zimmer out of the game, Alston shuffled his players, moving Jim Gilliam to second and inserting Sandy Amoros in left. Amoros, a small Cuban who was known for his speed, had played 102 games in left that year. Byrne was reduced to cheerleading. "I was one of those bench jockeys or tried to be. I was going to jack the guys up if I could from the bench." In the bottom of the inning the Yankees mounted a comeback, but when Yogi Berra lofted a fly down the foul line in left with two men on, luck once again came down in a Brooklyn glove. The left-handed Amoros raced across from left center, snared the ball in his fully outstretched glove, and sent Berra back to the bench. Would the right-handed and slower-footed Gilliam have made that play? Probably not. Alston had the Midas touch with his moves that day. Amoros iced the cake then by doubling off McDougald.

The Dodgers began to count the outs. Nine to go. In the seventh, Pee Wee Reese, the long-suffering captain of the Brooklyns, fielded all the outs in the inning himself, a grounder from Skowron, a grounder from Cerv, and a pop-up behind third from pinch hitter Mickey Mantle. Podres did not look tired.

In the eighth, the Yankees made a final charge. Rizzuto singled. Martin lined a ball into right, but Furillo grabbed it above his ankles. McDougald singled, to bring that perennial World Series hero Yogi Berra to the plate again. But he merely lifted a fly into right, leaving the task to Hank Bauer, the "Man of the Hour." Bauer took a ball. Then a strike. He fouled one back, then looked at another ball. Podres reared back and threw so hard he lost his balance. Bauer did, too, swinging and missing and sending the game into the ninth.

Podres stayed on the hill, energized by the nearness of victory. He got Skowron to hit a tapper back to the mound; one out. Then came a fly to left from Cerv; two out. Elston Howard stepped to the plate. He looked at the first pitch, a strike. He watched another go by, this one a ball, and then took a cut at the next offering . . . but missed. Podres, trying for the kill, threw a fastball but it rode high; 2–2. Howard caught a piece of the next pitch, fouling it off. Podres dealt again, another foul. Was Howard catching up to him? This time Podres went to his changeup. Howard swung hard but connected softly, topping the ball right to Reese, a man who had played in five World Series before now but won none. Two seconds later, the ball was safely in Hodges's glove, and he and the Brooks had finally won one.

All of Brooklyn dissolved into a joyous celebration, as thousands poured into the streets, parading banners up and down Flatbush Avenue and waving pennants from windows, dancing, singing, and chanting. But in the Bronx, the Yankees' clubhouse was somber. Casey Stengel sought out Byrne. "I believe if they had left me in there, we would have got some runs," Byrne said, thinking back on the game. "Later Casey came by my locker and said, 'I don't think I shoulda taken you out.' He was trying to say we'd had a great year." A great year that fell just short.

Extra Innings

- The joy over the Dodger win spread as far as St. Thomas in the Virgin Islands, where "5,000 people paraded for four hours . . . carrying banners that said 'At last—Brooklyn wins,'" reported Robert Creamer in *Sports Illustrated.*

- When his baseball career ended, Tommy Byrne returned to Wake Forest University to finish his degree. He would later become mayor of the town of Wake Forest and spur real-estate development in the area. Though the university moved to Winston-Salem, Byrne is still a resident of Wake Forest, and lives adjacent to a golf course he developed.

24

October 8, 1956: Brooklyn at New York

Imperfect Man

In which Don Larsen finds a ball in his shoe

The pennant winners of 1955 were back for a rematch, the Dodgers to try to defend their world championship title, the Yankees to get it back. A glance at the starting lineups showed why—both clubs had retained the cream of their talent. Reese, Snider, Robinson, and Hodges versus Mantle, Berra, McDougald, and Martin. Mantle was coming off his best year yet, winning the Triple Crown, belting 52 home runs, and winning the MVP award.

If the Yankees had a weak spot, though, it was starting pitching. Gone were the days of the "four aces" rotation. Although Whitey Ford was brilliant, winning 19 games, Tommy Byrne, Bob Turley, and Bob Grim all struggled at times. Don Larsen, a journeyman pitcher who led the league in losses in 1954 for the Orioles (3–21), split his time between the bullpen and the rotation. He made 20 starts and went 11–5 that year and found himself starting game two of the series at Ebbets Field. He was shelled. The Dodgers knocked him out in the second inning and trounced the Yankees, 13–8. Coming on the heels of their game one loss, the defeat put the Yankees into an 0–2 hole. But Whitey won the next day, and Tom Sturdivant the next. With game five scheduled to be the final game at Yankee Stadium before the Series returned to Ebbets Field, Casey Stengel pondered who should make the start, putting off any announcement until the day of the game.

Larsen, a 27-year-old from Southern California, found out he was Casey's choice when he arrived at the ballpark that morning. There was a baseball in his cleats, the Ol' Perfessor's way of indicating his choice. Stengel felt Larsen had a better chance of success in Yankee Stadium, which was more of a pitcher's park than cozy Ebbets. But Larsen had no inkling of how good he would be that day. "Everyone asks how I felt before the perfect game," Larsen told *Baseball Digest*. "You never feel bad when you're in the World Series." In September, the six-four Larsen had quit using his windup and produced good results—four wins—but coming off the game two loss, he couldn't be sure.

The first person who knew Larsen had his best stuff was Yogi Berra, who was his battery mate that day, and saw the difference in the very first inning. "Anything I put down, he got over. That was the best control he ever had," Berra said. He struck out Jim Gilliam looking to open the action. "He was only behind on one hitter, that was Pee Wee Reese in the first inning. 3–2. He never got to 3–2 again. He was always ahead." Reese, too, went down looking. Duke Snider made contact, lining the ball to Hank Bauer in right. In the second inning, Jackie Robinson almost reached base when his line shot went off third baseman Andy Carey's glove. But Gil McDougald was there backing up and nipped Robinson at first.

But let's not forget the opposing pitcher, 39-year-old Sal Maglie. Maglie had earned the nickname "the Barber" for the close shaves he threw at batters' chins, a known intimidator. Maglie was a New York native, from Niagara Falls, who had broken into the big leagues in 1945 but found himself banned from playing after he was one of several players who jumped to the Mexican League. In 1950, after the ban was lifted, he returned to the majors and pitched effectively for several years before injuries began to slow him. In 1956, Cleveland gave up on him in May, placing him on waivers. The Dodgers took him in and Maglie may have been the piece they needed to come out on top. Maglie pitched well down the stretch (including a no-hitter on September 25), and the Dodgers edged out both the Braves and the Reds on the final day of the season. The next day's *Herald Tribune* carried a headline, "Maglie Eager to Face Yankees." Indeed he was, beating Whitey Ford in game one and now looking to beat Larsen, too.

Maglie matched Larsen pitch for pitch through three innings. The first hit of the game came in the bottom of the fourth with two outs, when the Triple Crown winner Mantle stood in against the Barber. And homered. Now Larsen was working with a lead. "Wherever I put the glove, he hit it," Berra said. "Fast balls. Sliders. He got everything where it was supposed to be." The tall, gangly pitcher who earned the nickname "Gooney Bird" sent Dodger after Dodger back to the bench in a relentless stream. In the fifth the Dodgers came close— Hodges launched a ball that Mantle had to race hard to track down, snaring the ball with a backhand catch, and Amoros drove one deep but foul. But that was the limit of the Dodgers' hitting.

What was the difference between the Larsen of game two, who was wild in the strike zone, and the pitcher of game five? From somewhere he found a control he had never had before. "Maybe it was because he had the hell beat out of him [in game two]," Berra said. Larsen also placed his trust in his catcher, throwing whatever Berra signaled for. "All day long, Yogi led me through the maze of Dodger hitters," Larsen wrote in *The Perfect Yankee*. "He only shook me off twice," Berra told reporters after the game. "But each time, he finally signaled for the original pitch."

In the sixth the Yankees managed an insurance run. The number eight hitter,

Carey, opened the inning with a single. Larsen bunted him over to second. Hank Bauer came to the plate and singled Carey home. Joe Collins knocked a hit and Bauer went to third, but they would tally only the one run when Maglie got Mantle to hit into a double play. But the additional run did not reduce the mounting tension. Stengel, worried that Larsen might revert to his old ways, sent Whitey Ford down to the bullpen to warm up. Whitey remembered it well. "Our pitching coach, Jim Turner, and Casey Stengel, thought that Don always got tired after five innings. So I warmed up in the sixth, seventh, eighth, and ninth inning. Now from the bullpen at the old Yankee Stadium, you couldn't see home plate or the pitcher. You could only see the shortstop and the third baseman. So I didn't even know what was going on! The greatest game ever pitched in a World Series and I missed the last four innings!"

The Dodgers continued to go down. By this point, Larsen was simply too good for the Dodgers to touch. They hit fly balls, grounders, soft liners, nothing that came close to a hit. Larsen himself came up to bat in the eighth to a standing ovation. He struck out, but by that time no one wanted to see him run the bases anyway. Maglie struck out the side, but it hardly mattered.

Jerry Coleman was on the bench that day and recalled the mounting excitement. "Nobody was paying a lot of attention until the sixth inning. We knew it was a no-hitter but then in the eighth we realized, hey, it's a perfect game! And suddenly every guy on the bench became a manager. Everybody became excited and were anxious so we started saying hey you ought to play this guy over here, shade this guy that way—we wanted everything to be perfect—and Casey turned around and said, 'Goddamn it, I'm the only manager here!'"

Before the ninth inning, Billy Martin gathered the infielders together and told them "nothing gets through," but was so nervous himself that he bobbled one of the warm-up tosses Collins fed to him. Broadcaster Vin Scully intoned, "Let's all take a deep breath as we go to the most dramatic ninth inning in the history of baseball." Mantle wrote in his memoir of the 1956 season that "I never was as nervous as I was in the ninth inning of that game."

He needn't have worried. First up was Carl Furillo, known as a contact hitter and a tough out. Yogi wanted Larsen to stick with fastballs and sliders, no big breaking stuff. The key was location. For Furillo that meant staying away from his hitting zone, low and inside. Larsen threw the first pitch outside, and Furillo swung late, fouling the ball off. Larsen went a little farther outside for the next pitch, and Furillo fouled that one off as well. Larsen reared back to throw another hard slider, but this one sailed high, a ball. Berra called for a fastball, and Furillo again got a piece of it. Then fouled off another one. As the at-bat went on, the tension continued to mount. Then finally

Furillo caught up with one . . . a fly ball to right that Bauer gathered easily.

"The pitch of the crowd noise went up an octave," Larsen wrote. "I saw arms waving and people grabbing each other. The fans were going crazy." He had to put it out of his mind, though, and concentrate on Berra's glove. Roy Campanella came to the plate. He was the complete opposite of Furillo, a hitter who had trouble with the pitch inside. Larsen dealt him a fastball in; Campy fouled it off. Berra then called for a pitch away off the plate and Campanella went after it, grounding to Martin.

With one out to go, Larsen suddenly felt the tension lift. "A bit of a peaceful feeling came to me," he wrote. He had reached the point where the outcome was fate, "where I would find out if a miracle was truly going to occur." Sal Maglie was due to hit, but down to his last out, Walter Alston would surely send up a pinch hitter. Dale Mitchell, a veteran lefty hitter who played several good years with the Indians but who was mostly limited to pinch-hitting duty at this stage of his career, walked to the plate.

Larsen dealt. A bit outside, a ball. Mitchell had let it go by. Larsen came back with a fastball on the outside corner, just nipping it. Mitchell was in a tough position. If he let another strike go by, he would be down 1–2 without ever swinging the bat. The next pitch came and he took a big cut—and missed.

Now Mitchell would have to protect the plate. The next pitch headed for the outside corner and he fouled it off. Larsen dawdled a few moments on the mound, picking up the rosin bag and resetting his cap on his head. Yogi called for that outside pitch again. Larsen whipped the ball toward the glove as hard as he could. Mitchell took a half swing at the pitch but couldn't pull the trigger on the high fastball. Umpire Babe Pinelli's arm shot up to signal the third strike, and Yogi Berra leaped into Don Larsen's arms. "That was a perfect pitch," Berra recalled. "It was the outside corner. And I was happy!"

◆Extra Innings

- Babe Pinelli, the home plate umpire, was umpiring his final game behind the plate. He retired after the Series ended, closing out a 22-year career.

- A group of 34 Yankees fans from Mexico traveled to New York for the World Series. When their ticket broker did not produce tickets to the games at Ebbets Field, the fans were forced to go to court to get their refund of $1,787. The hearing took place on the morning of game five, and after the proceedings ran late, city officials offered their own cars to make sure the international guests arrived at Yankee Stadium in time to witness the historic game.

- Don Larsen's mother did not see her son pitch his perfect game from her La Jolla home. "I make it a rule never to watch Don when he pitches," the 61-year-old told the *New York Herald Tribune*. "Seems like every time I watch him, he loses. So I just don't do it."

- Maglie, who had pitched a no-hitter on September 25, told reporters after the game, "I knew just how [Larsen] felt in the ninth inning, and in a vague way I didn't want to see his no-hitter ruined. It would have been impossible, of course, but I wanted to see us win it without spoiling his performance."

- Mantle hit the homer using Jerry Lumpe's bat. Mantle had a habit of borrowing bats from his teammates. For much of the Series he used Hank Bauer's bat, but switched. As Bauer told Arthur Daley, "All a guy on this team has to say is 'Hey, Mickey, I got a good bat,' and Mickey will say, 'Let me try it.'"

25

July 23, 1957: Chicago at New York

With Fireworks, Too

In which Mickey Mantle thrills all

Mickey Mantle was born to play baseball. Raised in the mining town of Commerce, Oklahoma, Mickey was named after the Philadelphia A's star catcher Mickey Cochrane by his baseball-loving father. "Mutt" Mantle put a baseball into Mickey's crib and taught his oldest son to switch-hit, with help from his own father. "He and my grandfather, who was left-handed, pitched to me every day after school in the backyard," Mantle wrote in his autobiography, *The Mick*. "I batted lefty against my dad and righty against my granddad." He was discovered by the Yankees' legendary scout Tom Greenwade and was in New York by 1951.

With DiMaggio gone by 1952, Mickey assumed the mantle, naturally enough, of team star. At first some fans were reluctant, still clinging to their images of the graceful Yankee Clipper sailing through center field, but the talent Mantle displayed soon made him an icon revered throughout the United States, not just in New York. In 1956, he won the Triple Crown (52 home runs, .353 batting average, 130 RBI) and the Most Valuable Player Award, not to mention another World Series ring in the Yankees' defeat of the Dodgers. Later in his life, Mantle would lament that had he not been alcoholic, he might have achieved even more, but when the 1957 season opened, he was on top of the world.

A baseball season being what it is, though, Mantle had been in a bit of a slump when on July 23, the Yankees hosted the second-place White Sox. "There were no formal plans along these lines, but last night's opener of an 18-game Stadium home stand turned out to be Mickey Mantle Night," wrote Harold Rosenthal in the *New York Herald Tribune.* "With fireworks, too."

The fireworks started in the first inning. After Don Larsen had dealt with the White Sox (walking two, but otherwise no trouble), Mantle came up with two out in the bottom of the frame. He faced Bob Keegan, a pitcher who had originally come up in the Yankees' system, but didn't make the majors until he joined the White Sox in 1953. In 1954, he earned an All-Star selection, but then was hampered for two years by knee trouble. In 1957 he was back on track, though one might not think so, given what happened next. Mantle hit a ball straight into center field. Larry Doby squinted at the ball, unable to judge the angle on the flight coming right toward him, and the ball fell at his feet. Mantle got a double out of that, bringing the lefty-swinging Harry Simpson to the plate. Simpson homered into right center and the Yankees were up by two. Yogi Berra lined out to end the inning and the excitement, but not for long.

Mickey came up again in the third. Tony Kubek had opened the inning with a single to center, but had been erased when Gil McDougald lined into a double play. Thus the bases were empty when Mantle came to the plate. Keegan got behind on the count, 3–1, and served up something crushable. Mantle hit the ball so hard, the *Herald Tribune's* headline proclaimed, HIS HOMER ALMOST OUT OF STADIUM. The ball in fact hit two rows short of going out of the right-field bleachers onto River Avenue. "A hasty check of blueprints by Jim Thomson, the Stadium superintendent, indicated that Mantle's drive had landed about 465 feet from home plate."

The score remained 3–0 in the Yankees' favor until the White Sox half of the fifth. Larsen had never been renowned for his control, and this time the wildness cost him. After striking out Les Moss, Larsen walked Sammy Esposito, then threw a wild pitch that allowed Esposito to scamper all the way to third. He then walked the pitcher, Keegan. Jim Rivera knocked a base hit, scoring Esposito, and Nellie Fox lay down a bunt single, loading the bases. Stengel brought in Tommy Byrne, the "Wild Man," himself, who got two ground balls—one that scored Keegan, and one that ended the inning. 3–2 Yankees.

Jerry Coleman started the action in the bottom of the inning, doubling off Keegan, and scoring when Kubek singled to right. But the lead did not last long. In the top of the sixth, Byrne found his control had deserted him as well. With two out, he walked Moss and Esposito. Walt Dropo pinch-hit for

Keegan, and Byrne walked him, too. Then pinch hitter Ron Northey came in . . . and Byrne walked him as well, forcing in a run. At this point, Byrne headed for the showers, and Art Ditmar came on. Unfortunately, the first batter he faced, Fox, singled, scoring one, and then Earl Torgeson did the same, scoring two.

With the White Sox up, 6–4, Mantle did his best to get the Yankees back in it. He singled to lead off the bottom of the sixth, went to second on a base hit from Simpson, and then stole third, but was stranded there. But he came to bat again in the seventh. This time Elston Howard had led off the inning with a triple and scored on a wild pitch. Jerry Coleman drew a walk, and Enos Slaughter came in to pinch-hit for Ditmar. Slaughter walked as well. Kubek laid down a bunt for a hit, loading the bases for Gil McDougald. McDougald walked in a run, tying the score and leaving the bases loaded for Mantle, who needed only a triple to hit for the cycle. He connected for a "vicious liner, hit right-handed off Jack Harshman," wrote Joseph P. Sheehan in the *New York Times*. "The ball eluded Minnie Minoso's leaping grasp in the left-field corner." As the ball rattled around, Mantle legged his way to third. The hit cleared the bases, put the Yankees up, 9–6, and capped off a spectacular night for Mantle, which the *Chicago Tribune* called "one of the greatest games in the Oklahoman's career."

"His big night put Mantle back into American League leadership in batting with an average of .367, and in runs batted in with 69," reported the *Times*. The Yankees tacked on another run, of no consequence, in the eighth when Coleman, Kubek, and McDougald all singled, but Mantle grounded out to end the inning. These other guys "weren't bad either," wrote Rosenthal at the end of his game story, "[but] when it happens on a night like this, such information winds up way down here. Sorry, fellows." Mantle went on to win the MVP Award for the second year in a row.

◆Extra Innings

- When Mantle first came up to the Yankees, the organization viewed him as DiMaggio's successor and gave him the number 6 to wear (DiMaggio was number 5). Mantle struggled, and after a trip back to the minors, returned, this time to wear number 7, which he would wear the rest of his career.

- Jason Giambi, who signed with the Yankees in 2002, chose the number 25 because 2 + 5 = 7. Giambi's father was a huge Mantle fan who raised his sons in Southern California but taught them to love the Yankees. "Look, Pop," Giambi said as he got misty-eyed at his introductory Yankee press conference, "it's not 7, but it's pinstripes."

26

October 13, 1960: New York at Pittsburgh

Pittsburgh Stealers

In which a team that was thoroughly dominated nevertheless emerges on top

By the end of 1960, the Ol' Perfessor, Casey Stengel, was on his way out. He was in the last year of his contract, and the Yankees' lackluster performance in 1959 had started the front office grumbling. But with the recent additions of Roger Maris and Ralph Terry, the 1960 Yankees were contenders, despite the friction between the 70-year-old Stengel and his bosses. On August 1 the team was in second place, but soon went on a winning streak, finishing the year eight games in first place as Maris won the MVP Award. "Maris made them the Yankees again," wrote historian Glenn Stout in *Yankees Century.* "Or at least a reasonable facsimile of the team that had dominated . . . like no other." The Yankees went into October as they had so many times before, the heavy favorites.

The club they faced, the Pittsburgh Pirates, were in their first World Series since 1927, when their opponent had been Ruth's Murderers' Row Yankees, and they had been swept in four straight. Roberto Clemente, Vern Law, and Dick Groat were fine players, but few thought Pittsburgh would be able to stand up to the Yankee offense. With Mantle and Maris, not to mention Yogi Berra, the Yankees of 1960 had an imposing lineup as well. Moose Skowron was batting .309. Tony Kubek had knocked 155 hits. And indeed, in some ways, the outcome of the Series would be exactly as the bookies predicted: the Yankees would outscore Pittsburgh by a total of 55–27, and outhit them 91–60.

But baseball is an unpredictable game. Despite being outgunned by a wide margin, the plucky Pirates scratched out three wins to force a seventh and final game. One might think that Stengel had suffered from overconfidence, choosing to start Art Ditmar in the first game instead of World Series ace Whitey Ford. Ford notched wins in the third game and the sixth, staving off elimination. That left Bob Turley to start game seven. Turley had been a great pitcher at one point in his career, winning the 1958 Cy Young Award, the 1958 World Series MVP Award, and featuring a fastball that topped at 93 miles per hour. But in 1959, with bone chips in his elbow, he lost the zip on the fastball and began to rely on a curveball more. He had World Series experience, but could no longer inspire confidence.

Anthony Christopher "Tony" Kubek

He didn't last even two innings. In the first inning, with two out he walked Bob Skinner, and Rocky Nelson hit a two-run home run. Clemente popped out, but when Smoky Burgess singled to start the second, Casey yanked Turley in favor of Bill Stafford. Stafford immediately walked Hoak. Then Bill Mazeroski, an exceptionally fine defensive second baseman but who was considered a lightweight hitter, hit a roller in the infield to load the bases. Vern Law, the Pittsburgh pitcher who to this point had merrily dispatched the Yankees six-up, six-down, then tried to help his own cause with a hit. Instead he grounded the ball right back to Stafford, who threw home for the force-out there, catcher Johnny Blanchard then tossing to first baseman Skowron for the double play. One more out would get Stafford (and Turley) out of the jam, but the next batter, Bill Virdon, brought two runners home with a base knock to right. Groat grounded out, but the score after two was 4–0 Pirates.

The Yankees did not score until the fifth, when Skowron greeted Law with a solo homer. But the next three men went down in order. Meanwhile, Bobby Shantz was pitching for the Yankees, Stafford having been lifted for a pinch hitter, and Shantz was pitching well, though in pain. Each inning as he went out to warm up, he would signal Stengel in the dugout whether he could continue.

The Yankee bullpen remained active. Even Ford tried to warm up, but as he told Tony Kubek, as recounted in the latter's book *Sixty-One* (written with Terry Pluto), "I suppose I'm still shocked that I didn't start the opener. I pitched the third and sixth games . . . and Casey let me throw nine innings even though both games were blowouts. I could see that the seventh game was going to be a wild one, and I tried to warm up, but my arm was so stiff . . . I couldn't even get the ball to home plate on a fly."

The Pirates' bats remained quiet, and the Yankees mounted an assault in the sixth.

Bobby Richardson started things going with a single, and he moved into scoring position when Kubek walked. Maris popped out, but Mantle singled, bringing in Richardson and putting men on the corners. Yogi Berra then did what he had done in so many previous World Series. He homered, giving the Yankees a 5–4 lead. Shantz continued to set the Pirates down, and in the eighth it looked like the Yankees were pulling away. They added two more with two out when Yogi walked, followed by a string of Yankee hits: Skowron, Blanchard, Boyer. 7–4 Yankees, with six outs to go.

But in the eighth fate took a bad hop. Pinch hitter Gino Cimoli led off with a single. Virdon came up and hit a double-play ball right at Tony Kubek. The ball kangarooed off the Pittsburgh infield, which had been described as cinder-hard and littered with pebbles, and into Kubek's throat. Kubek remembers the incident unhappily in *Sixty-One*: "For nine years I played in the majors but I'm still known as the guy who got hit in the throat. . . . I guess everyone is supposed to be famous for at least ten minutes. The throat incident took about ten seconds, but that's what people remember. I meet a stranger [and] he'll say, 'Aren't you the guy who got hit in the throat?'" Kubek was taken to the hospital, and instead of two outs, there were two on and no one out. Groat singled into left, scoring Cimoli. Shantz gave way to Jim Coates, the Yankees' fourth pitcher of the day. Skinner bunted the runners over. Nelson flew to Maris for the second out, but Clemente beat out an infield hit as Coates was late to the bag, to bring in Virdon. The Yankees only clung to the one-run lead for one more batter. Hal Smith buried a Coates pitch in the seats, a three-run shot giving the Pirates a 9–7 lead. Down in the bullpen, Ralph Terry was already worn out, but he got the call to take the hill. "I warmed up five times that game," he explained. "I came in and got out Don Hoak. But I didn't have anything left. It's the seventh game, it's give your all or go home. So I threw hard, and after about the second time I warmed up, I was done."

Amazingly, the Yankees were not done. They tied the score as their relentless offensive machine kept churning. Richardson singled, pinch hitter Dale

Long singled. Maris popped out again, but Mantle singled in Richardson. Berra grounded out, a near double play that would have ended the game and the Series, but Mantle dove back to first and Long scored the tying run.

So the score was 9–9 going into the bottom of the ninth, and Terry went back out to the hill. With his arm as worn as it was, Terry could not get the ball down. He would face only one batter, though, as Mazeroski deposited his second pitch over the ivy on the left-field wall. Just like that, it was over, the first walk-off home run to decide a World Series.

The Yankees' clubhouse was a somber place after the loss. Mickey Mantle cried because he felt that the better team had lost. "You wonder what a manager tells a team that has been blown out as badly as the Pirates," wrote Mantle in his 1994 memoir *All My Octobers*. "[The Pirates' manager] Danny Murtaugh [told them] 'I looked in the rule book and it said the Series will be decided on games won, not on runs scored.' I wish it had been the other way."

Terry wasn't easy to console either, but Stengel found a way. Terry, who like most of the players sensed that Casey was on his way out, stopped into the manager's office. "I felt worse for him than for me because everyone knew it was his last year," Terry remembered. "He said, 'How were you trying to pitch him?'" Terry answered he had been trying to get the ball down, but it had hung up. "Well," Casey told him, "if you were trying to blow away a high-ball hitter with high fastballs, I wouldn't sleep too good at night. But when you follow the scouting report? Just forget it; come out and get 'em next year."

The next year Terry responded by going 16–3, but Stengel would not be in the dugout to see it. The era of the Ol' Perfessor had come to an end.

◆ Extra Innings

- Bill Mazeroski, home run hero of the 1960 World Series, was not inducted into the Baseball Hall of Fame until 2001. Maz was inducted on the strength of his defense, and he still holds several fielding records, including most double plays turned by a second baseman (1,706). On August 8, 2001, the day of his induction, he set a new record: shortest ever Hall of Fame induction speech, at 2 minutes and 30 seconds. "I got 12 pages but I might not get through all of them," he told the crowd before breaking down in tears, unable to say more than a few more words before sitting down to a standing ovation from the 23,000 present.

- Game seven of the 1960 World Series is unique for another World Series record, fewest strikeouts in a game: none!

September 20, 1961: New York at Baltimore

Racing Ruth (and Frick)

In which Roger Maris finds himself having the worst best season ever

Nineteen sixty-one was the year of the M+M boys, Maris and Mantle, batting third and fourth in the Yankee lineup for manager Ralph Houk. Mantle was the superstar, the heir to the crown previously worn by Joe DiMaggio. The Oklahoma boy had come up through the Yankees' system and earned his place as the glamour position player. Maris had come up with the Indians, then moved to the Kansas City A's in his second year. In 1959, Maris found himself headed to New York as part of a seven-player deal: Maris, Kent Hadley, and Joe DeMaestri came in exchange for Don Larsen, Hank Bauer, Marv Throneberry, and Norm Siebern.

Maris made an immediate impact. A good defensive outfielder with a strong arm and a left handed line-drive stroke, Maris played his first game as a Yankee on April 19, 1960, at Fenway Park, where he singled, doubled, and hit two home runs. Mantle finished that year with 40 home runs, Maris with 39. Maris also earned MVP honors in 1960. He also might have won a World Series ring if only Bill Mazeroski hadn't conjured some late-inning magic.

Houk, who took over managing the Yankees in 1961 after the ouster of that old improvisation artist Casey Stengel, preferred a set lineup, and his number three and four hitters feasted on American League pitching, both hitting a prodigious quantity of home runs. By August tension and excitement began to swirl around the two hitters, who were within hailing distance of Babe Ruth's hallowed record of 60 home runs in a single season.

Much has been made of the way Maris was hounded by the media, unprotected by the Yankees, and unable to meet the celebrity-hungry press's expectations that he would be as witty, interesting, or charming as Mantle, or even as appreciative of the media attention as some writers felt he ought to be. Maris did not appreciate the attention—he dreaded it.

An empathetic Bob Addie wrote the following in his column in the *Washington Post*:

Suppose you were the President of the United States and you had no Secret Service or other buffers to keep away the curious? How would you react? It is, perhaps, presumptuous, to compare a baseball player named Roger Maris to the President . . . but Maris stands as an exposed island in the hurricane of attention which has been his since he became a challenger to Babe Ruth's home run record. . . . It is almost funny to see the reporters and photographers, held in leash like greyhounds about to chase the mechanical rabbit, when they storm into the dressing-room after Maris. . . . There are dozens of reporters from all over the country . . . drawn by the drama of the home run race. Some have odd assignments like sticking with Maris all day to report on what he eats, what he says, and what he does up until game time.

In a game where a player's self-confidence may be his greatest tool, Maris found himself questioned at every turn. Some fans and writers believed that Mantle was a more worthy successor to Ruth and resented his success. And there were others who looked askance as Maris's pursuit of Ruth. Commissioner Ford Frick, the man who had ghostwritten one of Ruth's books on baseball, decreed that the record would be broken only if it were done within 154 games, which had been the length of the season in 1927 when Ruth had set the mark. "You don't break the 100-meter record by running the 100-yard dash," Frick reasoned. After answering the question "Can you do it?" for the seemingly millionth time, Maris began to succumb to the stress. His hair began to fall out.

But he continued to hit. At the plate and in the field he could still be the master of his own destiny. MARIS CONNECTS FOR NO. 57 read the headline in the sports section of the *Washington Post* on Sunday, September 17. Shirley Povich wrote in his daily column, "Ralph Houk, the Yankees' manager, has rejected a proposal that he move Roger Maris and Mickey Mantle to the top spots in the batting order so they could have additional shots at Babe Ruth's record. 'Ruth's record probably is the most glamorous of any ever made. The fellow who breaks it should receive no special help,' Houk said." Mantle, meanwhile, was slowed by an infection after an injection by a quack doctor and was out of the race.

On Monday, September 18, the *Post* headlined Maris again: MARIS INCHES CLOSER WITH NO. 58. The Associated Press reported that Maris had "smashed his 58th homer and missed another by a foot." The one he did hit cleared the wall in the 12th inning to give the Yankees an extra-innings victory in Detroit and to put their magic number at two. The next day Povich devoted his entire column to previewing the Yankees' upcoming series: "Maris Takes on Ghost of Ruth in Baltimore." The day's doubleheader, though—one win and one loss—produced no homers for Maris. "The magic game number for both the Yankees and Roger Maris is '1' but the Yankees have an infinitely better chance of achieving their goal than does Maris," wrote Bob Addie in the *Post*.

And so came game 154 for Maris, the day by which Frick had decreed the record should be broken, or else continue to stand. Baltimore's Memorial Stadium was not known as a hitters' park, and Maris in particular had not hit a home run there all year, unless one counted a shot he hit on July 17 that was wiped out by rain (Frick didn't). The Orioles started Milt Pappas. After a brief, three-game stint in the minors, Pappas had come up as an 18-year-old rookie in 1957 and proved to be too good to send back down. Although he was known to be somewhat hypochondriac (he earned the nickname "Gimpy" from his teammates), Pappas still averaged 15 wins a season in many of his years with the Birds. In 1961 he would end the season 13–9 with a 3.04 ERA.

Bobby Richardson opened the game by hitting the ball to Jerry Adair, who bobbled it, allowing Richardson to reach. Kubek followed with a fly to center, to bring Maris to the plate. On a 2–1 pitch, Maris lined the ball into right, where Earl Robinson hauled it in. Berra singled, but Johnny Blanchard grounded to first to end the threat.

The Yankees' Ralph Terry took the hill, and retired the O's on two quick ground outs and a strikeout. Most of the Baltimore crowd had come to see Maris, anyway. In the second, the Yankees mounted a small rally. With one out, Moose Skowron tripled. Clete Boyer singled to bring him in. That was as far as it went, though. Terry struck out, and Richardson grounded out.

Terry cruised through the bottom of the second as well, and Kubek opened the third with Maris on deck. Kubek grounded back to Pappas, who took the ball to the bag himself, and then turned his attention to Maris. Was Pappas winded, or distracted by the moment? Maris deposited his fourth pitch over the auxiliary scoreboard and into the right-field bleachers, for home run 59, and the question became, could he hit another in the three times at bat he was expected to have in the game? Pappas came unglued. Berra followed the Maris homer with one of his own. Then Blanchard singled and Elston Howard doubled, bringing Blanchard home. Dick Hall, a tall righthander with good control, replaced Pappas on the mound and escaped the inning without further damage, but the score stood 4–0 Yankees.

Terry continued to cruise, sitting down another three in the third. He struck out himself to open the fourth, and Richardson grounded out. But Kubek singled, bringing Maris up again. Hall did not give in, nipping the outside corner for a strike, then the inside corner. Maris looked at a ball and then swung for a sucker pitch, a high fastball, and struck out. In the bottom half, Terry gave up a hit, breaking up his perfect string on ten batters, but Adair was quickly erased on a double play. The O's went down in order in the fifth but came to life in the sixth. With one out, Ron Hansen singled to center and so did Hall, moving Hansen to second. Brooks Robinson followed with a single as well, scoring Hansen and moving Hall to second. Jerry Adair then hit a ball to short. Kubek fed Richardson to start the double play, but Richardson fumbled. Hall scored and Adair was safe at first. Terry struck out Jim Gentile to escape the jam, the Yankees still leading, 4–2, going into the seventh.

Tony Kubek led off the inning and grounded out. Maris stood in. He connected on a fastball, just a little early. The drive went deep into the right-field stands, but foul. "I knew the minute it jumped off the bat it was foul, and that's that," said Maris. The next one was fair, but about ten feet short of the fence. Berra grounded out to end the inning.

Maris got his final chance in the ninth. Hall had been lifted for a pinch hitter, so the noted knuckleballer Hoyt Wilhelm came on to pitch. Richardson grounded out and Kubek popped up, leaving only Maris. "The crowd gave the Yankee outfielder an ovation as he came to the plate," wrote Addie. Wilhelm dealt a knuckler and Maris fouled it back. In danced another, and Maris tried to check his swing, but the bat touched the ball and it squibbed weakly back to the pitcher, who retired him unassisted. "The bat never went, but my body did," Maris said about the at-bat. "I wanted to get three good swings whether I hit it or not. As it turned out, I didn't get one" (*New York Herald Tribune*).

"The Yankees were celebrating their second straight pennant, their sixth in the last seven years, and their 11th in the last 13. But Maris was still the big story," wrote Addie. "No other man except Ruth himself ever hit as many as 59." Maris had passed Hank Greenberg and Jimmie Foxx.

Maris, for his part, said he was "lucky I hit as many as I did, and now I'm completely relieved!" In the champagne celebration taking place in the Yankees' clubhouse he addressed reporters: "A thing like this takes a whole lot out of you," he said. "Let's face it. I would have liked to hit 60 or 61 within 154 games. I tried like the devil but all I got was one" (*UPI*). He also told reporters, "Commissioner Frick makes the rules. If all I am entitled to will be an asterisk, it will be all right with me."

Maris eventually did hit number 60 a few days later, and number 61 in the final game of the season at Yankee Stadium, for the only run of a 1–0 victory. Maris ended the year not only with the league lead in home runs (obviously), but also in RBI (142) and runs scored (132). He also won his second MVP Award in a row, and a World Series ring when the Yankees defeated the Cincinnati Reds. Major League Baseball eventually changed the record-keeping for all single-season offensive records to tally totals regardless of season length or games played. Maris's name stood at the top of the home run list longer than Ruth's, until 1998.

◢ Extra Innings

- During the game, the Yankees' bullpen tried to barter with Bob Reitz, the fan who retrieved the home run ball, offering him other balls and souvenirs in exchange. "At last report . . . he was holding out for two World Series tickets and perhaps a trip to Europe" (*Washington Post*). The day after the game, Maris went with former ballplayer Lou Grasmick, a Baltimore businessman, to negotiate for the ball. Reitz demanded $2,500, an offer Maris refused.

- Hank Greenberg, who had shared third place on the home run list with Jimmie Foxx at 58 in a season, watched Maris hit number 59 from a broadcast booth in Memorial Stadium. (Ruth occupied both first and second place on the list with 59 in 1921 and 60 in 1927.)

- Ford Motors tried to capitalize on home run fever by advertising "'61 HOME RUNS! You get a 'home run' deal on a great '61 Ford or Falcon right now!" The ads were not endorsed by Maris or the Yankees.

- In 1998, when Mark McGwire and Sammy Sosa chased Maris's record, Milt Pappas stated that he had told Maris the night before the game that if the game were not on the line, he would feed the hitter nothing but fastballs. Pappas disagreed with Frick's contention that the record would stand as separate from Ruth's if it took more than 154 games to achieve.

- Despite all the brouhaha about the game being the 154th contest of the Yankees' season, and therefore Frick's "deadline," the game was technically the 155th, though no one treated it as such. The anomaly came about because of a tie in the second game of a doubleheader back on April 22. Although the tie game did not count in the standings, it did count as far as individual statistics and "games played" when all stats were tallied at year's end.

28

October 8, 1961: New York at Cincinnati

Rough Year for Ruth

In which Whitey Ford breaks the Babe's favorite record

Ed Ford was a New Yorker born and bred. That made him different from the country-boy teammates who surrounded him, who came to the Yankees and

Edward Charles "Whitey" Ford

learned what the big city was all about. Whitey already knew. He grew up in Astoria, in a white working-class neighborhood where he played baseball in the summer with a local team, the 34th Avenue Boys. He wanted to be a first baseman, a natural pursuit for a lefthander, but pitched the 34th Avenue Boys to a 36–0 record in 1946. The Yankees signed him shortly thereafter, and in 1950 he joined the big-league club for good. He quickly became the ringleader of Casey Stengel's "whiskey slicks," including Mickey Mantle and Billy Martin, who were known for their late-night bar hopping. "Whitey's the chairman of the board, you know," said teammate Tom Tresh, who joined the club for good in 1962. "He just seemed to be the natural person to go to for the decision like 'what are we going to do tonight?' He was definitely a leader."

He was a leader on the mound as well. Upon being called up in 1950, Ford won nine starts in a row and capped off the year by taking a shutout into the ninth inning in the final game of a four-game sweep of Philly in the World Series. Stengel pulled him when he got into hot water, and Allie Reynolds sealed the Phillies' fate, but it was a bravura performance that would become nearly annual. In his 16 seasons in the bigs, the Yankees reached the World Series 11 times.

Ford was a deceptive pitcher in some ways. Listed at 5 feet, 10 inches and 178 pounds, the lefty didn't seem to have much of a fastball nor an intimidating presence on the mound—until a hitter had faced his array of curves and changes of speed. "Whitey got the ball and he didn't dilly-dally around on the mound," infielder Phil Linz recalled of the way the team loved playing behind Whitey. "He was a strike-thrower." Dave Kindred of the *Sporting News* would later compare him to Tom Glavine of the Atlanta Braves—not a power pitcher, but ruthlessly efficient.

In the 1960 Fall Classic, Ford pitched brilliantly as always, and many wondered why Stengel had elected to start Art Ditmar in game one instead of his usual October ace. Ford notched complete-game shutouts in games three and six instead. In 1961, Ralph Houk did not repeat Stengel's mistake, starting Ford in game one. The "Chairman of the Board" then pitched his third complete-game World Series shutout.

With all the buzz of the '61 season centering around Maris and Mantle's chase of Babe Ruth's home run record, who could have expected that one of Ruth's pitching records might be in jeopardy as well? As a hard-throwing lefty with the Red Sox, Ruth had set the standard for October mound magic, throwing 29⅔ consecutive scoreless innings in 1916 and 1918. With his three shutouts in hand, Whitey was at 27 innings and raring to go for game four, despite a stiff neck brought on by the air conditioning in his Pullman train car. "There was no pressure on me when the game started. The last thing on my mind was trying to break a record," Whitey said, explaining he was ignorant of the milestone he was about to reach. "I didn't even know Babe Ruth was a pitcher," he admitted. "There was no talk about me breaking his record. Then when I had pitched three shutouts in the row, all of a sudden something was in the paper about 'he has a shot,' but I didn't pay any attention to it."

Even though it was October, it felt like summer that afternoon at Crosley Field. John Drebinger in the *New York Times* called it a "day right out of July, with not a cloud in the sky, the temperature around 80 and the fans sitting in their shirt-sleeves in the sun-drenched bleachers." The Reds took the field trailing two games to one. Ford's opponent that day was 24-year-old Jim O'Toole, a fellow lefty whom he had beaten 2–0 in game one a few days before.

O'Toole handled the Yankees with ease to start, and Ford did the same, so no man reached until Moose Skowron opened the third inning with a walk. Clete Boyer followed with a ground ball to short, forcing Skowron at second. Whitey himself then grounded to second, forcing Boyer. He moved to third on Bobby Richardson's double, the Yankees' first hit of the game, but was stranded when Tony Kubek lofted a fly ball to center.

The Reds answered the almost-rally with one of their own. With one out, Darrell Johnson singled into left field, the Reds' first hit. Up came O'Toole, but he did as Whitey had, forcing the runner. Shirley Povich described what happened next in the *Washington Post*: "At 1:44 P.M. Whitey Ford thumbed up one of his soft, sly curves to Elio Chacon, and that little fellow from Venezuela became a part of American history." Chacon's grounder to Richardson ended the inning, and Ford had broken Babe Ruth's record, tallying 30 consecutive scoreless innings in World Series play.

Whitey would always remember the moment. "When I walked off the mound after the third inning [when] I reached thirty innings, the crowd sort of clapped, and I was wondering why is the crowd clapping for me in Cincinnati? I got back in the dressing room and the writers, who very seldom came down in the middle of the game, said did you realize you beat Babe Ruth? I said, really? That was when I realized Babe Ruth was a pitcher."

Now every scoreless inning added to the record, which was nice, but winning the game would still require some run support. Maris opened the fourth with a walk. Mantle, who was hitless in the Series and still suffering from the abscess on his hip that had landed him in the hospital at the end of the regular season, then singled into left center and Maris ran hard to third. "Actually it would have been a double for any other hitter," or so thought Shirley Povich, "but Mantle . . . could only limp with pain to first base." Mantle, his abscess bleeding, was replaced by Hector Lopez and was applauded by the Cincinnati crowd. Ralph Houk later told reporters that Mantle had been hurting for some time and he had "intended to take him out after that at-bat." Elston Howard followed, grounding into a double play, but Maris scored.

Maris moved to center and Lopez took Mantle's place in right, while Ford went back to the mound. Eddie Kasko started the action in the fourth with a base hit. Vada Pinson followed with a sinking shot down the left-field line that Yogi snared on the run, despite the slanting sun. Then Whitey hit Frank Robinson, but the threat had barely materialized when Wally Post grounded into a 6-4-3 double play.

The Yankee bats went back to work in the fifth. Skowron singled to right, but was erased on a double play, bringing Whitey to the plate. He battled O'Toole, fouling off pitches and eventually working a walk. Bobby Richardson knocked a hit into center, and Whitey held at second. Tony Kubek followed with another single to center. Pinson made a throw to the plate, but Whitey crossed safely ahead of the tag with the second run.

Whitey went back to work in the bottom of the inning. He retired Gene Freese and Gordy Coleman quickly, then allowed a single to Johnson. Dick

Gernert pinch-hit for O'Toole but grounded into a force play, pushing Whitey's streak to 32 innings. Frank Crosetti, a star infielder with the Yankees in the 1930s and '40s and then a longtime Yankee coach, asked home plate umpire Augie Donatelli to take the ball out of play, just in case.

"Old Crow" was prophetic. In the sixth, Jim Brosnan took O'Toole's place on the hill. Brosnan was a righty relief specialist who also was known for writing a frank and candid book called *The Long Season*, about his time in the National League. Brosnan got Lopez to stare at strike three, but Howard followed with a double, bringing Yogi to the plate. With first base open, Reds manager Fred Hutchinson elected to intentionally walk him and go after Skowron. Moose took a weak swing, but his slow roller up the third-base line was an infield hit. With the bases now loaded, Boyer came to the plate for one of those classic Yankee October moments. His double off the left-field wall scored two and brought Whitey to the plate for the second time in two innings. Whitey went up there hacking, and fouled a ball off his big toe. The foul hurt so much, Whitey fell on his backside in the batter's box, grimacing in pain. He ended up grounding out. With Richardson up, the Reds caught Skowron in a rundown to end the inning.

Though Whitey answered the bell for the sixth, the swelling and pain in his foot were too much. Chacon greeted him with a leadoff single. "Landing on that foot when I let the ball go hurt like blazes," he told reporters later. Houk came out to check on him after Chacon's hit and discovered how bad it was. As he walked off the mound, the fans gave him an ovation. Whitey had gone as far as he could, and left up 4–0, with the 32-inning streak under his belt and Jim Coates taking his place on the mound. Coates picked right up where Ford left off, allowing only one hit and no runs in his four innings of relief. The Yankees tacked on three more in the seventh, cruising to a 7–0 victory.

After the game, Ford was his usual ebullient self with reporters. "Maybe I'll get together with [hitting coach] Wally Moses next spring and work on my hitting so I can go after some of the Babe's batting records, too," he wisecracked. The Yankees wrapped up the Series the next day with a 13–5 drubbing of eight Reds' pitchers. Whitey's record carried into 1962, where he pitched 1⅔ innings to run the streak to 33⅔ before Willie Mays scored on a bunt in the second inning of game one against the Giants.

Extra Innings

- Announcer Mel Allen was fond of giving players nicknames that rhymed, such as "Hank Bauer, Man of the Hour." It was Allen who first called Whitey Ford the "Chairman of the Board."

Who Holds the Longest Scoreless Innings Streak?

Whitey Ford's streak of scoreless innings in the World Series was snapped in 1962 at 33⅔. Yet in 2000, Mariano Rivera was touted to have broken Whitey's postseason record by pitching 33⅓. How can this be?

In 1991 a special records committee was convened to revise Major League Baseball's official records. Seymour Siwoff, founder of the Elias Sports Bureau, was among the committee members. The committee determined, among other things, that fractional innings in scoreless innings streaks did not count, except in the case of a relief pitcher entering partway through an inning. The rationale was that if a pitcher starts an inning and then gives up a run, the inning as a whole cannot be considered as scoreless, and so should not be counted in the streak, even in part. By this, Whitey's record was officially truncated to 33 innings.

Mariano Rivera began his streak of scoreless relief pitching on September 29, 1998, and carried it through 25 appearances in postseason play until October 17, 2000. On that day, with his streak up to 33⅓ innings (the fraction having come as a part of games where he entered partway through the eighth inning), Mo entered game six of the ALCS against the Mariners and retired two batters—pushing his streak to 34 innings—before he gave up two runs. His final streak total, therefore, stayed at 33⅓. "I'm just happy to be part of the Yankees, breaking the record as a Yankee, because it was a Yankee that held it," Mo said after passing Whitey. "I've known Whitey Ford since 1993 in Yankees' spring training. He's a great human being, and he was a great player. And being a Yankee, I have the most respect for him."

Of course, Rivera reached the 33⅓ mark pitching in a three-tiered postseason, while Ford's record still stands as a World Series record alone. Mo's World Series scoreless innings streak ran to 14⅓ innings at its longest point.

◦ The Reds drew on baseball history for some eminent figures to throw out the ceremonial first pitch prior to each game. "Dummy" Hoy, then 99 years old and the oldest living major leaguer, did the honors before game three, and Bill "Deacon" McKechnie, who had managed Cincinnati to pennants in 1939 and 1940, followed in game four. Cincinnati also tried to muster up some luck with a song: "Tell Your Aunt Hattie This Year It's Cincinnati."

◦ Whitey Ford also tops the lists for eight other World Series pitching records: wins (10), losses (8), games pitched (22), games started (22), innings pitched (146), hits (132), walks (34), most Series played by pitcher (11), and strikeouts (94).

October 16, 1962: New York at San Francisco

Redemption

In which Ralph Terry finds himself on the mound for the final pitch of the season, again

In 1962, the Yankees once again felt they had what it took to win it all. The team was much the same as the one that had enjoyed the great run of 1961, and Ralph Houk was back as manager. Even when they fell three games back in June, no one worried. One of the reasons panic did not set in when Whitey Ford was injured early in the season was that Ralph Terry was there taking up the slack, racking up 23 wins by season's end. Terry thrived under the tutelage of new pitching coach Johnny Sain. After Mickey Mantle returned from a disabling leg injury at the end of June, the team began to click, and ended the year five games ahead of the nearest competitor, Minnesota. "I was 5–0 versus the Twins, so I did my part," Terry said. The team's only possible weakness was its bullpen. "[Luis] Arroyo had a great year in 1961, [but] with that screwball [he

Ralph Willard Terry

threw], his elbow would swell up. Then in '62 his arm went bad on him, so it was bullpen by committee." Rookies Tom Tresh and Phil Linz made big contributions as well.

Meanwhile, the two teams who had fled west, the ancient rivals the Dodgers and the Giants, fought in a playoff to see who would face the Yankees. The Giants prevailed. With Willie Mays, Orlando Cepeda, Felipe Alou, Willie McCovey, and 24-game-winner Jack Sanford, San Francisco leaped confidently into their first World Series since moving out of New York.

Giants manager Alvin Dark chose lefty Bill O'Dell to pitch game one, while Houk went with that old standby, Whitey Ford. Ford pitched the complete-game victory, 6–2. In game two, Terry faced Sanford in a pitchers' duel: Sanford, the 2–0 victor, gave up only three hits. The Yankees won game three behind Bill Stafford, but then dropped game four, Whitey's next start, when the bullpen gave up a grand slam and the lead in the Series. Rain delayed game five, and Terry and Sanford faced off for a second time a day later. This time Terry was the victor, the benefactor of a three-run home run by rookie Tom Tresh.

"Ralph was a very happy-type guy," according to Linz. "But he was a competitor, and once the game started, like all of us, he wanted to win. He threw strikes and he didn't waste any time. He got the ball and he didn't dilly-dally around on the mound. Infielders especially love that."

The fate of the Series ultimately may have hinged on the weather. Typhoon Frieda brought soaking rains to San Francisco. The Series, which began on October 4, was not wrapped up until October 16, with a four-day delay between the fifth game in New York and the sixth game in San Francisco. "Of course we loved the rain, because we were able to stay in San Francisco and eat in all the famous restaurants there," said Linz, who along with Joe Pepitone and Jim Bouton was experiencing his first World Series. "Every night we were out there we'd eat a nice dinner somewhere. Let it rain for another week! It was okay with us."

The delay meant that each manager could tap his best pitchers again, and both game one starters came back. With the Yankees leading the Series 3–2, Houk hoped Ford could seal another championship. But it was not to be. Whitey didn't survive the fifth, while Billy Pierce went the distance in a 5–2 win, forcing game seven.

Both managers kept their rotations in line, so Sanford and Terry faced off for the third time in the Series. The sun shone brilliantly on that final day, but the ground was still soggy, and Candlestick Park's infamous swirling winds were fed by 40-mile-an-hour gusts. Terry took the mound determined not to suffer the fate he had in 1960. "Nineteen sixty-two was my year," he said when describing his attitude. "I made my contribution to the team and I wanted to repay all the people who had rooted for me. The New York fans never really held that Mazeroski home run against me." With Sain's help he also had a few more weapons at his disposal. "I went to the cutter. I had an overhand curve that was pretty slow. So now I had two different speeds on breaking pitches, the curve and what they call the cutter now." The cutter Terry could throw like a fastball, but with late-breaking movement in toward left-handed batters and away from righthanders.

Sanford, of course, was no slouch either, as his three-hit win showed. The pitchers' duel commenced with two no-hit innings from each hurler before Kubek singled with two outs in the third. Richardson walked. But Tresh, though he was leading the team in hitting in the World Series, grounded out to end the threat.

The Yankees finally nicked Sanford for first blood, just barely, in the fifth. Moose Skowron opened the inning with a single to center. Clete Boyer followed with a single, moving Skowron to third and bringing Terry himself to the plate. Sanford then committed the cardinal sin of walking the pitcher. With the bases loaded, Kubek hit a hard grounder to short. A tailor-made double play, but Skowron scored on the play. Richardson then hit a foul pop to first, ending the inning, but the Yankees led by the slimmest of margins.

"A 1–0 shutout is probably the most tension you can bring to bear on two pitchers. That game probably shortened my career by five years," Terry recalled. "I had a perfect game into the sixth." With two outs, Sanford got his revenge. "Sanford got a hit. It was the first time all game I shook off Elston Howard, wouldn't you know it." But Sanford's hit was a small victory, as Felipe Alou grounded out to end the inning.

From then on it was a game of two-out rallies and tension. "We had a lot of frustration that game that we couldn't score more runs. It was like two heavyweight teams—power against power. The score should have been 5–2, but the defense [was] real good and the field was muddy," Terry said. In the Yankees' half of the seventh, Howard struck out and Skowron lined a ball to McCovey in left. But then Boyer singled. Terry himself singled. Could Kubek add an insurance run? No. Kubek hit a fly ball to left, and Terry went right back onto the mound. Second baseman Chuck Hiller tried to get on with a bunt, but looped the ball right into Terry's hands. Then Mays hit a ball on a deep line to left. Tresh chased it in the swirling wind and just snared it with one hand in the corner, an out whose importance grew when McCovey then tripled to center. Terry bore down to strike out Cepeda and strand the runner there.

In the eighth the Yankees tried again. Richardson got things going when he hit the ball to short and reached on José Pagán's throwing error. Tresh tried a similar approach, the hard-hit ball skipping off Pagán's knee for a hit. Mantle then singled to short right, loading the bases. Sanford said good night. Billy O'Dell, who had recorded the save in game four, came on. Maris hit into a force-out at home, Howard grounded into a double play, and the Yankees were turned back again.

But Terry sat the Giants down in the bottom of the eighth, three up, three down. The Yankees mounted no threat in the ninth, Terry himself making the third out, going down on strikes. The ninth inning was to open with O'Dell's slot in the lineup, and Alvin Dark went to a pinch hitter.

"Matty Alou led off and hit a pop foul," Terry remembered. "Elston went over toward the Giants' dugout and camped under it. He had one foot in the dugout—it was a ground-level dugout, no steps—and someone shoved him and the ball popped out of his glove. They said, 'We were trying to catch you,' but Elston said someone had hit him in the shoulder." Alou then dragged a bunt toward second, perfectly executed. The leadoff man was on.

He was followed by his brother Felipe, who tried to bunt him over. The first two attempts went foul. Terry, burning with determination, struck him out. Then came Hiller, batting .280 in the Series, leading his team in RBI, with more than half his hits for extra bases. Terry struck him out, too.

With one out to go, Terry faced Willie Mays. "My approach was to keep the ball inside on Mays, but then I had him 2–0, and I went low and away. It was a beautiful piece of hitting. He was expecting it inside and he went to right with it anyway. It went to the right of Maris—it was basically a long single as Maris pivoted, hit the cutoff man." If the Giants had tried to score Alou, "Matty would have been out by ten or fifteen feet." Instead they had men on the corners, two outs, and two future Hall of Famers coming up, Willie McCovey and Orlando Cepeda. Houk decided this was a good time to visit the mound and discuss who Terry would rather pitch to, McCovey or Cepeda.

Terry recalled his thought process. "The day before Cepeda had three hits and we thought maybe he was starting a hot streak. Plus, if I walk McCovey I've got bases loaded and a National League umpire. With the National League umpire, who didn't know my stuff, he could squeeze the strike zone. Stan Landes called a terrific game for Jack and myself, but you never know. And the Giants had got into the World Series by a walked-in run, in their playoff with the Dodgers. It just didn't seem like a good idea. All these things were going through my mind at that moment."

Houk tried to lighten the tension, joking to Terry, who recalled he said, "'I don't know what the hell I'm doing out here.' He had a good sense of humor in tough times. 'How you feeling?'" Houk then asked what Terry, who was known for sometimes talking to the baseball in his hand, what he wanted to do. "I said, 'Okay, my idea is to go after McCovey with my best stuff, rip it inside, outside, and if I fall behind in the count, then put him on.'" Terry wanted to give himself the best chance of getting that final out.

McCovey swung and connected hard with Terry's first pitch, bringing a gasp out of the crowd. But the wind knocked it down, and Terry remembers Maris coming in for the ball before the wind blew it foul. Would McCovey hit the ball to the right side again? At second base, Terry recalled, "Bobby played him in the hole the whole Series. He knew how to play behind me. He knew the hitter. A couple of times in the year I'd see him playing somewhere and I'd move him, and of course the next hit would go right through the hole where he had been. So I left him where he was."

On the next pitch, Terry pitched McCovey inside, but "he used his hands, put topspin on the ball and hit a sinking liner." The line drive shot right from McCovey's bat into a leaping Bobby Richardson's glove. Linz remembers the moment very clearly. "When Bobby leaped to catch that line drive, everybody on the bench leaped with him. There is a photo I saw once where we were all off the ground, the whole bench. We caught that ball, all of us." It was the play that prompted an anguished Charlie Brown to cry, "Why couldn't McCovey have hit the ball just two feet higher?" in Charles Schulz's *Peanuts* cartoons. McCovey was out. Richardson was stunned. And Terry had found his redemption from 1960. "I am a very lucky fellow and I certainly thank God for a second opportunity," he told the *New York Times* after the game. "You don't often get another chance to prove yourself in baseball or in life." He was named World Series MVP.

Extra Innings

- Ralph Terry was from the same area of Oklahoma as Mickey Mantle. "I was a batboy or a water boy or whatever, in eighth grade, when Mickey was a senior and our school played Commerce [Mickey's school]," Terry recalled.

- Terry started out his career as a catcher in high school ball. "I always wanted to pitch. I knew I could throw the ball back to the mound harder than they could throw it to me. One day our top three pitchers were all out for 'Senior Day' and didn't show up. So coach let me pitch. I gave up one infield single and struck out 21 men. Coach was like, 'Well, okay, I guess you can pitch.'"

- Ralph Terry on luck: "The night before the game we played poker, me, Elston, Hector Lopez, Yogi . . . Yogi had a king-high flush and I had a queen-high flush or something. He was building up the pot so I called him, and on the last card I got an ace of hearts. My ace-high flush beat him. Yogi was the luckiest guy who ever lived, so if you beat Yogi on the last card, that was an omen. I said, 'That's it! I'm going to bed!' They didn't like you to leave with all the money, but I figured it was a good omen and I went to bed. I slept like a baby."

30

October 10, 1964: St. Louis at New York

The Bulldog

In which a young "pheenom" and an old hero triumph

In 1970, Jim Bouton became a household name for writing *Ball Four*, the book that spawned the genre of the sports celebrity tell-all autobiography. Bouton chronicled his life as a pitcher trying to catch on with a first-year expansion team, the Seattle Pilots. Along the way, he recounted various episodes from his earlier time with the Yankees, including the after-hours exploits of his teammates. The baseball establishment was scandalized (so they said) by the tales of boozing and womanizing that tarnished the reputation of the game, and Commissioner Bowie Kuhn even tried to get Bouton to sign a statement saying these things were untrue. But the real scandal the book uncovered was just how poorly players were paid and how badly they were treated by management. The book hit the best-seller lists, and in 2000 was chosen by the New York Public Library as one of the 100 most important books of the century.

Mickey Charles Mantle

Bouton came up in 1962 with a crop of rookies that included Tom Tresh, Phil Linz, and Joe Pepitone. In 1963, Bouton won 21 games and was one of baseball's hottest "pheenoms" (his word), with a 2.53 ERA. "I thought we'd be in the World Series every year and I'd win 20 games every year," Bouton said. "I thought I was going to be in the Hall of Fame." Bouton was known for throwing so hard his hat would fly off. In 1964, the year started out tough for the young pitcher. "My arm bothered me the first half of the year and I wasn't sure what the problem was. But I had an impacted wisdom tooth removed during the All-Star break and when I came back I felt strong—won 11 games the second half, so I was throwing as well as I've ever thrown. By the time the World Series came around I was ready." But Bouton's timing was bad—the 1964 Yankees were no longer dominating the league the way they used to. Ralph Houk had been bumped upstairs and replaced by Yogi Berra. Critics felt Berra was too close to the players, and after the infamous "harmonica incident" few believed he could hold authority over the team.

The Yankees were facing the St. Louis Cardinals, behind the hard-throwing intimidator Bob Gibson. The Cardinals had been unable to get past the Koufax-Drysdale Dodgers in 1963 (the team that swept the Yankees four straight in the World Series), but in '64 Koufax was hurt. The Cardinals' owner, the hot-tempered and baseball-ignorant beer mogul August "Gussie" Busch, was impatient for a championship. Busch was the George Steinbrenner of an earlier generation: irascible, more apt to listen to his friends than his employees, and convinced money could buy a championship. Steinbrenner eventually learned otherwise; Gussie never did, but in '64 he had a team stocked with talent that included Curt Flood, Tim McCarver, and a young Lou Brock. With Mantle's skills in decline, Flood arguably rivaled Willie Mays for the role of best center fielder in baseball.

With the talent of the Cardinals and the banged-up state of the Yankees (Kubek's wrist, Terry's back and shoulder, Mantle's everything), the Series was predicted to be long and hard-fought. In the first game, Whitey Ford was shelled in a 9–5 loss. In the second game, rookie sensation Mel Stottlemyre took on Bob Gibson and evened things up with an 8–3 win, but Ford's arm problems would prevent him from pitching again in the Series. The ball came to Bouton, who felt confident. "I never had the sense when I pitched for the Yankees that 'uh-oh, we don't have our best guys in there.' That thought never crossed my mind. To me all of my thinking about a game had to do with my preparation and what I was thinking about, my mental preparation and my physical preparation. It could have been a high school team running out there behind me." By that stage in his young career, Bouton had perfected his technique of preparation. "That was the summer when I developed my double warm-up. If I had any trouble it was in the first inning, so that meant I wasn't into the game yet mentally. So I would warm up twice, to try to simulate an inning, pitching, resting, then pitching, so by the time I went out there it felt like the second or third inning. There's a level of concentration you can arrive at that is almost zen-like."

Nor was he distracted by the additional hoopla of pitching in a World Series. "I always found it easier to concentrate in the World Series. I didn't have to manufacture an importance about the game, which I did a few times during the season. I had to sit down at my locker and tell myself 'it's life or death, if I don't win tonight thousands will be starving in Africa.' I was out there pitching for the human race. But I didn't have to do that for the World Series; there was always that butterfly feeling in my stomach. I loved the whole atmosphere, the buzz in the stadium, the bunting." On October 10, 1964, Jim Bouton turned in one of the finest pitching performances of his life, facing a tough veteran pitcher named Curt Simmons. Simmons called himself "the poor man's Koufax." He did not have Koufax's mechanics—he threw with a herky-jerky motion—and at 35 years old he no longer had much zip on his fastball. But he had enough off-speed pitches to keep hitters off-balance. Bouton and the Yankees had their work cut out for them.

It began with a one-two-three inning, as Curt Flood flew out to right, Lou Brock popped up to third, and Bill White lined a ball into left that hung up for Tresh. Simmons responded with a one-two-three of his own, with two grounders and an infield pop. The Cardinals mounted a minor threat in the second, when with two outs Tim McCarver walked and Mike Shannon singled to put men on the corners. But Bouton came on with his hard fastball, and Dal Maxvill popped to third.

Phil Linz, starting at short because of Kubek's wrist injury, wasn't surprised to see Bouton bear down. "I liked playing behind Jim. [That day] he had great stuff. A real rising fastball, a good breaking curve—like a twelve-to-six curve. He was a competitor—his 'bulldog' mentality—a winning-type guy where winning was everything to him, as it was with all of us. We had confidence behind him. And he showed what he could do and what kind of courage he had."

Now it was the Yankees' turn to threaten. Mantle grounded out, but Elston Howard followed him with a single. Tresh popped up. But then Simmons suddenly had a hiccup with his control. He walked Joe Pepitone on four pitches, pushing Howard to second. "I missed the curve on 2–0 and then I missed the next one," he told reporters after the game. "It was unusual." Then he had Clete Boyer down 0–2, but the third pitch, which was supposed to be a fastball in on the hands, "didn't come in." The ball strayed over the plate and Boyer doubled into left, scoring Howard and moving Pepitone to third. The rally did not last, however, as Bouton himself swung hard at a ball, but hit a fly to left to end the inning.

Bouton had earned the nickname "Bulldog" for being such a tenacious competitor, and now he had a one-run lead to protect. He sat down the next six Cardinals in a row. In the fifth, though, McCarver opened the inning with a single to right, and made second when Mantle boxed the ball around. Shannon lined the ball hard into right and the runner had to hold. Then Maxvill moved him to third with a ground out, bringing Simmons to the plate. Simmons was a typical hitter for a pitcher (lifetime average, .171), but he connected for a single, bringing in the unearned run. Curt Flood then tried for more, but his grounder to short forced Simmons and the half-inning was over, the score tied at one.

Running the bases did not tire Simmons. He sat down three more Yankees in order in the fifth. Bouton, by contrast, found himself in a jam in the sixth. With one out, White singled. Although Ken Boyer, brother of Yankee Clete Boyer, flew to left, Dick Groat doubled, White moving to third. With first base open, Bouton elected to intentionally walk Tim McCarver, to face Shannon instead. Shannon grounded into a force-out, and the Bulldog escaped the jam. The bottom of the inning was eerily parallel for Simmons. With one out, Bobby Richardson singled, and after Maris flew to right, Mantle doubled, moving Richardson to third. Simmons loaded the bases with an intentional walk to Elston Howard, and faced Tresh. A pop-up in the infield ended that threat.

Simmons retired the next six Yankees in a row, while Bouton walked a tightrope but escaped, runners reaching third in the seventh and the ninth. The only run he had allowed was that unearned run back in the fifth, so when Phil Linz let a grounder get through him in the ninth, putting McCarver on first, the Bulldog wasn't going to let it happen again. Shannon grounded to first, moving McCarver to second. Bouton then walked pinch hitter Carl Warwick. Bob Skinner then batted for Simmons. Bouton got him on a fly to center, and Flood on a liner to right to end the inning and strand McCarver.

The Yankee bullpen was quiet, and although he had thrown 123 pitches, the Bulldog began preparing himself mentally to pitch the tenth. Simmons, on the other hand, was already out of the game. "A flagrant fumble by Phil Linz turned out to be the best defensive play the New York Yankees made today," wrote Bob Fachet in the *Washington Post*. During the ninth-inning rally Bouton had squelched, the Cardinals' manager, Johnny Keane, had lifted Simmons for a pinch hitter. Keane now called on Barney Schultz to finish the job.

Schultz hadn't thought he'd be in a World Series that year. He had come into pro ball in 1944 as a hard thrower, but after injuring himself in the minors found he could no longer fling the ball. He tried a knuckleball instead, and developed into a relief pitcher who could throw every day. In 1964, though, the Cardinals had planned to make Schulz a minor-league player-cum-coach, and he was enjoying a good year in Jacksonville with an ERA under 1.00. Keane wanted him for his own bullpen, called him up at the beginning of August, and fit one of the final pieces into the pennant-winning puzzle as Schultz pitched well down the stretch, appearing in 30 of the 59 remaining games, allowing only one home run.

Bouton sat in the dugout with the other Yankees, watching Schultz warm up. "I was sitting on the bench near the bat rack and Mickey was standing on the dugout steps. Schultz's knuckleball was dropping about a foot—knee high, drop to the ankles, knee high, drop to the ankles." Mantle's left-handed swing had a bit of an uppercut to it, and here was a pitch that would fit right into his stroke. "[Mickey] wasn't the type to be a big shot or make predictions," Bouton recalled, "but he called his shot. I overheard it—not a big announcement, it was just a statement of fact." Mantle knew what he was talking about. "He walked up to the plate, Barney threw his first pitch, and Mickey hit a seven iron into the upper deck."

The Yankees poured onto the field, no one happier than Bouton. "The minute he hit it we all knew it was gone, the only question was would it clear the roof? He actually hit it higher than the facade but it then dropped down into the stands. I thought that was great because otherwise I'd have to go out and pitch the tenth." The relieved pitcher was there to greet Mantle at home plate with his teammates, a thrilling moment for both men, one more image for the storybook of a championship era.

But it was an era that was over. Eventually the Cardinals did prevail in seven games. After the Series, Yogi was canned, age caught up with Ford and Mantle, and the Yankees took a nosedive. They would not contend for another pennant until 1976. Bouton had arm trouble and found himself in Barney Schultz's shoes, reinventing himself as a knuckleball pitcher, but eventually found the most fame in being an iconoclastic chronicler of the game.

◆ Extra Innings

- Brothers Ken and Clete Boyer faced each other for the first time in the 1964 World Series. Both third basemen, they became the first brothers to both homer in a World Series when Clete knocked one out of the park in game seven.

* "Bouton also set a personal record yesterday, losing his cap 37 times in nine innings, and surpassing the former record which was 19." (*New York Times*)

* Mantle's walk-off blast was the 16th homer he had hit in a World Series, surpassing Babe Ruth, who hit 15. Ruth did it while appearing in 41 games in 10 different Series. Mantle was in his 61st game.

* The "harmonica incident":

On August 20, after a four-game sweep at the hands of the Chicago White Sox that put the Yankees in third place, 4½ games out, the Yankees sat in their team bus on a humid, sticky afternoon waiting to go to the airport. Utility infielder Phil Linz decided it was a good time to try to learn to play "Mary Had a Little Lamb" on the harmonica. Yogi Berra, now the manager and an old-school Yankee who didn't feel that harmonica playing was a proper activity during a losing streak, barked from the front of the bus that Linz should stow it. Linz asked what he'd said, and Mickey Mantle mischievously answered that Yogi had said to play it louder. Linz played it louder, angering Berra, who charged back and slapped the harmonica out of his hands. The newspapers leaped on the story as if it were a major international incident, criticizing Yogi for his lack of authority with the players and probably sealing Yogi's fate. Perhaps the incident helped to spark the team—the Yankees went 22–6 in September—but after the game seven loss to the Cardinals, Berra was relieved as manager and replaced by the man he had faced, Johnny Keane.

"We younger guys especially were shocked that he was fired. Me especially," Linz recalled. "He never held the harmonica thing against me. It's true, Mickey Mantle said 'play it louder.' And I played it louder. And it's probably the best thing I ever did, [because] it made me famous." The next day Linz received a $5,000 endorsement contract from Hohner harmonicas, and found other offers coming his way as well. "The ironic part about that is that the harmonica is really the reason why my life has been so good. In the off-season, I had to go to do all these large banquets that paid in the thousands. All over the country, top sports banquets. I saved enough money that winter that I opened my nightclub on First Avenue, and I had that restaurant for 23 years. It was all because of the harmonica thing and making that extra money in the off-season. I only hit 11 home runs my whole career, you know. But I'm in all the books."

31

August 29, 1972: Texas at New York

Taking on the Mantle

In which another kid from Oklahoma shines

When Bobby Murcer came to New York as a 19-year-old, everyone wanted him to be the next Mickey Mantle. Like Mickey, he was from Oklahoma, had been signed by the legendary scout Tom Greenwade, and Yankee fans were accustomed to a constant restocking of their championship roster. In 1965 the team was coming off a seven-game loss in the World Series to Bob Gibson's Cardinals and had every expectation of being in the hunt, as they had been pretty much every year from 1947 on. But Murcer struggled to hit lefthanders, and the team had aged. They finished the year with a losing record (77–83) and in 1966 hit rock bottom; a period of mediocrity had begun.

By 1972, the team was barely above .500, racking up a 79–76 record and drawing just under 1 million fans, finishing fourth in the standings. Although

Bobby Ray Murcer

the team had a core of talented players, including Roy White, Thurman Munson, and Mel Stottlemyre, the indifference of corporate ownership under CBS had perpetuated the mediocrity.

But there were worse teams. In 1972 the Washington Senators started life anew as the Texas Rangers. Although they were managed by the great Ted Williams, the Rangers were awful in their inaugural season, losing 100 games and drawing only 662,974 fans to Arlington to see them. On August 29 they arrived in New York to play a four-game series, beginning with a doubleheader.

Mike Paul was a lefthander who had spent four years with the Cleveland Indians, starting about a dozen games every year but relieving in 25 to 35 more. In 1972 he went to the Rangers and had his best season on a bad team. Although his record was a middling-seeming 8–9, that was quite good for a team with an overall .350 winning percentage, and he would finish the year with a 2.17 ERA.

None of that mattered to the 26-year-old Bobby Murcer, who after two years in the military had returned to the Yankees in 1969 and had learned to hit left-handed pitching. He had hit two home runs off Paul in a 1970 game against the Indians—the homers coming after one in the previous night's final at-bat and preceding a game-tying long ball off Fred Lasher in the eighth, tying Lou Gehrig's previous record of four straight homers in four at-bats.

Paul started off well that day, retiring Horace Clarke on a grounder and Thurman Munson on a fly to left. Paul then struck out Murcer. The Rangers scratched an unearned run off Steve Kline in the third, and so, down one run in the fourth, with one out, Murcer came to the plate. This time he hit the ball into the deep recesses of the old Yankee Stadium center field, a triple that sparked a two-run rally. "A lot of guys when they hit for the cycle, normally they don't go single, double, home run, and then triple. They usually get the triple first or second," Murcer remarked when speaking of the feat. "The triple is the hardest part. If you get the triple out of the way early, you have a chance."

His chances increased in the fifth with a double off Paul, but the two-out rally fizzled.

The Rangers struck back in the sixth, when Ted Ford hit a three-run homer, making it 4–2 Rangers, and in the seventh they tacked on two more on four successive hits off Kline. But Murcer was not done yet. In the bottom of the inning, the Yankees answered with four straight hits of their own off Paul and then lefty reliever Paul Lindblad: Hal Lanier pinch-hit for Kline and doubled, Clarke doubled, Munson singled, and then Murcer singled. Casey Cox then came on to pitch and walked Roy White to load the bases, but managed to escape after giving up only one more run on an out. The outburst had brought the Yankees within one run of their opponent. Cox then batted in the top of the ninth, and as Murray Chass told it in the *New York Times*, might have been better off making out.

"Ted Williams, the Texas manager who appears to maneuver pitchers with less success than he hit them, had a hand in the Yankees' tying run. He did it with an off move involving Casey Cox, his third pitcher. Williams let Cox bat in the top of the ninth, but when he walked, the manager sent in a runner for him. That required a new pitcher in the last of the ninth, and the first man Steve Lawson faced was Murcer."

Lawson was a rookie, but left-handed, and he had struck out Murcer in a game earlier in the season. Bobby needed only to hit a home run to complete the cycle and to tie the game. The count ran to 2–2 before Murcer "electrified the incredulous crowd of 15,987" by doing so, according to Chass.

Murcer had a chance to win the game for the Yankees in the tenth, when he came up with two on and two out, but Williams elected to walk him intentionally rather than let the red-hot hitter take a hack, and Horacio Piña escaped the jam by getting Roy White to ground out. The Yankees got to Piña in the eleventh, though, when Ron Blomberg and Bernie Allen walked to start the inning, and Johnny Callison singled in the winning run.

The day was not a complete triumph, as the Yankees dropped the next game of the twinbill, 7–4, and made several gaffes in the field, but Murcer remained hot. He had become the first Yankee to hit for the cycle since the man whose shoes he was supposed to fill. He racked up two more hits, including another home run, raised his average to .294, and found his name next to Mantle's in the Yankees' record books at last.

Extra Innings

- When the Yankees dealt Murcer to the Giants before the 1975 season, they received Bobby Bonds in return.

- Murcer had three separate playing stints with the Yankees: 1965–1966, prior to his military service; 1969–1974, after serving; and 1979–1983, after playing for the Giants and Cubs. He is a Yankee for life. After retiring from the playing field, he began working as a color analyst for Yankees' radio broadcasts and kept that up through 1985. He then served a year in the Yankees' front office, as assistant general manager, before hopping to television, where he has announced Yankees games on Sportschannel, the MSG Network, WPIX Channel 11, and the YES Network.

32

October 14, 1976: Kansas City at New York

Chaos Unleashed

In which the Yankees unlock the Bronx Zoo

In 1976, the nation celebrated its 200th birthday, the Yankees their 74th season, and the Kansas City Royals their eighth. Ewing Kauffman had bought the Royals in the major-league expansion of 1969, the same year that the American League Championship Series (ALCS) was inaugurated. Eight years later, the Royals were the best of the West, and faced the Yankees in the five-game ALCS to decide the pennant.

The Royals began to win after Whitey Herzog arrived midway through the 1975 season, when he managed them to a second place finish. In 1976, stocked with talents the likes of George Brett, Frank White, and Freddie Patek, the Royals edged the Athletics for first place. In this, his third full season in the bigs, Brett tallied 215 hits and narrowly won the batting title over his teammate Hal McRae. White was developing into one of the best defensive second basemen of all time. When he wasn't playing, Cookie Rojas was, and with either one, Patek was a formidable double-play partner. The Royals' pitching staff was heavily left-handed, with hurlers such as Larry Gura (acquired in 1976 from the Yankees for Fran Healy) and Paul Splittorff. Splittorff had won 20 games with a weaker Royals team in 1973, and although he was only 11–8 with a 3.97 ERA in 1976, he remained very tough on left-handed hitters.

The Yankees, meanwhile, had fought their way back to the top of the heap for the first time in 12 years. In 1973, a new ownership group led by George Steinbrenner had purchased the team from CBS. In 1974 and 1975, the team had played at Shea Stadium while Yankee Stadium underwent $106 million in renovations, and in '76 the new-look team in their new-look home finished 10½ games up on their nearest competitor. "We led from start to finish that whole season," recalled outfielder Roy White, then the longest-tenured Yankee. "The lowest our lead got down to was about 5 games in August, and then we went on a winning streak and extended it back up to 9 or 10. So winning the [East] that year was kind of a cakewalk for us."

Like the Royals, the Yankees had found the manager who made a difference midway through the previous year, and in this, his first full year as Yankee manager, Billy Martin led them to a 97–62 record. Attendance also jumped to more than 2 million for the first time since 1950. The lineup was powered by catcher Thurman Munson (.302 and 105 RBI) and third baseman Graig Nettles, whose 32 homers led the league. Chris Chambliss at first had blossomed into a guy who could hit for average and power (.293, 17 homers, 96 RBI). The team was well balanced with speed as well, with table-setters Roy White, Mickey Rivers, and rookie Willie Randolph swiping 111 bases combined that year. The pitching staff was led by free-agent pickup Catfish Hunter, young Puerto Rican Ed Figueroa, and the veteran Dock Ellis. Lefty Sparky Lyle anchored the bullpen with 64 appearances, 23 of them saves. The *Kansas City Star*'s "scouting report" on the Yankees read:

"The Yankees this year made it to the top of the American League East without devastating power. The New Yorkers are more of a 'contact' club. Billy Martin's crew flashed speed, solid starting and relief pitching, a good inner defense and Thurman Munson, one of the game's best catchers. New York, nevertheless, outhomered the Royals 120–65."

But it was a team that had not yet been in postseason play. "It was such a novelty. It was difficult to put expectations on it," said Elliott Maddox. "Billy Martin was nervous as could be. He was just beside himself. He wanted to win so much, being a player under Casey Stengel, who was looked upon as the last great Yankee manager. Billy just wanted to join the ranks and be a winner in New York. Billy used to say New York was the only place to play baseball, in New York and for the Yankees. He loved the Yankee pinstripes." Martin was as hard-nosed a manager as he had been a player, exploiting every and any advantage, badgering umpires, and confronting his own players.

The Yankees took the first game in Kansas City, in a 4–1, briskly pitched affair by Catfish, who went the complete nine and allowed only one run despite his complaints about the rock-hard mound and artificial turf. The Royals came back against Figueroa the next day, though, winning a seesaw game, 7–3. The scene then switched to Yankee Stadium for all the remaining games in the best-of-five. Kansas City scored three in the first inning of game three, but Ellis and Lyle held them down the rest of the way and the Yankees pulled out a 5–3 win. In game four, game one starters Hunter and Gura came back for a rematch, and neither pitched as well as he had in game one. Both offenses knocked the ball around, including two home runs by Nettles, but the Royals came out on top, 7–4.

The final and deciding game was played on a Thursday night at the remodeled Yankee Stadium in front of 56,821 fans. In New York, it was a welcome return to the excitement that had seemed the birthright of the team since the 1920s, while in Kansas City the outbreak of pennant fever was so pervasive that the local hockey franchise, the CPHL (Central Professional Hockey League) minor league Kansas City Blues, canceled their opening night game.

Twenty-eight-year-old Ed Figueroa took the mound for the Yankees. He had narrowly missed being the first Puerto Rican pitcher to win 20 games, but had the best record of all the Yankee starters, at 19–10 with a 3.02 ERA. Ron Guidry described him this way: "Figgy was a good pitcher. He wasn't an over-powering guy. He was always around the plate. He wasn't flashy, wasn't dominant, wasn't a strikeout guy. He just won." Figueroa got off to a good start, retiring the first two men easily with a grounder and a strikeout. But George Brett doubled, and John Mayberry lifted a home run that just cleared the wall and Oscar Gamble's glove in right, his first homer in two months. Figgy didn't let it bother him, coming back to strike out Hal McRae and end the inning and let the Yankee bats take over.

The night before, Herzog had been undecided who to pitch. "It will be either Dennis Leonard, Marty Pattin, Al Fitzmorris, or Paul Splittorff," he told reporters, rattling off nearly his entire staff. "I'm leaning toward Leonard because he throws hard. But I think Splittorff will pitch along the way, although I don't think he will start." Whitey still had that idea in mind the next day when Leonard took the hill. The Yankee Stadium crowd roared with excitement when Mickey Rivers legged out a triple to open the action. Roy White then put on the speed for an infield hit that scored Rivers, and promptly stole second with Munson at the plate. Munson knocked a base hit into left, and Tom Poquette tried to catch White at third. White was safe, and Munson took second on the play. With two men in scoring position and three lefty hitters (Chambliss, Carlos May, and Nettles) coming up, Herzog yanked Leonard after he had thrown only nine pitches.

"I was hitting sixth in that lineup," Nettles remembered. "And he was gone by the time I got there. I was hoping to see the righthander. I thought it was kind of a panic move on Whitey Herzog's part to yank his starting pitcher so early." But in came Splittorff, Herzog's backup plan. Chambliss hit a long fly, deep enough to score White from third, and the Yankees had tied the game at two. A fly ball and a pop-up later, and May and Nettles were turned back.

The Royals were right back at it in the second. Jamie Quirk lofted a ball into left for the first out. But Cookie Rojas lined a ball into center, then stole second. Figgy struck out little Freddie Patek, but Buck Martinez followed with a single into right and Cookie scored. Al Cowens grounded to Randolph to end the threat, but the Royals had taken a one-run lead, which Splittorff protected with a one-two-three inning. Figueroa answered with three up and three down of his own, sending Tom Poquette, Brett, and Mayberry back to the bench.

In the bottom of the third, the table-setters came around again. Rivers singled, White walked, and Munson knocked Mickey in and put men on the corners. Chambliss grounded into a force-out, allowing White to score. May and Nettles reprised their first at-bats, a fly and a pop-up, but the Yankees had bootstrapped over the Royals by one.

Figueroa responded with another one-two-three, and the Yankee offense continued to roll in the fourth. With two out, Fred Stanley drew a walk, bringing the table-setters up again. Rivers had his third base hit of the game, and White walked again to load the bases. Herzog had seen enough. Marty Pattin came in to face Munson, and induced a fly to left to end the inning.

Figueroa gave up a hit in the fifth, but thanks to a double play, faced only three men. Herzog went to lefty Andy Hassler then, who walked a tightrope. Chambliss doubled, but May failed to move him over when he struck out. Nettles couldn't advance him either when he popped up in the infield. But Hassler loaded the bases on back-to-back walks to Gamble and Randolph. Stanley, a solid shortstop who batted ninth, then came up and lined a ball right to Rojas.

So the Yankees were unable to increase their lead until the sixth. Figgy had again gone through the heart of the Royals' lineup. Mayberry managed a two-out single, but McRae tapped a comebacker to Figueroa. Meanwhile, the top of the Yankees' order was once again ready to march. Mickey Rivers was known to many as a bit of an off-the-wall character, often making cryptic statements worthy of Yogi Berra, but no one could dispute his speed or hitting ability. He tallied his fourth hit of the night, this time beating out a bunt for a hit. Playing for insurance, White sacrificed him to second. Like clockwork, Munson then singled, scoring Rivers. Running aggressively, Munson tried to make second and was thrown out by right fielder McRae. Chambliss followed with a single and stole second. May then grounded a ball to third that Brett threw away—May was safe on the error and Chambliss crossed the plate. Sandy Alomar was sent in to run for May and was gunned out trying to steal second. The score stood 6–3 Yankees, but if not for the two outs at second, it might have been more.

Figueroa's focus had not changed. He allowed one harmless hit in the seventh. In the bottom half of the inning, the Yankees threatened again, Nettles reaching third, but Hassler was replaced by hard-throwing rookie Mark Littell, and the Bombers were turned back once more.

In the eighth, Figueroa faced Al Cowens leading off. He singled to left and Martin decided it was time to play the percentages with Brett coming up. "Figgy was getting tired," Martin explained. "He was going a little low with his arm." He lifted his starter for lefthander Grant Jackson. Herzog inserted Jim Wohlford to pinch-hit for Poquette, and was rewarded with a base hit. And so the American League batting champion came up representing the tying run. Nettles watched the reliever warm up. "Grant Jackson was usually a guy who was tough on lefthanders. We had all the confidence in the world in him if he was going to face Brett," Nettles recalled. "But Brett was just in a zone where he could hit anybody."

Brett, a left-handed hitter, pulled the ball down the right-field line into the short porch, just a few feet fair into the seats, tying the game with that one swing and stunning the crowd.

Willie Randolph wouldn't allow himself to get too deflated. "It became very nail-biting at the time. When he came up I thought 'oh, my God' and when he hit it I was like 'aw jeez. . . .' But when you're in the heat of the game you're just thinking: you're going to win, you're going to win, you're going to win." His teammates shared that optimism. "Brett had already hit us pretty good in that series so I kind of thought we were due to get him out," Roy White said. "I was kind of deflated a little bit when he hit that home run to tie it up right. But at least it was still tied, so you've got a shot to win." And after all, the top of the order was coming up again in the eighth.

But this time they didn't produce. Rivers flew to right. White grounded right to first. "When I hit against Littell in the bottom of the eighth, I was kind of hoping I'd be the guy to hit a home run," White remembered. "I think that passes through every hitter's mind when you're going to the plate in this sort of ball game. And I actually did hit him very hard, but it was sort of a one-hop right to first." Munson struck out.

Dick Tidrow came on to pitch for the Yankees. The righthander had been moved to the bullpen in 1975 and had been an effective set-up man for Lyle in 1976 and also earned 10 saves himself. "He was the only player consistently dirtier than Thurman," recalled teammate Elliott Maddox. "He looked like he would take a shower and then go and roll around in the dust somewhere." And so Tidrow's nickname was "Dirt," not only for his appearance but also for his down-to-earth approach on the mound. Dirt got two quick grounders from Rojas and Patek. But the Royals were not quite ready to quit. Martinez singled and Tidrow, working cautiously, then walked Cowens. Wohlford then hit a high chopper to short. Stanley had to wait to grab the ball and flip it to Randolph for the force at second. A close play, but second-base umpire Joe Brinkman ruled Cowens out. "I'm not saying Cowens was safe and I'm not saying he was out," philosophized Herzog after the game. "But a safe call would have filled the bases for us and who knows what would have happened?"

Littell went out to warm up for the bottom of the ninth. The big rookie was known for his blazing fastball and he had impressed Herzog, and opposing batters, with it all year. But the rowdy Stadium crowd, anxious and heady, began to throw bottles at McRae in right. The game was delayed while order was restored. The grounds crew cleaned up the debris, and Littell stood and watched the scene. In the dugout Willie Randolph watched Littell. "I remember thinking at the time, even then, that [the wait] might have affected him a little bit. Because pitchers usually like to get the ball and throw it and go after guys. I thought, 'Gee, I wonder if this guy is going to stiffen up. I wonder if he's going to lose his concentration.'"

Other Yankees were thinking about Chambliss. "Mark Littell was the perfect pitcher for Chris to bat against," in Maddox's opinion. "He became such a good fastball hitter, he could make a fastball look like a changeup. Well, Littell had a good fastball, so we figured, 'this is perfect.'" Maddox had roomed with Chambliss when the first baseman had first come to the Yankees. "Chris was extremely quiet. At one point he was not viewed as a good fielder; he was looked on as below average. In 1974 and early 1975 he was platooned. But the manager at the time was Bill Virdon, he saw how hard he was working to improve his fielding, so ultimately he was given the opportunity to play first full-time." Under Martin, Chambliss played almost every day, and both his fielding and hitting prowess had risen.

Sandy Alomar and Nettles stood by the on-deck circle as Chambliss stepped into the batter's box, his manner quiet as always. But the fans were going crazy with anticipation. Maddox remembered "that night, the air was light, a nice fall evening, low humidity, and all that lefty had to do was get it up in the air and it was going to go." Littell threw his signature pitch, a high fastball that Chambliss had failed to handle earlier in the series. "I challenged him," Littell told the *Kansas City Star.* "The other night he swung at the same pitch and missed." This time Chambliss connected.

Roy White watched the outfielder running back to the wall. "I remember the towering ball out into right center. Al Cowens, with his back to the wall, jumped, and when he came down [the ball] wasn't in his glove. That was a great moment for me because I'd been with the Yankees for nine years. I was the longest standing member of the Yankees there, and had never been in a World Series, after expecting to be in it every year like when I was a kid. So I was one of the happier guys when that ball disappeared over the fence."

Murray Chass called the homer "a blow that rivaled Bobby Thomson's 1951 home run for stunning drama" in the *New York Times.* As the ball went into the stands, the fans overflowed onto the field. Nettles found himself swept up in a human tide. "The ball flies out and the first thing I see is all the people coming on the field. I ran up and grabbed Chambliss's bat, because I knew the fans would grab the bat. So I stand there just kind of waving the fans away with Chris's bat. I did save the bat and gave it to Chris later."

Meanwhile, Chambliss was engulfed close to second base by what Bob Addie called "a mass of screaming, howling, jumping humanity" in the *Washington Post*. "By the time he got to first, about half the stands were on the field. He gave one guy a nice elbow," Maddox recalled. The fans were tearing up the bases and carrying them away. Chambliss soldiered on, but even if he had wanted to touch third base, it was no longer there to be tagged.

Rookie Willie Randolph ran onto the field as well, to try to help Chambliss in his circumnavigation. "I just remember that when I was a kid they always said if you don't touch all the bases it doesn't count. I remember losing my cool at the time, thinking 'Oh, my God, he's not going to be able to get to home plate. They're going to call it back like a do-over.'" Randolph came near his teammate. "I just remember trying to make a path for him, knocking people out of the way and people were grabbing at me. Somebody grabbed my hat, somebody pulled a lock of my hair out of me, then I was running after him thinking, 'Forget this. This is crazy.' It was scary. Finally we just ran, like run for the hills, protect yourself."

Gerald Eskenazi wrote in the *New York Times* that in addition to the bases, the jubilant mob took hunks of the field, "but not nearly with the thoroughness or destructiveness that marked the Mets' memorable World Series victory in 1969. There was more grass than holes remaining at Yankee Stadium."

Eventually the umpires called for Chambliss to return to the field, with a phalanx of police and players, to touch the spot where home plate had been. He probably never came close to third. But Herzog did not challenge the validity of the home run. The Royals were beaten and there was no turning back the tide of fans, nor the brimming over of a joy twelve years suppressed. In the clubhouse the traditional champagne showers were inflicted on one and all. "I remember pouring bottles of champagne over the head of Cary Grant, who was in the clubhouse," Maddox remembered. "We were just celebrating. I wasn't a big drinker, but I still don't know how I got home that night."

But the hard-fought series and its climactic ending drained the Yankees. Roy White thought, "I don't think we had enough time to kind of sit back and enjoy the fact that we'd won a playoff and regroup and get prepared for a World Series against the Cincinnati Reds. The very next day we were on a plane to Cincinnati, and we got in, we had to work out in like 35 degree temperatures, and then the next day we're standing out there for the national anthem." The Reds, who had swept the Phillies in three straight, were well rested and ready to roll. They swept the Yankees in four games. But a new generation of Yankees had a taste of October, and the hunger for more had been stoked.

Extra Innings

* Howard Cosell and Keith Jackson provided the play-by-play announcing for the ABC television broadcast of the Series. In the booth with him to provide color commentary was then-Oriole Reggie Jackson. Cosell, a longtime disparager of baseball, and Jackson argued at some length over baseball strategy, which prompted writers to say that Cosell's dislike of baseball was based on his lack of knowledge of the game.

33

October 9, 1977: New York at Kansas City

Royal Treatment

In which George Brett and Kansas City experience déjà vu all over again

In 1977, the New York team that won the pennant the year before kept its core of players and added a few more, including shortstop Bucky Dent and pitcher Mike Torrez. Of the newcomers, two men could not be more different than Ron Guidry and Reggie Jackson. Guidry was a homegrown rookie, a skinny left-handed power pitcher who weighed a slight 160 pounds, quiet and laid back. Jackson was George Steinbrenner's free-agent splurge for the year, an outspoken, charismatic slugger who had been an important part of Charlie Finley's world championship dynasty in Oakland, winners of three in a row from 1972 to 1974. He clashed often with Billy Martin, but he produced. Meanwhile, the Kansas City Royals, too, had kept their core, while second baseman Frank White grew into an everyday contributor. And despite what meager threats arose in the regular season from their competitors, at the end of the season the Yankees and Royals once again stood atop their divisions, like two heavyweights fighting for a title shot.

And once again they exchanged blows in a hard-fought series. With the help of three home runs (Hal McRae, John Mayberry, and Al Cowens), Kansas City easily took the first game, 7-2, behind Paul Splittorff, the lefty who had earned the nickname "Yankee-killer." But New York bounced back in game two, behind their own lefty Guidry, who pitched the complete game and won, 6–2. The Royals came back with a 6–2 win behind Dennis Leonard and looked to eliminate the Yankees in game four in Kansas City. But the Yankees rallied for a 6–4 win, with Sparky Lyle contributing 5⅓ innings of scoreless relief, to force the deciding game five.

Billy Martin had his hands full deciding who should play. The Royals would be going with Splittorff, and Martin removed Roy White and the lefty-hitting Jackson from the lineup. "Billy had a chance to sit me down, and he took it," Reggie remembered. "I bit my tongue. The media was all over me about not playing and stuff, but I just said hey, if that's what they want to do, that's what we'll do." For his pitcher, Martin decided to tab the man who had, thus far, not disappointed him, and that was Guidry on only two days' rest. "I don't say he's the best man I've got," Martin told reporters the night before the game. "I say he's my hottest pitcher right now." It was ironic that the Herculean task of putting the Yankees in the World Series should fall to Guidry, especially after pitching the complete nine innings in game two, because the Yankee organization had considered Guidry too frail to be a starting pitcher. They didn't believe he had the stamina to be a starter and had intended him to be a bullpen ace.

"I was the closer at Columbus in Triple-A," Guidry recalled. "When I got called up in '75, of course I went in the pen, and in '76, too. But I never got a chance to do the same thing in New York as I had in Columbus because of Sparky Lyle." Guidry was used mostly as a long man in mop-up duty, and hung around with the other relievers. "What happened to me was that in the time I spent in the bullpen I actually learned another pitch from Sparky Lyle. I always had a good fastball, but I never really had a great breaking ball. But I learned to throw a great slider from Sparky. He's the one that taught me how to throw the slider because we threw so much alike." Early in 1977, Guidry finally got a chance to show off that slider when injuries, doubleheaders, and roster moves made it necessary to slot him in as an emergency starter several times. After the third emergency start in which Guidry pitched into the ninth and came out with a win, Martin finally called him into his office and said they were putting him in the rotation.

"I think the biggest thing that they were concerned about was because of my size, being so small, whether I would be able to stand up to the strain of pitching a lot of innings," Guidry said. "I only weighed about 152 pounds. But from my side, it actually never took a lot out of me to throw a ball, because of my mechanics. I could throw 20 pitches a day or 150 a day. It wouldn't matter. They thought I wasn't going to be able to stand up to the strain and I proved them wrong." The soft-spoken Cajun from Louisiana, called "Gator" by his teammates, racked up a 16–7 record and a 2.82 ERA, with nine complete games.

But durable as Guidry was, October 9 wasn't his day. "It was one of those games that you think that you have good stuff, but it's either too good or not good enough," he said in retrospect. The Yankees had gone down meekly in the top of the first, and Guidry came out to face the Royals. "I remember the first couple of batters, right-handed batters, hit balls to the right side, so I know I'm throwing okay, because they're hitting the ball late." Freddie Patek grounded out, but McRae worked a full count before singling to right. Gator had Brett 2–2, before George, swinging late, dropped a triple into the left-field gap just beyond Mickey Rivers's outstretched glove, scoring McRae. When Brett slid hard into third base he and his nominal rival, Nettles, scuffled, the tension of the elimination game and the bad blood that had been brewing between the teams from earlier knockdown plays boiling over. "It was just a heat-of-the-game-type thing," Nettles explained. "I guess you'd say at that time we were the two top third basemen in the league; there was a little minirivalry going. We were good friends, even though we got into a fight. It was just the heat of the situation and the tension." Brett knocked Nettles' hat from his head with a haymaker and then found Guidry's arms wrapped around him from behind. The benches and bullpens emptied, but no more blows were thrown. Guidry went back to the mound, and neither Nettles nor Brett were ejected.

Rivers, watching his pitcher from the outfield, shook his head. "He always looked the same," Rivers remembered. "You couldn't tell if he didn't have it that day or if he had it that day. But he just couldn't get strike three." Cowens grounded to third and Brett scored. Amos Otis then hit the ball back to Guidry, but reached. Guidry then struck out John Wathan to escape the inning, down by two.

Splittorff handled the Yankees without much difficulty. Although Lou Piniella doubled, Cliff Johnson, Graig Nettles, and Chris Chambliss were unable to move him along. Guidry came back to get the Royals, and his teammates went to work on Splittorff in the top of the third. With two out, Mickey Rivers was at it again, singling and stealing second. Willie Randolph walked. Thurman Munson knocked Rivers in and sent Randolph to second with a single, but Piniella grounded out to end the rally. 2–1 Royals.

If Guidry was not tired in the third, it was because the Royals didn't give him time to tire. McRae doubled on the first pitch. Brett grounded to first, moving McRae to third, and on the very next pitch, Cowens singled to left. 3–1 Royals. Martin had seen enough and sent Guidry to the showers. Mike Torrez came hot out of the gate, struck out Otis and Wathan, and stopped the momentum. "That was the oddity of the game," Guidry explained. "I had beat them already once, pitched a dominating game, and Torrez . . . they hit him all over [in game three]. And yet when I went out there [in game five], they hit me, and Torrez came in and pitched four, five innings of shutout ball. He just shut the door. That's the thing about the game, you just never know."

But the Yankees were still fighting an uphill battle with Splittorff. They put the leadoff man on in the fourth and fifth but were unable to cash in. The score remained 3–1 through seven innings as Torrez kept the lid on the Royals.

In the eighth, Randolph led off. "Even though Splittorff was the so-called 'Yankee-killer' of the time, I remember hitting him pretty well," Randolph recalled. "He had a good overhand curveball, and he liked to ride the high fastball and try to get you to pop it up. He was crafty." Willie concentrated on getting a ball down in the zone he could handle and lined the second pitch he saw into center, and Herzog went to the mound to talk it over with Splittorff. "It was just a question of what we thought we could do with Munson," Splittorff told reporters after the game. "Three different times [Munson] had seen me and I'd done something different every time." Herzog, Splittorff, and catcher Darrell Porter mulled over the situation. "We decided to go with the percentages, right-hander against right-hander," Splittorff explained.

Herzog brought in Doug Bird, a tall righty who had notched 14 saves on the year, and at first the move seemed wise when Bird struck out Munson. But Piniella smacked the first pitch he saw into right and Randolph scampered to third. With a righthander pitching, Martin no longer had an excuse to keep Reggie Jackson on the bench. "He got his point across, which was that he was the boss, and that was that," Jackson said. "The camera kept watching me the whole ball game, so I wanted to make sure not to do anything to make myself look foolish [in the dugout], until I wound up getting in the ball game." Jackson looked far from foolish in the batter's box. He took the first pitch for a ball, and then fouled off two pitches as he sized up Bird and waited for his pitch. It was the next one, and Reggie lined it into center. Randolph scored and Piniella moved to second. Bird gave way to lefty Steve Mingori. Nettles stroked a liner into right, but right to Cowens. Chambliss then smashed a ball, but Frank White made a diving backhand stop and flipped it to Patek for the force. The inning was over, but the Yankees had cut the lead to one run.

Torrez now had the heart of the Royals' order to deal with again. An easy grounder to Dent made one out. Cowens's line shot to Rivers made two. But then Amos Otis walked. He stole second on Torrez's second pitch to Pete LaCock, and then LaCock walked as well. It was time for Sparky Lyle.

Lyle had pitched so well in 1977, he became the first relief pitcher in the

American League to win the Cy Young Award. A free-spirited lefthander, he was known as much for his devastating slider as for his throwback mustache and cheekful of chaw. Lyle was accustomed to taking charge late in games; he'd just done it the day before in an early, fourth-inning appearance, and finished the game to seal the victory. He faced the veteran Cookie Rojas with his usual aplomb, and Rojas went down on strikes. Sparky went back to the dugout to see what his teammates could do for him in the ninth.

Herzog just needed three more outs and he would have managed the Royals into the World Series. As fans chanted "We're number one! We're number one!" as the Royals took the field, he called on Dennis Leonard, the staff ace, to come in and close the door. Leonard had racked up 20 wins and 244 strikeouts in 1977. The same man Whitey had tabbed to start game five the previous year, he now wanted to finish things. Paul Blair, who was only in the lineup because Martin had benched Jackson to start, greeted Leonard with a little looper into center. "Blair will never forget that single and he will never forget that Martin let him hit it," wrote Murray Chass in the *New York Times*. "It was the most pressure I ever had on me and I was afraid I would let him down," Blair later said. "I'm so glad I came through for him."

Martin now inserted Roy White, a switch-hitter, for the light-hitting Dent. "Every game was a tooth- and nail-biter with those guys. We were battling and battling," White remembered. His own at-bat was a small battle itself. "The count went to 3–2, and I fouled off about four or five pitches, and I ended up getting a walk." Perhaps Herzog then remembered what had happened to Leonard the previous year—he didn't record an out then either—or perhaps he was playing the percentages with lefty-righty matchups. Out went Leonard, in came Larry Gura, a lefty who was mostly a reliever, but whom Herzog had chosen to start against the Yankees the past two years, never with good results. Gura had been a Yankee, had feuded with Billy Martin, and bore a grudge, and Herzog kept hoping this would motivate the lefthander to beat his former team.

Mickey Rivers stood in against Gura. The count went to 2–2 but Rivers slapped a single that scored the tying run, while White took third. "You know I was just lucky against Gura because he was looking great," Mickey admitted. Herzog seemed determined to empty the bullpen, bringing on that hard thrower Mark Littell to face Willie Randolph. Randolph drove the ball to Otis in center, but deep enough to score White and allow the fleet-footed Rivers to advance to second. 4–3 Yankees. Littell came back to get Munson out, but Rivers advanced to third on the ground ball to short, bringing Piniella to the plate. Lou bounced the ball to Brett, who airmailed the ball over first baseman Pete LaCock's head, allowing the ever-important insurance run to score.

Reggie grounded out, but the score stood 5–3 Yankees as Sparky went back to the hill to finish the job.

On the first pitch from Lyle, Porter popped up to short, but the Royals gave one last gasp. On an 0–2 pitch, Frank White singled to left, to bring the tying run to the plate. Nettles got up on his toes, thinking double play. "Sparky always got a lot of ground balls. If he didn't strike 'em out, then it was a ground ball. He threw a lot of sliders, so I knew whoever was up was going to hit it down on me or to shortstop." Fast Freddie Patek stood at the plate. "Patek ran really well, so we had to turn it pretty quick." Fred Stanley and Randolph cheated toward second, with the double play in mind as well.

"I remember it very vividly," Randolph said. Patek connected on a Lyle slider to put the play in motion. "It was kind of a big chopper to Nettles, I just remember thinking, 'give me the ball.' Graig was pretty quick. He didn't have a strong arm, but he was quick on getting rid of the ball. I knew going around the horn wasn't going to be easy, so I just remember keeping my composure, not getting too anxious, waited back on the ball, and when Graig gave it to me it was one of the quickest times I've ever turned [a double play] in my life. I just made sure I squeezed the ball, got rid of it with a good throw, and Chris made a nice play stretching out at first. I just remember it happened really fast, almost like it was fast motion—this was an opportunity for me to end the game and get it over with. I don't know where I got the speed from." White was out at second, Patek at first, and the Yankees had beaten the Royals with a ninth-inning comeback for the second year in a row.

"It wasn't quite as dramatic as the Chambliss walk-off home run, because you know, it was a bunch of singles and some doubles," Roy White said in retrospect. "But it was just as rewarding."

Extra Innings

- Sparky Lyle credits none other than Ted Williams for his success as a pitcher. The two met in 1966 when Lyle was pitching in the minors with a curveball that he couldn't control. "I believe in Ted Williams," Lyle told Derrick Jackson of the *Kansas City Star*. "He told me that a slider was the one pitch that he couldn't hit. If he, one of the greatest hitters in the game of baseball, tells me that he couldn't hit a slider, you're going to be darn sure I started trying to throw the slider."

- According to the *New York Times*, Billy Martin, the hard-drinking, tough-as-nails manager of the Yankees, told Bill White prior to game five, "I even went to church this morning," prompting a comment from someone in the clubhouse, "You'll stop at nothing to win, eh?"

34

October 18, 1977: Los Angeles at New York

Mr. October

In which Reginald Martinez Jackson joins the ranks of the exalted

The year was 1977. Jimmy Carter sat in the White House, *Star Wars* reigned at the box office, and everyone was discoing down with the Bee Gees' *Saturday Night Fever* sound track. New York suffered that year from a weak economy, a record heat wave, a massive summer blackout that set off a wave of looting and arson, and a psychotic killer calling himself the "Son of Sam," who preyed on attractive women at random. Despite all these disasters, the Yankees stormed into their second straight World Series, ready to face an old enemy from their historic past—the Los Angeles Dodgers.

The Dodgers had been in California for two decades already, but '77 was a year of change for the men in blue. For 23 years, seven first-place finishes, and four world championships, they had been managed by Walter Alston. But in the final week of the '76 season, the reins were passed to scrappy Tommy Lasorda.

Lasorda, a career minor-league pitcher who lost his spot on the major-league roster to make room for Sandy Koufax, had been part of Alston's coaching staff for several years. After taking over as manager, Lasorda quickly gained a

Reginald Martinez "Reggie" Jackson

reputation as a fiery but benevolent manager who could motivate his players to be their best. Lasorda professed belief in the Big Dodger in the Sky and said if you cut him, he would bleed Dodger blue. His club boasted four 30-home-run hitters: Dusty Baker, Ron Cey, Steve Garvey, and Reggie Smith. Tommy John, his arm and his career resurrected by the surgery that would bear his name, had led the staff with 20 wins.

But if Lasorda was the Dodgers personified, Billy Martin was the same for his club. "If you cut me open, you'll see the 'NY' on my heart," Martin told

New York sportswriter Phil Pepe. "And when I die there will be pinstripes on my coffin." Billy Martin was a Yankee through and through, from his game-saving, heads-up play in the 1952 World Series against these very same Dodgers, to his steering the club to back-to-back pennants for the first time since 1963–1964. Martin had spent the year feuding with the press, his players, umpires, and the Boss, George Steinbrenner, but Martin's combative personality fueled the team's competitive fire, and he was blessed with the same luck that shone on his mentor and idol, Casey Stengel. Stengel was never afraid to sit a player down, and for 11 years his moves always seemed to work (until the fatal miscue of failing to start Whitey Ford in game one of the 1960 World Series). Martin's benching of Reggie Jackson in game five of the ALCS took on mythic proportions as both Jackson's replacement, Paul Blair, and Jackson himself in a pinch-hitting role, had notched key hits in the victory.

Winning was the best balm for the fractious Yankees, and Martin pledged to start Jackson in every game in the World Series. Reggie responded by hitting .450. The Yankees won the first game in 12 innings, then dropped the second as Catfish Hunter, plagued by injuries, including a hernia that had kept him off the mound since September 12, gave up three homers in three innings and the Dodgers won, 6–1. Mike Torrez stemmed the blue tide somewhat in game three (a three-run homer to Baker his only major lapse), while the Yankees launched ten hits for a 5–3 win. Reggie led the team to a 3–1 lead in the Series with a double and a home run in game four. He was still hot in game five, but the Bombers were unable to clinch the championship as four worn-out Yankee pitchers gave up thirteen hits in the 10–4 loss. Jackson had launched a solo shot in the eighth inning that hit the right-field foul pole at Dodger Stadium; the sound of the ball hitting the pole was still in his ears as the Series shifted back to New York.

Mickey Rivers summed up the feeling on the team. "The guys were playing a good brand of ball. The Dodgers were a good team, their guys could hit. But we really wanted to win. You know after we lost to Cincinnati in '76, I said if we get that close again, we have to make sure we win. If we get that close again, we're going to win." With the October temperature a cool 51 degrees, 56,407 spectators hoped to see the Yankees bring the first world championship in 15 years to the Bronx. At home, another 30 million or so folks—according to ABC half of all television sets in use were tuned to the game—settled in to see what might be the finale of baseball's year-long soap opera.

The Yankees felt good with Mike Torrez taking the mound. After his terrific relief appearance in Kansas City and his strong showing in game three, the team was ready to roll. But Torrez got into trouble in the first inning. With two out, Reggie Smith hit a ball to Bucky Dent at short, but Dent juggled the ball. Smith then took second on a passed ball and Cey walked. Steve Garvey, who had batted .297 with 33 homers and 115 RBI that year, laced a pitch into the right-field corner. When the dust had cleared, Garvey stood on third with a triple, and two unearned runs had crossed the plate. Torrez bounced back, getting Dusty Baker to stare at strike three, but the Yankees were clearly going to need some offense to accomplish their mission.

They would have to do it against Burt Hooton, the Dodgers' starter who sported the lowest ERA in the rotation (2.62) and who had allowed the Yankees only five hits and one run in his game two start. Hooton had a decent fastball and change but was known for his knuckle curve. Dodger catcher Steve Yeager described Hooton's weird breaking ball in the *Sporting News* as "one hellacious pitch when it's right" because of the unpredictable way it moved from side to side. Mickey Rivers had a bad swing at it and popped a ball foul, but Baker was able to snag it leaning into the stands. Willie Randolph and Thurman Munson both grounded easily to short.

Torrez and the defense were solid in the top of the second, retiring the seven, eight, and nine hitters to bring Reggie Jackson to the plate. Jackson didn't swing the bat once, watching Hooton's bender dip in and out, never hitting the strike zone. Four pitches later, he stood on first and Chris Chambliss walked to the plate, promptly launching a home run into the bleachers in right center, tying the game.

The lead didn't last long. With two out in the third, Torrez again faced Smith and again did not get him out, though this time there was little the defense could do about it. Smith homered near where Chambliss had, and it was 3–2 Dodgers.

Reggie Jackson was about to change that. In the fourth, Munson led off with a single. Reggie was still waiting to see a strike from Hooton. "Our scouting reports were so detailed," Jackson recalled. "It was Birdie Tebbetts and Gene Michael with the ball club at that time. I spent a lot of time understanding their pitchers and how they would pitch me. The word was to pitch me in and that helped me to see the ball and hit it. The big thing that happened to me that night was they threw me strikes." He got one on the first pitch, and with one swing sent the Yankees ahead, 4–3, burying a line drive into the right-field seats. Hooton then fell behind Chambliss, 2–1, and Lasorda called for Elias Sosa. Chambliss dropped a ball into short left field between Baker and shortstop Bill Russell and legged out a double. Graig Nettles grounded a ball to second, moving the runner along, and Lou Piniella brought him in with a sac fly to left. Sosa then walked Dent, and the rally might have continued if it had not been one of those alternating years where the National League rules were in place for the World Series, meaning the pitcher, Torrez, had to bat. He grounded to short, but went back to work in the top of the fifth up 5–3.

In the bottom of the fifth, Rivers started the action with a base hit. Randolph then tried to bunt him over, but Yeager snagged the ball in front of the plate in time to catch Rivers at second. Munson lined a ball hard into center, but right to Rick Monday.

And here was Reggie again. Sosa was more of a strikeout pitcher than Hooton, a fireballing reliever with an ERA of 1.98. But he suffered the same fate as Hooton. He threw one pitch, Jackson hit it out, and Sosa left the game. Doug Rau came on to get Chambliss out, but the Yankees were now up 7–3, and pulling away. Torrez sat down Dodger after Dodger, and in the eighth, when Davey Lopes managed a single off him, Lopes was erased with a double play.

But the show was not over yet. Charlie Hough, a more orthodox knuckleballer than Hooton, was on the mound in the eighth when Jackson came to bat one more time. "Nobody really had to tell me what Charlie Hough was going to do," Reggie remembered. "I couldn't believe they were going to bring in a knuckleball guy since I had had so much success against them in the past." The pitcher had changed but the script had not. One pitch, one homer. "This one didn't take the shortest distance between two points," wrote Red Smith in the *New York Times*. "Straight out from the plate the ball streaked, not toward the neighborly stands in right but on a soaring arc toward the unoccupied bleachers in dead center, where the seats are blacked out to give batters a background. Up the white speck climbed, dwindling, diminishing, until it settled at last halfway up those empty stands, probably 450 feet away." Three home runs in one World Series game tied the record set by none other than Babe Ruth, and five in one World Series set a new standard. That four of the home runs, dating back into game five, came on four successive swings, defies belief. Jackson circled the bases to the familiar chant of "Reg-gie! Reg-gie!" and was called out of the dugout for a curtain call by a standing ovation from the fans. After his performance, not much seemed to matter. The other three Yankees to bat in the inning made out quickly, as if eager to get into the field and finish the game.

The home-run-hitting Dodgers were beaten at their own game, it seemed, and futilely reverted to National League–style little ball in the ninth. Cey went down looking against Torrez. Garvey beat out a hit to deep short and moved to second when Baker followed with a single. Monday flew out to deep right for the second out and Garvey tagged and moved to third. Vic Davalillo stood in to pinch-hit for Yeager and dropped a bunt down the third-base line. Nettles scooped up the ball and threw to Munson, but Garvey beat the play and scored. Pinch hitter Lee Lacy followed with another bunt attempt, this one popped in the air. "I saw the thing go up," Torrez told reporters. "And I said 'C'mon ball, I got you.'" Torrez squeezed it in his glove and the Dodgers were done, Jackson's bravura show of power ending with a strange little off-key grace note. The Yankees had won their first world title since 1962.

Reggie was selected MVP of the World Series and also set several other records in addition to his home run marks. He topped Gehrig and Ruth's previous high for runs in a Series with 10 to their nine, and his 25 total bases passed Lou Brock and Duke Snider. Reggie's heroics drew praise from all corners. "Reggie Jackson, an integral part of the Yankees' season-long storm, rose to his inimitable dramatic best last night," wrote Murray Chass in the *New York Times*. "[He] provided a remarkable conclusion to a year in which Jackson was scrutinized and dissected as perhaps no other baseball player has ever been." The Dodgers were equally impressed. "Reggie rose to the occasion," Steve Garvey told the *Times*. "I think he released a lot of emotional tension from the season into one game. I think all the turmoil throughout the season helped him in the Series, helped him tonight, helped him to perform in a way to release that tension. That's his way."

Years later, Reggie's teammates still talk about it. "We all kind of expected Reggie to do things like that in the playoffs and World Series," Roy White said. "We always knew if the game was on TV, he was gonna be great. He always seemed to hit home runs on the *Saturday Game of the Week* or whatever. Being in the spotlight, Reggie was a better hitter. He had more concentration, more discipline, and was able to succeed on many occasions under those circumstances. It was certainly a part of history sitting there watching him hit all those home runs you knew it was a special moment to be there and see that." Graig Nettles agreed. "It's the defining moment of his career. And it helped us win the World Series. I was happy about it."

Extra Innings

- In 1977, Reggie Jackson drove in 110 runs, the most by a Yankee since Mickey Mantle drove in 111 in 1964.

- Ruth and Reggie:
    The two men who have hit three homers in a World Series game have some striking similarities. Both played right field and hit left-handed. Both were 31 years old when accomplishing the feat for the first time (Ruth did

it again two years later). Both brought their total of World Series homers to seven with the third shot. Both came to the Yankees in ballyhooed deals, having won world championships with previous employers. Both had their uniform numbers retired by the Yankees, and both entered the Hall of Fame as Yankees.

- "Playing here in New York, the press has been like a cobra in the jungle. I've been attacked. In Oakland, they made fun of all the controversies. Here, you get whipped. Maybe they whipped me into having a good year and I owe the press part of the credit": Reggie, in the *Sporting News*.
- Red Smith on Reggie: "In his last nine times at bat, this Hamlet in double-knits scored seven runs, made six hits and five home runs and batted in six runs for a batting average of .667 compiled by day and by night on two sea-coasts 3,000 miles and three time zones apart. Shakespeare wouldn't attempt a curtain scene like that if he was plastered."

October 2, 1978: New York at Boston

Dented

In which Carl Yastrzemski has reason to kick the Green Monster

In 1978, the New York Yankees were still "the Bronx Zoo," with all the bickering, hoopla, and dog-eat-dog mentality that nickname implied. Several of the characters who had been agitating to leave the previous year had left, including Mike Torrez, who went to the Red Sox, while others, such as Mickey Rivers and Thurman Munson, stayed put. Boss George's big catch of the winter free-agent season was fireballing relief pitcher Rich "Goose" Gossage (a move that upset Cy Young Award winner Sparky Lyle). Otherwise, the cast was largely the same, headed by the increasingly paranoid and drunkenly belligerent Billy Martin, whom sportswriter Dick Young described in the *New York Daily News* as the man with "the *I'm the boss* chip on his shoulder."

Gossage did not flourish under Martin's confrontational style, and both he and the team struggled in the early going. Lyle did not pitch often enough to sharpen his slider. Don Gullett and Catfish Hunter tried to pitch through injuries, but Gullett made only eight starts and Andy Messersmith five before both were shelved for the season with injuries. Ed Figueroa added himself to the list of players who did not get along with Billy. Pretty much the only pitcher who didn't struggle was Ron Guidry, who won eleven straight starts on his way to a 25–3 record and a minuscule 1.74 ERA. Guidry hit 95 on the radar gun with his fastball and also had perfected the slider, which he could throw at two different speeds and use it to saw off the bats of righties at the handle. Strikeouts were so frequent when he was on the mound that the Yankee Stadium faithful began the rhythmic "two-strike clap" every time another K seemed imminent.

Meanwhile, in Boston, two future Hall of Famers, Carlton Fisk and Carl Yastrzemski, were the heart of a team some called the best Red Sox squad since Pesky-Williams-Doerr-DiMaggio. Jim Rice was having a .315, 46 home run, 139 RBI season, and Fred Lynn wasn't far behind (.298, 22, 82). Rick Burleson, Dwight Evans, and Jerry Remy (along with Rice, Fisk, Yaz, and Lynn) were all All-Stars that year. The Red Sox also snagged free agent Mike Torrez after his World Series victory. Torrez racked up a respectable 16–13 record, but the stars of the staff were Dennis Eckersley, who won 20 and had an ERA of 2.99, the twirling Cuban Luis Tiant, and "Spaceman" Bill Lee. It looked, for much of the season, like for once the Red Sox had the talent and the drive to bury the Yankees. At the All-Star break the Yankees were 11½ games back, in third place. Kansas City, their western rival, came to town shortly thereafter and swept three games. On July 17 the Yankees were in fourth place, 14 games behind.

But some curious things can happen in a 162-game season. Gossage eventually found his groove and his 98-mile-per-hour heater. Catfish's shoulder began to come around after he had the adhesions in it popped. And Martin's whiskey-loosened mouth finally got ahead of him when he uttered the now infamous words referring to Jackson and Steinbrenner, "The two of them deserve each other. One's a born liar, the other's convicted," and within 24 hours he was gone, replaced by calm and affable Bob Lemon (himself fired by the White Sox). And in mid-August, the day Reggie was installed at cleanup, the pressmen's union went on strike, meaning the *New York Times*, *Daily News*, and *Post* disappeared from the newsstands, and with them their constant advancement of the Yankee soap opera. The griping did not stop, but it was no longer public, and Lemon directed the team's focus from personalities to playing. Figgy went 11–2 after Lemon's arrival. And the Yankees won 12 of 14 games on their way to a four-game series in Boston.

When the Boston Red Sox opened the gates to let the Yankee ballplayers off their bus and into the cramped grounds of Fenway, they held a four-game lead over New York. But injuries were hampering the Sox just when the Yankees were surging. Evans was still dizzy from a beanball, Remy had broken his wrist, and Fisk and Yaz were both still playing but with cracked ribs and other nagging ailments. But it was New York's performance, in which they outscored the Red Sox 42–9, that led to nicknaming the four-game sweep the "Boston Massacre." By the end of the season both teams had identical records, 99 wins and 63 losses—Boston winning on the final day and New York losing. American League rules stipulated that the tie must be broken with a one-game playoff.

A coin toss determined that the game should be played at Fenway Park. Guidry went to manager Lemon and asked (some say demanded) to start on three days' rest. "The mood of the team was great," Guidry remembered. "The team was playing well, we had gone up to Boston in September, and we had beat them four in a row, and we knew we could beat them. There was no 'Oh, no, we gotta go play in Boston.' We weren't afraid to go there." Lemon gave him the ball, telling reporters his plan was to let Guidry go as long as he could, and then bring in Gossage, who had led the league in saves. Reggie was one of those who was glad to hear it. "Guidry taking the ball was a big emotional lift for our ball club. A big psychological lift. We knew we had our best—the best in baseball—pitching for us. And so that was very comforting." In the other camp, Red Sox manager Don Zimmer decided to go with none other than former Yankee Mike Torrez.

"When you think about it," said Graig Nettles, "[It was the] third year in a row that we were in a win-or-go-home situation—us having been through that situation the last three years probably gave us a little edge. You never know. The best thing about that game was we played it the next day and we didn't have to think about it for three or four days or a week. We just went right up and played it like it was just one more day on the season."

The game was scheduled for the afternoon of a crisp and bright New England fall day. The action began like so many big games for these Yankees before, with Mickey Rivers getting on base. "I don't know why, but I always liked the feel of playing there [at Fenway]," Rivers said. "The intensity of that stadium and the intensity of the ballplayers, I loved it." He walked on four pitches, then stole second. Although it was true that Torrez knew the Yankees, both their signs and their hitters, these Yankees also knew him. Torrez then faced his former battery mate, Munson, and struck him out. Piniella grounded a ball to third, and Reggie skied a ball to the opposite field, where it was headed over the Green Monster until the wind knocked it toward Yaz, who tracked it down with alacrity in the corner. "Maybe that was Mr. Yawkey's breath helping us out," pitcher Bill Lee told Thomas Boswell of the *Washington Post*, referring to the Red Sox' late owner. Apparently getting to Torrez would take an act of fate.

Guidry responded with two strikeouts in the bottom half, Munson's mitt popping loudly with each fastball. Torrez sat down Nettles, Chambliss, and White in the second. Guidry then faced Yastrzemski. Yaz had been born on Long Island, but had been a Red Sox his whole professional career. Drafted out of Notre Dame, he had made the bigs in 1961 and won the Triple Crown and the American League's MVP Award in 1967. But here, in his 18th season in the major leagues, he had only his third shot in postseason/playoff baseball. The crowd was tense and quiet. Guidry's second pitch was up and Yaz, a lefty hitter, put a hard swing on it, pulling it hard. The ball sailed into right and past "Pesky's pole" for a home run. The uptight fans exploded with relief.

Guidry teetered, but Roy White and Mickey Rivers were able to snare deep line drives from Fisk and Lynn. Butch Hobson grounded to Nettles. But Boston had the lead, and Torrez defended it. A hit here or there had no impact on him. "Mike Torrez was really pitching great, he had great stuff that day," Roy White recalled. "And I started thinking, wow, we might not win this game the way he's throwing. I didn't think we were going to get to him." But Guidry settled down as well, allowing only two hits until the Red Sox came to bat in the sixth.

Rick Burleson opened the inning with a double. Zimmer, sensing the low-scoring vibe in the air, played for one run. Remy dropped a sacrifice bunt down, and Jim Rice came to the plate. Remy, as it turned out, had given himself up for nothing, because Rice's following single would have scored Burleson anyway. Yastrzemski grounded to Chambliss, and Rice moved up a base. With first open, Guidry gave a free pass to Fisk and went after Lynn. Out in right field, Lou Piniella was thinking that Guidry didn't look so hot. In fact, he figured there was some chance that Fred Lynn might even be able to pull the ball, just as Yaz had in the second. So he positioned himself much closer to Pesky's pole by 40 or 50 feet.

Lynn did pull the ball, a sinking liner that on any other day would have rattled around in the corner and scored two men. Sweet Lou ran and met the ball with a basket catch. Inning over.

With that ball, Piniella also grabbed the momentum for the Yankees. With one out in the seventh, Chambliss and White knocked back-to-back singles. "I was actually looking for a slider," White said. "He had been throwing a good, hard slider that was breaking in, so I was kind of looking for that slider, thinking that I would be the one to hit one out. And Mike threw a fastball, over the middle of the plate . . . and I got a base hit up the middle." With two on, Lemon called back Brian Doyle, playing today only because of Willie

Randolph's hamstring, and sent slugging Jim Spencer to the plate. Spencer took a big cut but flew out. Now came Bucky Dent.

Dent had come to the Yankees from the White Sox in exchange for Oscar Gamble, two minor-league pitchers (LaMarr Hoyt and Bob Polinsky), and $200,000 cold, hard cash. Dent had heartthrob good looks—a light-hitting, slick-fielding shortstop with nothing controversial about him. He had hit only four home runs all year and sported a lifetime average of about .250. But having just used a big pinch hitter and being short on infielders because of Randolph's leg, Lemon, who knew Dent from his time in Chicago, sent up his shortstop to swing away. Guidry knew the pitcher's mentality. "You kind of forget about a guy like Bucky, who was a good contact hitter. Not a power hitter, but a contact hitter."

Dent was thinking about Torrez. "When you play behind a guy for a long time, you understand him. Plus I had faced him before with Oakland and Baltimore. I was familiar with what he had." After taking a ball, he looked for the slider, got it, but fouled the ball off his foot. While Gene Monahan, the Yankees' trainer, tended to Dent, treating his foot with anesthetic spray, Gene "Stick" Michael, coaching first, struck up a conversation with the runner on base. "Roy White was on first base and I said to him, do you think he can handle Torrez? He said, nah, not unless he hangs him a slider."

Meanwhile, Mickey Rivers in the on-deck circle had noticed something: Dent had a cracked bat. "So I told the batboy, 'Here, bring this to my homey'—I called Bucky my homey—'and give him this bat,' and I gave him a good bat." Torrez had stood there watching while Dent went through the motions with the trainer and then the batboy—Torrez later admitted he may have lost his rhythm. When the former teammates were once again set, Torrez on the rubber, Dent in the batter's box, Torrez wanted to come back with the same pitch again. But what Dent got was a fastball over the plate. "After I fouled that ball off my foot I was just thinking to hit it hard someplace and drive in a run." He put a good swing on it, and Bill White, announcing the game on television, shouted, "Deep to left!"

The wind, which had held up Reggie's ball in the first, was now blowing the other way. Yastrzemski went back to haul the ball in, but it kept carrying, carrying, right into the netting above the Monster. As Dent circled the bases, Yaz leaned against the battered green wall and kicked at the ground dejectedly. The Fenway crowd, which had become raucous after Yaz's homer, now was shocked to near-silence. 3–2 Yanks.

Roy White remembered the silence. "That was how I knew it was out. I didn't think it was going to be a home run when he hit it, but I figure it's going to be off the wall, and I'm running as fast as I can, watching Carl Yastrzemski, and as I'm rounding second I'm thinking if he misses the carom as it comes off the fence, maybe I'll score. I'm thinking score from first. And then all of a sudden I see no reaction from Carl except for his shoulders kind of slumped and I didn't hear the ball hit the fence, and there was this kind of silence. So I knew it was out." Dent himself didn't know it was a home run at first either. "I lifted that ball down the line and I never did see it go in the net, it wasn't until I got around first that I saw the second-base [umpire] signaling. That and the dead silence. As I rounded third I remember how quiet it was except for the sprinkling of Yankees fans in the stands. It was like the fans were stunned."

The *Washington Post* reported, "It was a sudden-death playoff, and sudden death was what Yankee shortstop Bucky Dent seemed to bring to the Red Sox."

Torrez was stunned, too. He walked Mickey Rivers for the second time that day, thinking ahead to Munson, whom he had struck out three times already. But Zimmer wasn't taking any chances with a pitcher who had just been beaten by the number nine hitter. He called for Bob Stanley, a big righty who had been a strong bullpen contributor all season. Munson took the first pitch while Mick the Quick took second base. On the next pitch he doubled in the gap between Yaz and Lynn; Rivers scored. That was four runs on four hits in the inning, and the Yankees had gone from a two-run deficit to a two-run lead.

Now it was Gator's turn to go back out there and see if he could keep Boston from bouncing back. He struck out Hobson to start the inning. But George Scott singled, and Lemon had the best reliever in the game warmed up in the bullpen. "I didn't want to come out of the game when Lemon took me out," Guidry said. "I didn't want to come out. [Scott's hit] was away, a right-handed batter hit a ground ball away. I still had good stuff, I didn't want to come out, but he said Goose was ready, and he brought Goose in."

Goose was hyper, keyed up. He hadn't slept well the night before, imagining Yaz coming to the plate. It was actually Bob Bailey standing in there, to pinch-hit for third baseman Jack Brohamer. (It was Bailey's last game and last plate appearance in the majors.) Goose threw a wild one (scored a passed ball on Munson), and Scott took second. But 98 miles an hour is 98 miles an hour, and Bailey struck out. Burleson went down on a grounder to short, and Gossage went to catch his breath in the dugout.

Meanwhile, it was Mr. October's turn to face Bob Stanley. "I said, 'Wow, this guy throws the ball down, he's a fastball pitcher. It's really going to be strength against strength,'" Reggie remembered. "I like the ball down. And I don't think it was very many pitches, either the first or second pitch, and I hit the ball into the center-field seats. No doubt straight away." The ball landed several rows deep into the bleachers in center, and the Yankee lead was now three runs.

They were going to need them. Goose never did catch his breath. Remy doubled to lead off the bottom of the eighth. Rice put a pretty good swing on a ball, but it was a fly to right. Then there was Yaz, whom Gossage had envisioned. Yaz knocked the ball into center for a single, and Remy scored. Then Fisk singled, sending Yaz to second. Then Lynn singled, scoring Yaz. The lead was down to one. Gossage tried to concentrate. Hobson lofted another fly for Piniella, two out. That left Scott. Goose reared back for the strikeout and got it.

The Yankees could not light another fire in the ninth, so it came down to getting the final three outs. Zim sent up Evans, still plagued with vertigo, to pinch-hit; he flew out to left. But Burleson walked. The bright October sun was slanting behind the third-base stands now. Remy came to the plate and hooked a ball into right field, where Lou Piniella stood, squinting. "It was almost by him, because he was blinded by the sun," Reggie remembered. Piniella later told reporters that he never saw it. Instead, he decoyed the runners, pounding his glove as if he saw the ball, and then stretching out his arms like a soccer goalie on a penalty kick. The ball hit the turf in front of him and bounced up, right into his glove. Lou then uncorked a throw to third that held Burleson at second base.

Guidry, icing his arm in the clubhouse as usual after a start, in case he had to pitch again in a few days' time, was watching on the clubhouse television. "The play of the game was Lou's play in right field that he cut off to hold Burleson at second," he said. "If that ball gets by we probably lose, and if he doesn't cut it off, you know that guy's going to score eventually." The next hitter, Jim Rice, also hit a ball to right, the biggest part of the ballpark. This one Piniella saw and plucked out of the air deep in right. If Burleson had been on third, he would have scored easily on the sacrifice fly. Instead he tagged up and advanced to third on the play.

"And lo and behold Carl Yastrzemski is up at the plate," Roy White remembered. "Goose is out there and you know Goose is throwing fastballs. Yaz knows it, and everybody in the ballpark knows it, so you're kind of holding your breath on each pitch." New England held its breath for a miracle, for Yaz to break through 60 years of frustration.

Peter Gammons wrote in *Sports Illustrated* that it had to come down to this: "one final two-out bottom-of-the-ninth shoot-out between Gossage, the premier fastball pitcher of his time and Yaz, arguably the premier fastball hitter of his." Gammons turned to someone and said, "Yaz always wins in these moments."

That thought was also going through the head of Graig Nettles, standing a hundred feet or so away from the 39-year-old left fielder. "I had been with the Minnesota Twins 11 years earlier, in 1967," Nettles recalled. "And we went to Boston the last weekend of the season. All we had to do was win one of two games and we would have won the pennant. [But] Boston won both games and Yaz went like seven-for-eight and just killed us. So here it is 1978, 11 years later, and Yaz comes up with men on, and I think, 'Here he goes, he's going to do it again.' In the back of my mind I'm saying, 'Yaz is going to get us again.'"

Gossage threw a fastball, low. Yaz let it go by. Fans screamed, and everyone on the Yankees' bench clenched their jaws. Goose toed the rubber, and reared back for another scorcher. This one had plenty of hop. Yaz swung, hard, for the fences. But the bat didn't connect where he wanted it. Roy White unclenched his jaw. "Carl took that swing, that big swing that was going to knock the ball about 500 feet if he connects with it. And he just misses it, just gets under it a bit, and it's that high foul. It seemed like it was up there forever. If that pitch was four inches lower, I think Carl would have hit it out. But it was just a little bit too high for him."

Nettles watched it rise, the wind drift it toward foul territory. "I was thinking I was glad that it wasn't a real high pop-up." He backpedaled, backpedaled, and finally squeezed it in his glove at his shoulder. "Finally! I could just see Yaz having one of his typical big moments, and he just popped it up at the right time.

He pops it up to me and I say, 'Now we finally got Yaz out!'"

A new generation of Boston baseball followers had been indoctrinated into the legacy of heartbreak. And a generation of baseball writers turned over the gem of a game in their hands almost with disbelief; they had just witnessed an instant classic. Boswell called it a "game as rich and multicolored as the season-long battle that preceded it." Bill Madden wrote that the comeback would not have been complete without "a side portion of controversy, theatrics, and history." Maury Allen called Dent's blow "almost as dramatic as Bobby Thomson's homer against the Dodgers in 1951." Phil Pepe was as pragmatic as he was emphatic about the ending. "After seven weeks of spring training, 26 weeks of the season, after 162 games, it came down to the final inning, the final batter." The Red Sox had authored another tragedy, the Yankees another triumph.

The Yankees went on to face, and beat, their "other" rival, Kansas City, in the ALCS, and then a rematch with their "other, other" rival, the Dodgers, in the World Series, which the Bombers also won. Bucky Dent hit .417 in the World Series and was named Series MVP. Ron Guidry won the Cy Young Award and set a new franchise record for strikeouts in a season at 248, beating Jack Chesbro's 239, which had stood since 1904.

◀ Extra Innings

- Red Sox Manager Don Zimmer endured a further humiliation from Dent's home run when he became a Yankee coach in 1982. He rented Dent's home in New Jersey when the shortstop was traded to Texas, and photographs of the home run adorned the walls in every room. Zim turned them all around for the duration of his stay.

- Both teams played short an All-Star that game. Willie Randolph was out with a hamstring and Red Sox right fielder Dwight Evans was still groggy from being beaned earlier in the year.

36

August 6, 1979: Baltimore at New York

Captain, My Captain

In which Bobby Murcer memorializes a close friend with the game of a lifetime

In the spring of 1979, the Yankees had every reason to believe that their championship run would continue, but none could foresee the tragedies that would affect the team from off the field. Shortly after their World Series win of 1978, Bob Lemon's son Jerry suffered a fatal car accident. Lemon's equanimity was shattered, and the team played .500 ball for several months. Rich Gossage hurt his thumb in a clubhouse scuffle with Cliff Johnson and missed 12 weeks. (Johnson was sent packing shortly after the fight.) Reggie Jackson also was hurt. So were pitchers Catfish Hunter and Ed Figueroa. To juice up the offense, the Yankees traded Mickey Rivers to Texas for Oscar Gamble and also reacquired Bobby Murcer. Three months into the '79 season, Lemon knew his heart wasn't in it anymore. He was replaced by none other than Billy Martin. The team began to gain some ground, getting to 10 games over .500 by the end of July, but the Red Sox, Orioles, and Brewers were even better. Although the Yankees would have been only three games back if they played in the West, in the Eastern Division they were behind the first-place Orioles by 14. Still, this was a team that had overcome a similar deficit the year before, and they expected their annual surge into September, while other teams would begin to wilt.

It never happened. The Yankees' hopes for the season came crashing down just short of a runway in Canton, Ohio, where the team captain, Thurman

Munson, was practicing landing his jet plane when one of the plane's two engines lost power. The date was August 2, an off-day between a Yankee road trip to Chicago and the beginning of a home stand in New York. Munson had held a pilot's license for several years and had bought the plane, hoping it would allow him to visit his wife, Diane, and their three children more easily. At times he had said he wanted to be traded to the Indians to be closer to home, but at others it seemed impossible for him to picture himself as anything but a Yankee.

George Steinbrenner and Billy Martin had named him captain in 1976, the first Yankee captain since Lou Gehrig, another Yankee who had died before his time. But in the eyes of his teammates, Munson was already their leader. "No one else even attempted to assume the role of the leader," said Elliott Maddox. "Thurman didn't try to assume the role of leader, we just gave it to him. Many times a catcher is looked upon as the leader because he's the only one looking out. Everyone else is looking in toward home plate." The players responded to his toughness on the field, the pitchers to his understanding and fine game-calling skills. "I developed a really nice bond with Thurman because I got a chance to pitch to him and he was so good behind the plate," Jim Kaat said. "He called it 'pitching backwards,' but it was really pitching the right way. I wasn't a very hard thrower, so he said, 'Now when we're ahead, we're going to use fastballs because they won't be looking for them, and when we're behind, we'll use the curve.' Now that's really the right way to pitch. The few times I had a chance to pitch to him we had a lot of fun. He'd be giving signs and laughing behind the plate."

Gene "Stick" Michael had been Munson's roommate for five years and got to know him well. "He had that gruff appearance, but he wasn't that way at all. That was just a thing to get people to keep their distance. He was really a softie. He had big compassion for children and animals. It was all a false exterior." Michael also esteemed him as a player. "He was a tough guy, mentally tough, physically tough, and he learned how to hit. His first year he hit .300, but he started the year oh-for-40 or something like that, and from there on he hit three-something to get his average up. To me that was the best example of how tough he was mentally." Thurman never looked back. Although his lifetime career average was a laudable .292, in three World Series he amassed 25 hits and a .373 average. His clutch performances in the postseason only raised him in his teammates' estimation. And the fans loved how hard he played, even through injuries, how much dirt he had on his uniform, and the swagger that became a champion. In 10 full seasons in New York he was elected to the All-Star team seven times. He was the American League's Rookie of the Year in

1970, won the MVP Award in 1976, and won three consecutive Gold Gloves from 1973 to 1975.

All those numbers lost their meaning on August 2. Bucky Dent remembered hearing the news. "When you lose a captain of your team, an integral part of your team and the organization, it's stunning. I was at the World Trade Center, eating at Windows on the World. We had an off-day. I came down to get my car and the attendant said, 'Oh, it's a shame what happened to Thurman.' I didn't know, because I wasn't watching the news or anything. I said, 'What are you talking about?' He says, 'He got killed in a plane crash.' And I had to go sit down in my car. It was like someone had just punched me in the head. I just backed up and sat down. Driving home I still didn't believe it. You just don't believe it can happen." The next day the Yankees had to start a four-game series with Baltimore and lost, 1–0.

On August 5, Munson's body lay in state at the Canton Civic Center, in a room named for President William McKinley, who had similar last rites performed for him in the same city. More than 200 floral arrangements covered the floor, and for four hours, thousands of fans paraded by to pay their last respects. The next day at 7:40 A.M., the entire Yankee team took a chartered flight to Ohio for the private funeral. Two Orioles who were former Yankees, Rick Demspey and Scott McGregor, went on the plane as well as many baseball dignitaries, including Commissioner Bowie Kuhn, American League president Lee MacPhail, and Mets manager Joe Torre.

Also on the trip was an old Yankee, now back in the fold after stints in San Francisco and Chicago, Bobby Murcer. When Munson had come up for a cup of coffee at the end of 1969, Murcer had been installed in the Yankee outfield. They became fast friends. "I put him on his jet Wednesday night," Murcer told the *New York Times*. "After the game in Chicago. He wanted my family and me to fly home with him that night, but I had some things to do in Chicago, where I still have an apartment." Murcer was called on to read a eulogy at the funeral. "Lou [Piniella] and I both gave eulogies," he recalled. "Before the funeral started, Lou and I went back in a gymnasium there at the community center, and we just sat back there and gathered our thoughts about the eulogies." Piniella read from Ecclesiastes. Murcer quoted philosopher Angelo Patri, but made his own remarks as well. "He was number 15 on the field and he will be number 15 at the doors of Cooperstown. Loving, living, and legend, history will count my friend as number one."

The shock and enervation persisted through the flight home and the team's preparations for that night's game. They had been up at 5:00 A.M. to catch the charter, and at 2:00 P.M. many players tried to catch a little sleep in the clubhouse or trainer's room. By all accounts, Bobby Murcer should have been one of them. He and his wife, Kay, had flown out to be with Diane Munson a day early, and they had stayed up all night talking. But Murcer did not want to rest. "Billy had told me when we got back to Yankee Stadium that I wasn't going to play that night. He said, 'You know you're tired. Take the night off. It's been a long few days for you,' because, you know, I'd been in Canton with Diane and the family. I told Billy, 'I don't feel tired and I think I should play.'" Murcer wouldn't take no for an answer. "Billy wasn't even going to play me that night but there was just a sense inside me that said I needed to play in that game. And he said okay, fine." Thurman's locker stood untouched, his uniform hanging empty on a hanger in its usual place.

The fans knew the funeral had been that morning, and 36,314 showed up at the Stadium. Another 36 million watched on television on ABC's *Monday Game of the Week*, the highest viewer rating for that night, and second highest ever for a regular-season baseball game on ABC. "That was probably the toughest game I ever played," said Reggie Jackson. The Yankees took the field before the national anthem, and then a tribute to Thurman was played. Jackson continued, "The standing ovation went on so long when they had his picture there on the television in center field, that everyone was basically kind of crying. I remember just kind of crying in the outfield. It seemed like it went on for half an hour, though it was probably five or six minutes."

In the end the Yankees put their best team on the field. "Getting out there on the field was a way to get our minds off it for a few hours as best we could," Graig Nettles said. "I wouldn't have wanted to sit out that game. I wanted to get back on the field and try to think baseball again." The lineup looked like an All-Star team with Jackson, Nettles, Dent, Chambliss, and Randolph all playing, and Ron Guidry on the mound. And then at catcher, Brad Gulden. "The only thing I remember about that night was turning around after the national anthem for my warm-up pitches," Guidry recalled. "The national anthem was played first, and turning around to throw my warm-up pitches and not seeing Munson there was . . . I remember turning around and knowing he was never going to be there again. And I was wondering how I was going to get through the rest of my time because he made pitching so easy." Guidry retired the Orioles on a strikeout and two easy grounders, bringing Willie Randolph up to lead off for the Yankees.

"I was just so wrapped up in thinking about Thurman. It was tough," said Randolph. "Guys were crying. Guys were down. In some sense we didn't even want to play the game but we had to play. We all kind of felt like we wanted to go out and play for him and win it for him, and all that, too. We had gone through an exhausting day, and we were just running on adrenaline and fumes and emotions. It was one of the toughest days I've ever had to experience as a player, with a heavy heart and everything, and not having your captain, your leader, there, to lead you, and you have to go on." He slapped a single into center and stole second. But there were heavy hearts and heavy bats coming up. Dennis Martinez, the Orioles' starter, usually struck out two to three men per game. Here he fanned Murcer, Chambliss, and Jackson in a row.

Guidry then had two down in the second when Lee May homered. The score remained 1–0 Orioles for several innings as neither team seemed highly motivated. Then the O's notched another, when May doubled to lead off the fifth, moved to third on a ground out, and came in on a sac fly. They tacked on two more in the sixth when Ken Singleton hit a two-run homer. The team with the best record in baseball seemed well on its way to another win.

But some vestigial memory of championships and performing under pressure lurked in the Yankees' tired bodies. With two out in the seventh, Bucky Dent, batting ninth, worked a walk. The bench instinctively sniffed the air— was Martinez getting tired? losing his control? Randolph followed with a double, and Dent went to third, bringing Bobby Murcer to the plate. "Dennis had a good fastball, a great curve. Good control—you had to be on your toes," Murcer remembered. But this time he made a mistake, delivering a "picture perfect high fastball out over the plate," as Angus Phillips described it in the *Washington Post.* The man who had once been seen as the heir to Mickey Mantle in New York had been back with the Yankees for more than a month at that point, and had not hit a home run since his return. Perhaps he just hadn't seen a pitch that good; Murcer sent it into the right-field stands, a three-run home run. The Birds' lead was down to one.

Dennis Martinez gave way to Tippy Martinez (no relation), a bullpen specialist who was tough on lefties, and he held the score there. And Guidry's arm kept doing its job. Another strikeout, another grounder, another strikeout, and the Orioles were gone in the eighth. Martin sent up three pinch hitters in a row in the bottom of the inning—to no avail, all made out against Tippy—and then it was back to Guidry. A single, a force-out, a man caught stealing—Jerry Narron now catching, still looking like a stranger, gunned the ball to Dent—and then Lee May again. This time Guidry struck him out, too.

The bottom of the ninth had arrived. Again, a walk to the number nine hitter, Dent. This time Randolph tried to bunt him over, but Tippy Martinez rushed his throw and fired the ball past first. Willie scampered to second, Dent to third. Murcer knew the situation. "That was kind of towards the end of my career and normally Billy would pinch-hit for me, being that a left-handed pitcher was in the game and the game was on the line." But Martin let him hit. As Murcer went to the plate, "I just didn't feel like he was going to get me out," he said in the *Washington Post*. Even a fly ball would have brought the tying run in, but Murcer smashed the ball down the left-field line. Dent crossed the plate, the speedy Randolph right behind him. The Yankees had won the game.

Murcer's teammates were amazed. "There you have Murcer reading the eulogy and then coming in and driving in all the runs in the game," Nettles marveled. "That was quite an ordeal for Bobby."

"It was just a really emotional night with the fans, a lot of people crying and weeping and depressed," Roy White remembered. "And Bobby ended up having this really electrifying night."

But Willie Randolph felt it was almost to be expected from a man with a pinstriped lineage. "I wasn't surprised. Bobby had been around a long time, he was a veteran guy, he knew how to handle himself, a good, solid hitter. And you know it was a storybook the way it ended the way it did. He knew how to keep his composure in tough situations." After the game, though, many players' composure crumbled. "I just remember being happy and sad at the same time," Randolph said. "A wealth of emotions and things that went through my mind. It wasn't like the game wasn't important, we still wanted to win, and we still wanted to end the day on a positive note. It was a weird ending to a surreal day."

Guidry was awarded the win, thanks to Murcer's heroics. "It was fitting that it worked out that way," Guidry said. "Because they were close friends, Murcer and Munson, their families were very close. Murcer was almost finished anyway. He was going out the door. But for him to come and have that kind of a game, on that kind of emotional day, it was just fitting that it was him that did it. He rose above all of that day, and he had one of his best games that he had had in years. He threw all of that adversity aside—and it wasn't like we had never gone through adversity, we had been doing that for years you know?—and what he did upheld the tradition of the New York Yankees."

The Orioles went on to win the East, then beat the California Angels for the American League pennant. The Yankees' season, though, was over. Although Tommy John won 21 games and Ron Guidry led the American League in ERA with a 2.78 mark, an exhausted Yankee team finished with a forgettable 89–71 record. "I think from that day the whole rest of the season we were just kind of numb," said Jim Kaat. Munson's locker still stands as it was left that night, his number 15 jersey never worn again by another man.

◀ Extra Innings

- In the first game after the plane crash, the Yankees took the field for the national anthem but left the catcher's position vacant. Backup catcher Jerry Narron stood on the top step of the dugout while the anthem was sung, and then took up his spot behind the plate. The Yankees would do so every game for the remainder of the season.

- *Bobby Murcer*: "After that game I never did use that bat anymore, I gave it to Diane Munson. That was the only game that I used that bat in."

- *Jim Kaat*: "The last time I saw Thurman, we had been out in Chicago on a Tuesday night with Bucky, and Goose Gossage, Nettles, and myself. We had an Italian restaurant there that Bucky and Goose and I had frequented when we played for the White Sox: Traverso's. And they loved Thurman. So we took Thurman out there and Mama Traverso cooked up a bunch of food and stuff for us, on Tuesday night, and of course Wednesday night was get-away day, and then Thursday I'm at home and I hear the news over the air."

- Brad Gulden is known for being traded for himself. In November 1980 the Yankees traded him to the Seattle Mariners for Larry Milbourne and a player to be named later. In May 1981, Seattle completed the trade by shipping back Gulden as the player to be named later.

July 4, 1983: Boston at New York

Prince Righetti

In which we enjoy heat in the mid-nineties

In the early eighties, the Yankees still had strong teams, though they won no more championships. In 1980, the Royals finally beat them for the pennant, and in the strike-shortened season that followed in 1981, the Yankees won the first half and then faced their now-habitual foes, the Dodgers, in the World Series, only to lose. Other teams were becoming savvier about playing the free-agent market, while the Yankees let Reggie walk away. By 1983 the previous championship dynasty was over. The "new" team still included some holdovers from the championship years—Lou Piniella, Willie Randolph, Graig Nettles, and Ron Guidry—but the cast was largely new. Dave Winfield, Don Baylor, and Ken Griffey Sr. were the latest free-agent sluggers, while the catching duties were shared between Rick Cerone and Butch Wynegar.

David Allan Righetti

One thing that had not changed: the rivalry with Boston. "It was very intense in 1983," Nettles said. "It was intense before I got to the Yankees, even though I didn't know about it, but I soon learned. I learned that's an intense rivalry. The whole time I was there it was very intense and it still is to this day." The Red Sox came into town July 1 for a four-game series, and although the Yankees won a messy opening game, 12–8, the Red Sox had slammed 14 hits and four home runs. The Sox then pummeled them, 10–4, and 7–3, on the next two days. On July 3, before the game, Baylor spotted the next day's starting pitcher, Dave Righetti, sitting on the dugout steps in 94-degree heat. Baylor said, "Rags, you're young and wise. Why don't you get off this bench, go inside, and relax? You might need that energy tomorrow." Righetti went to the clubhouse.

The finale came on America's birthday, the celebration complete with parachute jumpers landing in center field before the game, and Chuck Mangione playing the national anthem. Despite the crushing losses, "the spirit in the Yankees' clubhouse is all cool confidence," said Mangione during a visit to the radio booth.

Taking the mound for the Yankees that day was 24-year-old lefthander Dave Righetti. Righetti was a Southern California native whose father, Leo, had played in the Yankees' minor-league system in the fifties. Some had tagged Righetti "the next Ron Guidry" because when he came up in 1981, the lefty was clocked at 95 miles per hour. (Never mind that Guidry was still around, and would win 21 games for the Yankees that season.) In the Texas Rangers' minor-league system, Righetti had once struck out 21 men in a game and racked up 127 strikeouts in 91 innings. The Yankees acquired him as part of the trade that sent Sparky Lyle to Texas, and after being called back from the minors in 1981, Righetti earned the American League Rookie of the Year Award with a 2.06 ERA and an 8–4 record. If anything had hampered his early success, it was a lack of control, but by 1983 those problems were behind him. His previous start was a five-hit shutout in Baltimore. He went into July 4 with a 9–3 record, reasonably confident of his abilities.

But behind Righetti was a somewhat unfamiliar infield. Roy Smalley played shortstop. At first base was the rookie Don Mattingly, wearing the number 46, who had known Righetti in an instructional league. "More than anything I remember it was the Fourth of July," Mattingly recalled. "We had been to a concert the night before—Willie Nelson, a big concert at the Meadowlands— and then here it was, a hot day, and Rags just kept getting better and better." At second base was André Robertson. "Billy had a habit of resting guys [when we had] night game-day game," Willie Randolph explained. "It was a real hot, hot day. I had played that night, so he gave me the day off." Graig Nettles also was out of the game. "I had pinkeye and I couldn't see. I just couldn't see. When you get pinkeye it sometimes lasts for a couple of days and that happened to be one of those days." He was replaced at third by steady utility infielder Bert Campaneris, because whenever Righetti pitched, third base was indeed the hot corner. "I always got a lot of work at third base because he threw a lot of sliders," Nettles said of the days when Rags took the hill. "Right-handed hitters always pulled that slider down on me. And I expected a lot of strikeouts."

Rags conformed to those expectations exactly, striking out the side in the first inning, though he did walk Jim Rice. In the second he struck out two more, and two more in the third, making seven of the first eight outs strikeouts. In those early innings, he used his fastball almost exclusively, a pitch that had so much movement on it that day, it left the Red Sox shaking their heads. When he struck out Glenn Hoffman for his seventh K in 2⅔ innings, radio announcer Phil Rizzuto couldn't contain himself. "This is unbelievable!" he enthused. The crowd was excited to see the dangerous Red Sox lineup, which had hit 9 homers and 38 hits in the previous three games, wilt under Righetti's heat.

But it was Righetti who was starting to feel the heat. "In those first couple innings I was striking out a lot of guys," he later told interviewers. "I knew if I was going to last in the game I had to throw fewer pitches." In the fourth he and catcher Butch Wynegar varied their strategy. On just five pitches he retired the side: Wade Boggs lined to center, Rice to right. Tony Armas grounded the slider to Campaneris at third, just as Nettles had predicted, but weakly. Campy had to charge it to make the pickup, but his throw to first nipped Armas. In the fifth, Righetti struck out Dwight Evans, even though Evans choked up on the bat to shorten his swing, but then walked Reid Nichols. Rags helped erase the mistake himself, picking Nichols off first to stifle any excitement on the Boston bench.

Meanwhile, the Yankees weren't gaining any ground on John Tudor, the Red

Sox starter. Tudor and Righetti had faced off at Fenway earlier in the season, and Tudor had held the Yankees to two runs in a 5–2 win. Tudor was a lefty with good control who did not throw as hard as Righetti but did average five strikeouts a game. He had a deceptive arm motion and would sometimes come sidearm, sometimes three-quarters. In the fifth, the Yankees pecked away at him. With one out, Steve Kemp, Smalley, and Robertson hit successive singles—all ground balls that made it through the infield—for one run. Campy then walked to load the bases. But Mattingly and Winfield whiffed, and one run was all the Yankees got. "It was a real close game," Mattingly said. "1–0, 2–0, you couldn't relax."

Righetti carried on as if it were 0–0, sitting down three more, while the crowd grew more and more tense—as did the ballplayers. "As soon as we got to the sixth inning," Campaneris recalled, "we said, 'He's got a chance.'" In the bottom of the sixth, the Yankees doubled their score when Don Baylor hit a home run. "Then it was the seventh," Campy said, "and he's got a *good* chance." Mel Allen, who was calling the game on television, went through tongue-twisters to tell the folks at home what was happening without using the words "no-hitter" for fear of jinxing it, while the camera repeatedly zoomed in on the scoreboard showing zeros. The only person who would talk to Rags at all after the sixth was Nettles. "Right after that was the start of the All-Star break," he remembered. "I said to him, 'Get this thing over with,' because we were going to Atlantic City that night." The fans began to cheer with every pitch, then went berserk when Kemp leaped high against the sidewall in right field to snare a foul ball out of the stands. "I wanted to make the play because Evans is such a good hitter, and you don't want to give him another shot," Kemp told Larry Whiteside of the *Boston Globe*. "I was fortunate that no fan blocked me. But I was going to do anything to get that ball." Righetti, who had been tiring, was rejuvenated by the play. With every out the cheering intensified. Nichols flew to center, and Dave Stapleton popped a foul that Mattingly squeezed near the tarp on the first-base side.

With only three outs to go, the last thing anyone wanted at that point was a prolonged inning. But the Yankees put up some insurance runs. With one out, Dave Winfield started a rally by beating out a hit to shortstop. Lou Piniella popped up, but when the Red Sox catcher, Jeff Newman, had to dive into the stands to make the catch, Winfield tagged and moved to second. The inning ground to a halt, though, as the home-plate umpire, Steve Palermo, had slipped while following Newman to the wall and banged his head. Yankee trainer Gene Monahan tended to him as quickly as he could. Tudor then walked Baylor intentionally. The pace of the inning crawling, Bill White and

John Gordon, now in the radio booth, struggled for something to talk about. Every time White recounted the score, and said "Red Sox, no runs, no hits . . ." he would hiccup a little as if to stop himself. They began to talk, with forced casualness, about the previous no-hitters pitched by Yankees: Don Larsen, Allie Reynolds, Sad Sam Jones, George Mogridge. . . . Meanwhile, Butch Wynegar walked to load the bases, bringing Steve Kemp to the plate. Kemp lined the first pitch into right, bringing in Winfield and Baylor and knocking Tudor out of the game. Bob Stanley came on and retired Smalley on a grounder to first, and the final act of the Righetti show took the stage.

It was all Wynegar could do to keep his pitcher contained. Righetti was throwing so well, his ball had so much movement, it was hard to keep it in the strike zone. He went to a full count on Newman, who walked. Glenn Hoffman then grounded a ball to short. Smalley fired to Robertson at second, who turned and fired to first. "I was on the bag," Mattingly insists to this day. "He was out. He should have been out." But Hoffman was called safe, as it looked like Mattingly had been pulled off the bag by the throw. He slid his foot back to touch the bag again, but the umpire didn't see that. "I think he was out, but what can you do? It was a double-play ball but we didn't get the call." Mattingly, the rest of the Yankees, and 41,077 fans in the stands hoped the bad call would not turn the tide.

Jerry Remy came to the plate but grounded easily to second. That left only Wade Boggs standing between Dave Righetti and immortality. No lefthander had ever thrown a no-hitter in Yankee Stadium, and the last no-hitter in the Stadium had been Don Larsen's perfect game 27 years earlier. "We were definitely on our toes, because Boggs was a great hitter," Mattingly remembered. "Tough on lefties, and he was a tough out all the time. The last guy you'd wanted up there." The year before had been Boggs's first in the league and he had batted .349 and only struck out 21 times—an average of once every 16 at-bats. On July 4 he was leading the batting race with a .357 average, 101 hits, and on his way to winning the crown with .361. "The toughest out in baseball," said White as Boggs dug in with his back foot in the batter's box. In the dugout, Billy Martin did something he had never done before during a baseball game—he said a "Hail, Mary."

"The only thing I guess was that Rags had a good breaking ball that day, which really gave him the advantage," Mattingly remembered. Boggs, who almost never swung at the first pitch, took a ball. Then he took another: a strike. The third pitch he swung at and missed. Now he had to protect the plate. He fouled off the next pitch and then evened the count at 2–2 by taking a ball. The crowd groaned. Wynegar thought it over. "I was going to call a fastball again," he told reporters after the game. "But when I got down into the crouch, I figured, what the heck, let's fool him with the slider."

Righetti agreed. "I didn't think Boggs would be looking for it." He threw the slider. The ball zoomed toward the heart of the plate, and then just as Boggs's bat moved forward to meet it, gave a little dip and wrinkle, as if moving to avoid contact. Strike three, and the crowd exploded like a pack of firecrackers.

"After Boggs swung and missed, I went blank for a second," Righetti told the *Sporting News*. "Then I saw Butch coming at me and I grabbed onto him. I didn't want to be knocked down." He felt like crying as the tension he had held for so many hours flowed out of him, but he kept himself together. The pair were quickly engulfed by their teammates; then the scrum broke up near the dugout and Righetti raised his arms to the crowd. He raised his cap, tiredly, in his left hand and walked up and down in front of the dugout while the ovation went on and on. Then he went down into the dugout and into the clubhouse where the media were massing, waiting for him. Out in the stands, the crowd chanted "We Want Dave!" but already Righetti was no longer theirs; from the moment Boggs swung and missed, he belonged to history.

◀ Extra Innings

* Home plate umpire Steve Palermo asked Butch Wynegar before the fourth inning for the ball they had been using to warm up. Palermo inspected the ball for nicks or any signs of doctoring before tossing the ball to Righetti to start the inning. There was so much movement on Righetti's fastball and slider that Palermo must have wondered if it was "all natural."

* Bert Campaneris holds the record as the position player who has appeared in the most no-hitters. Righetti's was Campy's 11th in his 19-year major-league career. The man he subbed in for on July 4, 1983, Graig Nettles, never appeared in any. Campy also set an interesting record when he played all nine positions in a game on September 9, 1965, when he was with the Kansas City A's. (Three other major leaguers have done it since: Cesar Tovar, September 22, 1966, for the Minnesota Twins; Scott Sheldon, September 6, 2000, for the Texas Rangers; and Shane Halter, October 1, 2000, for the Detroit Tigers.)

* "Even I was rooting for him at the end."—John Tudor, in the *Boston Globe*.

* George Steinbrenner celebrated his birthday at the Stadium that day with his guest Richard M. Nixon.

Sticky Situation

In which a game is lost, won, and lost again

The East-West rivalry between the Yankees and the Kansas City Royals burned hot starting in the mid-seventies. The two teams had met in the playoffs four times (1976, 1977, 1978, and 1980), and plenty of bad blood had passed between them. With Billy Martin, the king of the confrontation, in charge in 1983, sparks were expected to fly any time the rivals faced each other. What no one could have predicted is that one particular kerfuffle would brew in the back of Billy Martin's mind for more than two weeks.

The Royals came into Yankee Stadium for a weekend series on July 22. The Yankees won the first game of the set after the Royals had tied the score in the top of the ninth, with a run in the bottom of the ninth. The next day Larry Gura faced Ron Guidry, and once more the Yankees got the better of Gura, winning 5–1. Having won the first two games, Billy Martin wanted the sweep. "He didn't like to lose," said Yogi Berra, who was serving as first-base coach that day. "He'd try to beat you any way he could." The Yankees put Shane Rawley on the hill to face Bud Black.

The Royals drew first blood in the second inning on a walk to first baseman John Wathan; a single sent him to third, and a ground out sent him home. Dave Winfield answered that with a solo homer in the bottom half of the inning.

Wathan started another rally in the fourth with a base hit. Leon Roberts then singled, but was caught at second trying to stretch it into a double. Frank White then singled in Wathan and put the Royals up by a run. They tacked on another in the sixth on back-to-back triples by White and Don Slaught, knocking Rawley from the game. Dale Murray relieved and the one was all the Royals got, making their lead 3–1.

The Yankees replied with a rally of their own. Bert Campaneris, playing second that day in his final major-league season, singled to spark the action. Graig Nettles struck out, but Lou Piniella followed with a base hit. Lou and Campy both scored when Don Baylor tripled, and Winfield brought him in with a base hit.

The 4–3 lead would last until the ninth inning. Murray, still pitching, got two quick outs, but then U. L. Washington singled, and Billy made the call to the bullpen for one more out. Hard-throwing Rich Gossage came on to face the ever-dangerous George Brett. Although the Yankees had beaten the Royals for three different pennants in the seventies, it was a homer off the bat of Brett that had finally sunk the Yanks in their most recent playoff meeting, in 1980. Goose threw—what else?—a fastball, on the outside part of the plate, and Brett hit it deep but foul down the left-field line. The next pitch was farther in, and Brett wasted no time planting it into the upper deck in right. The two-run shot would put the Royals up 5–4, but this was the moment when the idea Billy Martin had kept in his mind for more than two weeks surfaced.

Martin jumped out of the dugout and went to the home plate umpire, a tall, mustachioed fellow named Tim McClelland, picked up Brett's bat from where it lay in the grass, and showed it to him. "What he's talking about, Frank," said Bobby Murcer to his broadcast partner Frank Messer, "is that he's got too much pine tar on the bat. They might have a legitimate gripe here." The Yankees themselves had been victims of the rule. On July 19, 1975, in a game that the Yanks lost, 2–1, to the Twins, Thurman Munson had an RBI single nullified in the first inning when it was ruled that the pine tar on his bat exceeded the 18-inch limit.

Martin ambled behind McClelland, who took the bat in one hand and went to confer with the other umpires, Joe Brinkman, Drew Coble, and Nick Bremigan, all veteran arbiters. Crew chief Brinkman was one out away from going on his annual two-week vacation, and planned to fly home to St. Petersburg, Florida, right after the game.

Brinkman and his team were familiar with this situation. Two weeks before, working a Red Sox-Indians game in Cleveland, the Tribe's manager, Mike Ferraro—a former Martin coach and disciple—asked Brinkman to check Jim Rice's bat after a double, but the tar was two inches below the trademark and therefore legal.

Graig Nettles joined the confab. "I noticed it when we were playing in Kansas City the series before, because I knew the rule," Nettles said. "I had seen it happen before in a game so I knew it was a stupid rule, but it was a rule: you can't have pine tar up too high on the bat. I told Billy about it and he said let's just wait and see if he gets a big hit against us. And he didn't do anything against us in Kansas City, but then we came back the next week in New York and he was using that same bat, or one that had even more pine tar on it." Brett did not wear any batting gloves, which was typical for the time, and used the sticky resin to improve his grip on the bat. The umpires conferred, looked at the bat for several minutes, feeling it with their hands to determine if the colored areas were sticky, while Brett stood on the steps of the third-base dugout, watching warily. "I've seen it called before," said Murcer on the air. "This is going to be an interesting call."

The umpires then moved off by themselves and conferred for a few more minutes. Brett sat down on the Royals' bench, accepting handshakes from teammates but unsure of his fate. "Somebody said they were checking the pine tar, and I said, 'If they call me out for using too much pine tar, I'm going to kill one of the SOBs,'" Brett said in 1998.

The umpires went to home plate, which is 17 inches across, and McClelland lay the bat across the plate to measure how far up the bat the pine tar went. "I knew it at the time when they started measuring the bat," said Nettles. "Goose didn't know the rule, but I knew the rule. I was there telling Goose, 'Yeah, we got 'em! It's a rule. They gotta call him out.'" McClelland then stood, pointed with the bat at Brett in the dugout, and raised and clenched his right fist to signal "out."

Brett charged out of the dugout like a man possessed. Royals manager Dick Howser and two umpires cut him off just before he reached McClelland, and it took three umpires and three Royals to restrain him from doing something he might truly regret. McClelland stood stoically, watching the outburst.

"There goes the vacation, I figured," said Brinkman.

"I knew he'd be upset but I didn't expect him to go crazy like that," said Nettles. "I tried to say to him, 'George, don't hurt yourself, don't do anything stupid.' I thought he was going to take a swing at one of the umpires. I was ready to help calm him down, but he was too far out of it so I just backed away."

As the melee went on, Kansas City pitcher Gaylord Perry, himself no stranger to on-field chicanery, sneaked up behind the group and took the bat. He tossed it to Royals designated hitter Hal McRae, who passed it on to Royals pitcher Steve Renko. Renko was noticed just as he reached the Royals dugout, where he broke into a run up the tunnel. An umpire and a Yankees' security man ran after him and retrieved the bat. Messer informed his viewers, in his erudite way, "The fact that they have tried to secrete the bat lends credence to the umpire's call, in my estimation."

And so it appeared that the Yankees had snatched victory from the proverbial jaws of defeat, and that Goose had been awarded a save when the only batter he faced had hit a home run. But the weirdness was not over. A series of battles with Lee MacPhail, American League president and son of former Yankee president and general manager Larry MacPhail, ensued. The Yankees lost every battle. MacPhail overturned the umpires' call four days later. It was the first time in 10 years that MacPhail overruled his umpires. He reinstated the go-ahead home run, and ordered the end of the game replayed on August 18 at 6 P.M., the one off-day the players were to have in a stretch of 31 straight games.

A wild two weeks of legal battles ensued as the Yankees sought to win in court what they had been denied in MacPhail's office, even sending famous lawyer Roy Cohn to wage their paper fight. The appeals were denied as the judge wrote a two-word decision: "Play ball!" Further, the American League order of a 6:00 P.M. start time for the resumption of the fractured inning enraged Steinbrenner further—he claimed he had planned events for day camps around the spectacle, and now had to cancel them because of the late start.

So at 6:00 P.M. on August 18, 1,245 fans came to the Stadium to see what might be just four outs. By that time the trading deadline had passed, and many players in the original game were no longer with their former teams. Also, Brett, Howser, Perry, and Rocky Colavito were all ejected at the time of the original Brett outburst. (Brett, having been ejected, watched the game from an Italian restaurant in New Jersey.) Even a new umpiring crew was needed, and fortunately Davey Phillips and his crew were in town already to work a series.

With Campaneris on the disabled list, Martin moved Mattingly from first base to second and inserted Ken Griffey Sr. at first. Jerry Mumphrey had been in center at the time of the home run, and Butch Wynegar behind the plate. Both were gone, so Rick Cerone came in for Wynegar, but who to tab for center field? How about Ron Guidry?

The final substitution was George Frazier (no, not *that* George Frazier) for Goose. Martin ordered Frazier to throw the ball to first, then second, then third, making the claim that Brett had failed to touch the bases in his home-run trot.

Phillips denied Martin's appeal. Billy ran out to argue, claiming that the umpires present were not the ones on hand in the previous at-bat and could not state personally that they had seen Brett round the bases. But the umpires were ready for Billy. Dick Butler, supervisor of American League umpires, had provided Phillips with signed affidavits from Brinkman's July 24 crew attesting to the fact that they had seen Brett touch the bases. They didn't tell the Yankees about the affidavits, and sprang them on Martin, who had played his last card. The game went on.

Frazier faced Hal McRae with two out and the restored score 5–4. McRae struck out.

Now it was the Yankees' turn to bat. To win the game, they would have to score two runs, but by this time, very few players felt that the win was worth very much. The only thing potentially at stake was Don Mattingly's rookie hitting streak. Donnie had hit in 12 straight games prior to July 18, and then also hit in 12 more starting on the 19th. "It was one of those years where somebody was giving whoever had the longest streak like a thousand dollars or something like that. When I was a young player that was a lot of money!" Don recalled. But he had not gotten a hit on the 18th, so now, in a weird twist of fate, if he could get a hit almost a month later, his streak would officially be considered intact at 25 games. Unfortunately, Mattingly hit a fly ball that was tracked down in center field by Pat Sheridan. Roy Smalley followed with another fly out, and then Oscar Gamble pinch-hit for Ron Guidry and grounded out. After a delay of more than a month and an additional nine minutes and 41 seconds of play, the "pine tar game" was over, and the Royals had officially won it, 5–4.

Extra Innings

- The controversial bat was held by the American League office for about a week after the game, then returned to Brett by air courier. He wanted it back because it was, he said, one of the best bats he had ever had. In Detroit, he took it to the plate and found Tim McClelland there. The umpire had a sense of humor, and jokingly asked Brett if he wanted the bat checked for pine tar. About two weeks later, in a game against Milwaukee, Brett broke it. The bat is now in the National Baseball Hall of Fame and Museum in Cooperstown, New York.

- After the pine-tar incident, Kansas City entrepreneur Tom Leathers began printing bumper stickers that read "I Pine for George!" with a heart logo and smudged bat. The stickers, which sold for a dollar each, were popular with female Royals' fans, many of whom considered Brett Kansas City's most eligible bachelor. All proceeds from the sale of the stickers went to a medical center's program for fighting—what else?—Lou Gehrig's disease.

- Ron Guidry played center field one other time in his Yankee career, recording the final out of the lost 1979 season.

- Nettles on MacPhail's Ruling:
    "They actually made the right call. They let common sense take over. Because it was a silly rule on the books. Pine tar cannot help the ball go any farther. We all knew it was a silly rule, so that was one way of getting a stupid rule out of the book."

- The governor of New York, Mario Cuomo, was once a minor-league player before he gave it up to go into law. Upon hearing the outcome of the game, he commented "Congratulations" to New York's manager.

One other Yankee would miss the game when it was resumed. Utility infielder André Robertson had an early-morning car accident that day on the West Side Highway. The accident effectively ended his career.

September 30, 1984: Detroit at New York

Photo Finish

In which David and Goliath do battle under the glare of the media

In 1984 the Yankees finished in third place, but what kept fans watching to the end, checking the papers daily, and going to the park, was a different race. The two racers were young, popular, homegrown Don Mattingly, and veteran free agent Dave Winfield, who some fans never warmed to. At the All-Star break Winfield was batting over .370, while Mattingly was putting up an impressive .332. That doesn't look like much of a contest. But Winfield's average began to

Donald Arthur Mattingly

come back to earth as the summer wore on, and Mattingly's crept up. By September there was clearly a contest in the making between these two very different players.

Don Mattingly, a native of Evansville, Indiana, was drafted by the Yankees in the 19th round of the 1979 amateur draft. Other teams had skipped over him because they didn't feel he had enough speed, but Yankee scout Jax Robertson saw more potential.

He opened the eyes of his teammates when he came up for a cup of coffee in late 1982. "From looking at him then, hitting off those pitchers who had been throwing all year, we thought we had something," recalled Ron Guidry. "He wasn't gun-shy, he wasn't afraid." The next spring, Mattingly was noticed. "At the end of spring training it was, they would take either Mattingly or me, and they took Mattingly," said veteran utilityman Bert Campaneris. "So you knew he was good. Oh, yes. He was so good in spring training that they decided they had to keep him." In 1983, Donnie hit .283 as a part-time player appearing in 91 games. "One thing that really impressed me about him early was that for a rookie, for a young player, he didn't seem intimidated by where he was," Willie Randolph remembered. "You could tell just by the way he carried himself that he felt like he belonged."

But he was only getting his feet wet. In 1984, as a full-time player, Mattingly took a full dive into the talent pool of the best hitters in the league.

Dave Winfield had come to the Yankees from the San Diego Padres, where he had starred for eight years. Winfield had made his mark immediately after being drafted. In 1973 he had pitched the University of Minnesota into the College World Series, and went right to the bigs without doing time in the minors. But in New York, Winfield was always at a disadvantage, not because he wasn't a great player, but because he wasn't Reggie Jackson. Mr. October was a hard act to follow, yet George Steinbrenner, and the fans, expected him to fill the gap Reggie left. When Winfield hit .045 (only one hit in six games) in the 1981 World Series, Steinbrenner bitterly labeled him "Mr. May." Winfield wasn't Jackson, but he was an astonishingly talented athlete, in his career a 12-time All Star, seven-time Gold Glove winner, six-time Silver Slugger, and first-ballot Hall of Famer. In 1984 he was only halfway through his career, but his superstar credentials were well established.

"It was almost like a David and Goliath situation," Randolph said of the race and the story that developed around it. "What was made of it in the media, I guess it was just more dramatic, more Hollywood, to kind of look at this as a story about a young kid coming up as the challenger. I think it was uncomfortable for both of them to be teammates through that, and uncomfortable for us." Randolph explained that the batting race became something of a white elephant in the clubhouse. "No one wanted to talk about it, because there was so much made of it in the media. It's hard whenever you get two teammates fighting for it, because you'd almost rather one guy going against someone [on another team] so you could get behind him. So there wasn't a lot of talk about it. We just tried to win ball games." Other than an early conversation where the two hitters agreed between themselves that there would be "no friction," Winfield and Mattingly, too, did not talk about the race except when prompted by the media. They let their bats do the talking.

As September heated up, the players sensed that the fans had chosen the underdog. "I felt that," Don Mattingly said. "The fans got behind me. But if it had been reversed and I had been the 10-year guy, and there was a young guy coming up, I think it would have been just the opposite. They would have been for the young guy. Because you always like to see the young guy nobody knows about, come out of the minor leagues, as opposed to the other guy. I think it was natural that people rooted for the younger guy."

Mattingly, for his part, felt no pressure. "For me I had nothing to lose. The worst that would happen to me is I hit .340 or .335 or something. So I was just happy as could be to be swinging the bat the way I was. I was starting to get some confidence in the things I could do, so I had nothing to lose. It was fun, you know, for me." On September 24, Donnie got his 200th hit, becoming the first Yankee to tally 200 in a season since Bobby Richardson's 209 in 1962. On the 25th he doubled for the 42nd time, last done by a Yankee by Tommy Henrich in 1948. "I think it will go down to the last day of the season," he told reporters after that game. "We're both swinging the bat well." Of course, the very next day, Mattingly went 0-for-4 while Winfield collected one hit, putting their averages mere percentage points apart, .34184 for Mattingly, .34177 for Winfield.

The final series of the season would be against the Detroit Tigers, who had wrapped up their incredible wire-to-wire season already, on their way to 104 wins and the world championship. With the Yankees in third place, long since eliminated, all attention in New York focused on the final four days of the batting race.

In the opening game, the Yankees squeaked out a 2–1 win over the powerful Tigers, but the batting race drew even closer. "Mattingly, after twice relinquishing the lead in the game at Yankee Stadium, moved back ahead after getting one single in one official time at bat, with one walk. Mattingly is now hitting .341809. Winfield was at .341715 after going 0-for-1 with two walks, one of them intentional, and a sacrifice fly," reported Michael Katz in the *New*

York Times. "The tension could be felt on calculating machines throughout the Bronx."

Winfield had hit only .184 over the previous 11 games, but went 2-for-5 (both doubles) in the second game of the series, while Mattingly went 1-for-4. Dave had pulled his average .0005 higher than Mattingly's with two days left, and on the next day, with one hit to Donnie's none, pulled ahead, .341 to .339. "I guess I can't rest them tomorrow," joked manager Yogi Berra to the *New York Times.*

Winfield was not as lighthearted. "Honestly, it's been a trying year," he admitted. "I'll be glad when it's over." But about the pending race to the finish line, he added, "I'm sure we'll both think about it tonight and get up and go to church and then go 4-for-4." If they did, Winfield would win, .346 to .344. In fact, Don's only chance of overtaking Dave was to get four hits, while Dave got fewer than three.

Sunday morning came. "When I woke up this morning," Mattingly told the *Times,* "my wife gave me a big smile and said 'I love you.' I couldn't ask for more than that." Mattingly also may have gotten a boost from being such a young player because the Tigers' starter that day, Randy O'Neal, was a late-season call-up. "I faced him somewhere in the minor leagues. He was a new guy too, just coming up." Mattingly knew O'Neal's style and knew he could succeed against him. "He was a pretty good guy for me to hit."

As was usual, Mattingly batted third that day, Winfield fourth. Don came to the plate in the first inning after the first two batters reached, on a single and a walk. "I wanted to bring them in," Mattingly recalled. "Game situation." The lefty-swinging Mattingly blooped a single to the opposite field. "I kind of flared one in there, hit a little dinker. And then I kind of relaxed because I was like, 'Well, I hit one.'" The duck snort loaded the bases for Winfield. Winfield pulled a ball from O'Neal, but the grounder to third was an easy force-out at home plate. The bases remained loaded for big Don Baylor. Baylor doubled, bringing in two runs and moving Winfield to third. O'Neal, young and rattled in Yankee Stadium, then threw a wild pitch that brought in Winfield. Ken Griffey Sr. then walked, but O'Neal escaped when Butch Wynegar grounded into a double play.

The Tigers got a run back in the top of the second, but anyone filling out a scorecard was looking at when Mattingly and Winfield would come around again. They did in the third. On the first pitch he saw, Mattingly pulled a ball to right field that hit the wall for a double. "I swung early in the count because normally I was taking a lot of pitches at that time [and I thought] maybe pitchers were trying to get ahead of me, so I took advantage of that." Winfield was more patient, but it may have worked against him because he drew a walk. Then Griffey walked before O'Neal settled down. Mattingly scored on a ground out to make it 4–1 Yankees.

The twosome came around again the very next inning, with two out and a man on second. Mattingly again swung at the first pitch and this time cracked an RBI double down the line in right. Winfield followed with a single, and Mattingly moved to third. Baylor followed with a double that scored both men and knocked O'Neal from the game with the Yankees up 7–1.

The Yankees added two more runs in the fifth, but without any help from Mattingly or Winfield. Wynegar singled. So did Mike Pagliarulo, followed by a walk to André Robertson. Omar Moreno hit a sac fly that scored a run and advanced both runners. Toby Harrah grounded out to bring in one more and to bring Mattingly to the plate. He tagged the ball hard, but it was just a fly ball to center to end the inning.

But Winfield opened the next inning with the same move, a hard-hit ball to Chet Lemon in center. The Tigers managed back-to-back doubles in the seventh, to make the score 9–2 Yankees, but with their berth in the ALCS secure, they hardly needed to worry about a seven-run deficit. In the eighth they sent bullpen ace Willie Hernandez out to pitch, to give him a final tune-up before the playoffs.

"Appropriately, the duel between [them] went down to the players' final at-bats of the season's final game," wrote Moss Klein in the *Sporting News*. Mattingly smiled inwardly. "I couldn't believe it was coming down to the last at-bat," he told the press. "But I felt there was no way I could be a loser because I wouldn't have looked at finishing second to Dave as losing."

Mattingly was due to lead off the inning against Hernandez, who was en route to an MVP and Cy Young Award that season. "He was just nasty on lefties," Mattingly remembered of Hernandez. "He had that slider—he was tough. He had a great year that year and he had given me trouble all year long. So he was one guy I didn't necessarily go up there expecting to get a hit off him." Mattingly looked at two pitches first, a ball and a strike, and then pulled a bouncer toward second baseman Scott Earl. The ball hopped up and over his glove and on into right field, a single, Donnie's fourth hit of the game, the hit that he knew would clinch him the title. "I didn't hit it that good," Don said. "Just lucky." Winfield followed with a grounder that forced Mattingly at second. Mattingly walked off the field to a tremendous ovation. Berra then inserted a pinch runner for Winfield. As he came off the field, Mattingly went out to greet him, and the two shook hands and walked off the field together to more applause and cheers.

"It was good that we could come off together," Mattingly told reporters after the game. Winfield had ducked out of the clubhouse before the media arrived. "Dave has been a great person through this whole thing. He handled himself like a gentleman and I have great respect for him."

Mattingly finished the year with a .343 average, 23 home runs, 110 RBI, and 207 hits in 603 at-bats, leading the league in hits and doubles. It was the first batting title for a Yankee since Mickey Mantle won the Triple Crown in 1956. Winfield tallied .340, with 19 homers, 100 RBI, and 193 hits in 567 at-bats.

Extra Innings

- Mattingly's 1984 salary was $80,000. He earned a $50,000 bonus for appearing in more than 110 games.

- Dave Winfield was born on October 3, 1951, the day that Bobby Thomson hit the "Shot Heard 'Round the World" walk-off home run to beat the Dodgers and win the pennant for the Giants.

- Don Mattingly became only the fourth Yankee to bat .340 or higher, hit 20 homers, 40 doubles, and drive in 100 or more runs in a single season. The previous three were Babe Ruth, Lou Gehrig, and Joe DiMaggio.

Date	Mattingly	Winfield
9/25	.344	.341
9/26	.344	.342
9/27	.34184	.34177
9/27	.341809	.341115
9/28	.3412	.3417
9/29	.339	.341
9/30	.343	.340

40

July 1, 1990: New York at Chicago

No No No

In which a tough-luck pitcher's luck gets even tougher

Nineteen ninety was one of the less illustrious years in Yankee history. "That was one of *those* teams," as Don Mattingly described it. "That was when we started going downhill. They kind of dismantled our team after 1988 and started over." The team was simply not very good, but on July 1, in Chicago, it hit an emblematic low point. Thirty-year-old righthander Andy Hawkins took the hill against the White Sox. He had come to the Yankees in 1989 as a high-priced free agent and had been expected to become the ace of the staff. But his struggles at the start in 1990 had been so bad that at that point in the year, Hawkins wasn't even supposed to be a Yankee anymore. A month earlier he had lasted only one third of an inning against the Red Sox. The next day manager Bucky Dent was given his walking papers and a few days later, Hawkins (and his 8.01 ERA) was given the choice of demotion to the minors or outright release. He chose to be released, but Mike Witt injured his elbow in a game against the Orioles, and Hawkins was kept to take Witt's slot in the rotation. After the reprieve, he recorded a 1.95 ERA in the next three starts, lowering his overall ERA to 5.80. But despite how well he pitched, he gained no victories, and his record remained 1–4. On July 1, he hoped once again to change that.

It was another windy day in the Windy City, with bright sun, and Chicago celebrated the 80th anniversary of the opening of historic Comiskey Park, which was seeing its final year.

Hawkins's counterpart for the White Sox was a lefthander named Greg Hibbard, a lefty changeup artist in his second year in the big leagues. Hibbard was having a decent year—he would end up with a 3.16 ERA, with a 14–9 record and 211 innings pitched. In a six-year major league career, those would turn out to be his career bests. But both pitchers engaged in a duel that began in the first inning. Hibbard sat down 16 men in a row, Hawkins 14, before giving up walks. The Yankees broke up Hibbard's no-hitter in the seventh, with two outs, when Jesse Barfield and rookie Jim Leyritz both singled. But Mike Blowers flew out to end the inning, and in the bottom half of the seventh Hawkins kept up the no-hit pace using his best pitch, a diving forkball. "He was the type of guy who always grinded it out," remembered teammate Rich Monteleone. "But it seems like every year there's a pitcher who is what you call snakebit. A pitcher is sure of his performance and his ability, but also you have to have a little luck on your side." Maybe, thought Monteleone, as the outs piled up, maybe Hawkins's luck was finally about to change.

In the eighth, Barry Jones replaced Hibbard, but the Yankees were no more effectual against the new pitcher than they had been against the old, and the game remained scoreless. Hawkins got two quick infield pop-ups to start the bottom of the eighth.

So it was that Hawkins had retired 23 men without surrendering a hit, when the events would unfold that would cause Michael Martinez to write in the *New York Times*: "Their season has been part folly and part frustration, but today the Yankees found a new low to their crazy summer." The next batter, Sammy Sosa, who then played right field for the White Sox, grounded a ball to third for what should have ended the inning. But Mike Blowers blew it, dropped the ball he tried to field on the backhand, and Sammy beat the late throw with a headfirst slide. An overanxious scoreboard operator recorded it as a hit, but the Yankee bench erupted, waving towels and arms toward the press box. The official scorer ruled the play an error. Sammy then stole second, and Hawkins lost Ozzie Guillen, who walked on a 3–2 pitch. He then walked Lance Johnson on four straight to load the bases.

Robin Ventura came up, swung late on a pitch, and skied a ball into left field, toward Jim Leyritz. Leyritz had played only three games in left, a position manager Stump Merrill had put him in to keep his bat in the lineup while Mel Hall had a day off. Leyritz turned the wrong way in the tricky wind, dove for the ball, but it went off his glove. All three men scored, and Ventura stood on second. Then, as if to prove that fate was truly against Hawkins, Jesse Barfield lost the next fly ball in the sun. "I knew I was in trouble as soon as he hit it," the outfielder said. "I saw it go up and I tried to stay with it. I almost caught it right in the tip of my glove." Ventura scored on that error, the third of the inning, making it 4–0. Hawkins then retired Dan Pasqua on a pop fly to short.

The Yankees, now facing rookie Scott Radinksy, did not make a dent. Mattingly flew to center. Steve Balboni reached on an error by Ventura, but they could not capitalize as the next hitter, Barfield, grounded into a double play.

Hawkins sat in the dugout not knowing how to feel. In the previous 48 hours, two other no-hitters had been pitched, one by Dave Stewart of the Oakland A's in Toronto and one by Fernando Valenzuela of the Dodgers in San Diego. "I'm stunned that I threw a no-hitter, and I'm stunned that I got beat," said the confused pitcher. "I'll have to sleep on this."

The fans at Comiskey Park applauded Hawkins and his teammates congratulated him, but he didn't feel the joy he expected. "This is not even close to what I envisioned a no-hitter to be. You think of Stewart and Fernando coming off the field in jubilation, not this."

Two of those who congratulated Hawkins after the game were teammate Dave Righetti and manager Stump Merrill. "I told him just think of it as a no-no," said Righetti, who had pitched his own no-hitter just seven seasons before. The manager was pragmatic. "We gave them six outs in an inning. He pitched a no-hitter for me."

In his very next start, Hawkins pitched 11⅔ shutout innings, but lost 2–0 in the twelfth, dropping his record to 1–6.

"Everybody on the team was proud of his performance. We were all professionals and every pitcher knows he can't control what goes on behind him," Monteleone concluded. "Just a tough-luck pitcher." On July 12 he faced the White Sox again and this time lost a rain-shortened game in which Chicago's Melido Perez gave up no hits! A tough-luck pitcher, indeed, Andy Hawkins retired from baseball after two more seasons.

Extra Innings

* Three pitchers have tossed losing no-hitters in baseball history, and Hawkins's was the most lopsided in favor of the team that didn't hit. On April 24, 1964, Ken Johnson pitched a no-hitter for the Astros, but lost, 1–0, to the Cincinnati Reds on two walks and two errors. Hawkins's was the second, and the third was by Matt Young on April 12, 1992, when the Indians scored two unearned runs to the Red Sox' one. Steve Barber and Stu Miller also combined on a no-hitter for the Orioles, though Barber allowed 12 base runners, 10 via the base on balls and 2 hit by pitch. The Tigers beat the O's that day, 2–1, scoring both runs in the bottom of the ninth.

* Major League Baseball recently revised the rules regarding no-hitters. To add insult to injury, Hawkins's game was thrown off the list because although he pitched the complete game, he pitched only eight innings (because the home team did not bat in the ninth, having won the game).

* Perhaps the brightest spot in Hawkins's career came in 1984, when he notched the sole victory in the Padres' World Series history, against Detroit.

41

September 4, 1993: Cleveland at New York

One for the Books

In which a courageous pitcher defeats his opponents single-handedly

Jim Abbott was one of those rare prodigies, who came into Major League Baseball without working his way through the minor league system, joining the California Angels in 1989 right out of the University of Michigan. At the time, detractors of the Angels and their lack of talent hinted that Abbott was there only as a publicity stunt. But Abbott stuck in the majors, and after four years with the Angels had notched one 18-win season, and although he had gone 7–15 for a pretty bad ball club, he had lowered his ERA to 2.77 in 1992.

Why would a good, young pitcher establishing himself in the majors be considered a publicity stunt? Because Jim Abbott had been born without a right hand.

The Yankees traded J. T. Snow, Jerry Nielsen, and Russ Springer to acquire Abbott in the winter of 1992. Manager Buck Showalter and general manager Gene "Stick" Michael were rebuilding the club, and the team began to move in the right direction. But although Abbott pitched fairly well in his first two months as a Yankee, the team averaged only 2.8 runs a game for him, and his record stood at 1–5 on May 8. He found the transition to New York difficult, and suffered some sleepless nights. It would not be until July 27 that Abbott would reach .500, at 8–8. "Our team was coming around, so we were starting to have some better teams, a good bunch of guys. Those guys were just starting to turn the corner," said Don Mattingly of a time when the team was beginning to contend but didn't quite have all the pieces. Going into September they were 75–58, neck and neck with the Toronto Blue Jays at the top of the division.

On September 4, a damp afternoon at Yankee Stadium, "the Yankees handed the baseball to Abbott, their struggling lefthander, and asked that he simply keep the team competitive in this pennant-race game against the Cleveland Indians" (*New York Times*). In his previous start against the Indians, just a week before, Abbott had his worst outing of the season, lasting only 3⅔ innings while giving up 10 hits and 7 runs. The day did not have an auspicious beginning, either, as Abbott walked the speedy Kenny Lofton to open the game. Fellow pitcher Rich Monteleone watched from the bullpen. "I played with him when he was with the Angels first coming up," said Monteleone, who was rooting for his friend and knew what was going through the pitcher's mind. "Pitchers tell themselves subconsciously, okay, it's the first inning, I have to hold that guy there and not let him score. You think, oh, I made the mistake, the primal sin of walking the leadoff batter. So my job is to keep this run on the base and keep him from scoring. You just go after the next batter as hard as you can and don't make the same mistake." Abbott did, inducing Felix Fermin to ground into a 5-4-3 double play.

That day Paul O'Neill was playing right field for the Yankees. He described Abbott as "a cutter ball pitcher. He just cut the ball in on righthanders on every pitch. Lefthanders had to take him away. He was almost like Andy Pettitte. Whenever he was on the mound, you knew it was going to be pretty slow out there [in the outfield]." Dion James must have been pleasantly surprised, then, to catch the final out of the inning in left. Carlos Baerga, a switch-hitter who had been frustrated by Abbott's cutter, had decided to face him from the left side, to keep the cutter from bearing in on him, but all the Indians' leading hitter could get was a routine fly to the opposite field.

The Yankees didn't look much better against a big Cleveland righthander, Bob Milacki. The first man to reach was Bernie Williams, who walked in the second inning with two out, only to be stranded. Meanwhile, Abbott was throwing hard, striking out Albert Belle and Candy Maldonado, while hoping that today the Yankees would put some runs on the board.

They did in the third, helped by two Cleveland errors. Mike Gallego, playing second base for the Yankees that day, walked to lead off the inning. Randy Velarde then tried to bunt him over but hit a pop foul. Wade Boggs singled, putting men on first and second. Dion James then sent a ball into center that was mishandled first by Lofton, then by Jim Thome in the infield. When the ball finally came to rest, all three Yankees had scored, two unearned.

Abbott forged ahead, getting grounders from Fermin, Baerga, and Belle. Then another leadoff walk—another double play. "The outs were so unspectacular that the game just sort of rolled along," wrote George Vescey in the *New York Times*. "Because I walked some guys, it did not seem effortless by any means," Abbott said. As a ground-ball pitcher, "I give up a lot of hits," he explained. "I never expected to pitch a no-hitter."

Velarde hit a solo homer in the fifth to make it 4–0 Yankees, and Abbott was mostly concerned with keeping the lead. But in the sixth inning, some excitement began to creep into the crowd, a mere 27,225 on a day when it had rained in the morning. Thome, the Indians' hard-hitting lumberjack of a first baseman, connected on a cutter away, but right at Velarde. "It was like a seed sinking at my feet," Velarde told the *Bergen Record*. "That was a tough play." Abbott then walked his third man of the day, but Lofton flew out to left and Fermin grounded to third.

"I was sitting down in the bullpen, focused on the game. In the seventh inning, I just happened to look up at the scoreboard," recalled Monteleone. "I didn't say a word. I didn't want to jinx anything." The crowd could see the scoreboard, too, and they began to clap for every pitch. Abbott's other teammates ceased talking to him as well. "Early in the game, catcher Matt Nokes talked to his pitcher after every inning, trying to build his confidence," wrote Jennifer Frey in the *New York Times*. "[But] in the late innings, Nokes knew it was time to shut up."

But Abbott himself was starting to feel a wee bit tired. Baerga grounded to first for out number one of the seventh. Belle then grounded a ball into the shortstop hole. Velarde moved to make the play, but realized that with his position and angle, so deep in the hole, if he made a clean play he would still never catch the runner at first. As these thoughts flashed through Velarde's mind, Boggs flashed into his field of vision from the right. "If Velarde has to field the ball there's no way he can throw him out," said Boggs. "I went as far as I could go. I stretched and made a desperate effort." Boggs made a full-length dive to stop the ball, scrambled up, and the throw beat Belle by a clean half step. The Stadium crowd came to life with roaring cheers. The next grounder also came to Boggs, an easier one, but with an even louder cheer, as it meant Abbott had only six outs to go. "I felt a little tired in the seventh," Abbott admitted later, "but in the eighth and ninth, with the crowd, I didn't feel it at all."

What most of the Yankees were feeling at that point was tension. "As a position player, you start really concentrating and you start taking every pitch a little more seriously," said Paul O'Neill. "You don't want to be the one who loses the ball in the lights or gets a bad jump. You try to block out those things." Showalter sent Gerald Williams to left for defensive purposes, but Williams was a mere spectator in the eighth. Energized by the crowd, Abbott struck out Manny Ramirez and Candy Maldonado before losing a battle with Jim Thome, who walked. Cleveland manager Mike Hargrove sent Sandy Alomar up to pinch-hit, but this inning ended the same way the seventh had, with a grounder to third and a roaring ovation.

As Abbott came out to pitch the ninth, the crowd was on their feet, and the infield was on their toes. "I looked over at Mattingly and [Gallego] and they were bouncing up and down," said Velarde. "But my legs wouldn't move. I was like, 'Come on, feet!'" Meanwhile, Showalter and pitching coach Tony Cloninger relieved some tension on the bench with some humor. "I had to go to the bathroom for four innings but I didn't dare," Showalter said. Instead, he called the bullpen, told them to send in Lee Smith, the Yankees' closer, and hung up. "Watch how quickly that phone rings," Buck said to Cloninger. A second later, it did, Mark Connor, the bullpen coach, screaming on the other end, and the bench dissolved in laughter.

The mood in the stands was darker, as Kenny Lofton went up to the plate looking to bunt to break up the no-hitter. A common legend about Abbott was that when he was a high school pitcher, one team thought bunting on him was a good strategy, because they could take advantage of his one-handedness. In the legendary version, Abbott fielded nine bunt attempts and threw every man out. In real life it was "probably only five or six," according to Abbott. In real life, Abbott would pitch with his left hand, and then at the end of his natural follow-through, switch his glove from his stump to his left hand, as ready to pick up a bunt or stab a comebacker as any other smooth-fielding pitcher. If he did field a ball, he could switch back to throwing just as smoothly. "I can't even tell you how he did it," said Don Mattingly, who received many throws from Abbott at first base in his career. Rich Monteleone remembered Abbott's fielding prowess well. "He was better than anybody else out there. Mel Latzman was the pitching coach with the Angels and I remember he would always hit to us pitchers. And we used to have to catch 10 in a row. If you caught nine, and then you missed one, you started all over. Jim seemed like the only one who always caught 10 in a row. He was just so quick, it was just amazing how he could turn the glove over and be ready to field the ball."

According to Hargrove, Lofton was not trying to exploit a weakness by bunting, but trying to do what he could to keep his team in the game. If he had bunted back to the mound, he would probably have been out. We'll never know for sure, though, since after his bunt attempt went foul and the Yankee Stadium crowd began calling for his head, he chopped a grounder to second for the first out of the inning. "Donnie kept yelling at me about how big his goose bumps were," Gallego said. "He kept yelling about how the hair on his neck was standing on end." Two outs to go, and Felix Fermin stepped in. Fermin, with only three homers in his career to that point, was not feared as a power hitter, but he sent a ball soaring high and far into center field. Bernie Williams, the fastest center fielder the Yankees had seen since Mickey Rivers, chased it down and made the catch on the warning track 390 feet from home plate. Phew.

That left only Carlos Baerga to retire. Velarde still felt like his feet were stuck in the mud as the crowd roared on a called strike. The sound was so loud, even with the Stadium only half filled, that he could hear neither the pop of the ball in the mitt, nor the sound of the ball hitting the bat as, on Abbott's second pitch, Baerga grounded a ball toward short. "I really wanted the ball to come my way," Velarde told reporters later, "but I wanted it to be hit hard." Instead it was a soft grounder. Velarde charged in. "You always want the ball in a situation like that," Velarde explained. "If you don't, it's going to find you anyway." He scooped the ball out of the grass and threw to first, completing Jim Abbott's unbelievable feat.

"I remember watching Baerga ground out to Velarde to end the game and the first thing that came to my mind was that Jim Abbott had one arm, and here he is with the Yankees throwing a no-hitter," said Paul O'Neill. "It couldn't be more amazing." O'Neill ran in to join the throng of teammates around Abbott. Catcher Matt Nokes had his pitcher in a bear hug.

"I didn't know how to react," Abbott told reporters. "I didn't know whether to be supremely confident or supremely thankful. I guess a little bit of both." He tipped his cap as he went into the dugout, but the crowd stamped and shouted for a curtain call. As he came back onto the field, Abbott grabbed

Nokes by the jersey and pulled him onto the field to share the credit for the performance. "He deserved to be out there as much as I did," Abbott told the *Washington Post.*

The rounds of congratulations continued in the clubhouse. Then there was a press conference, where Abbott thanked another person, his wife. "She knows how much of an adjustment it's been to come here, and she's listened to more than her share of sleepless-night talks, irrational talk, and she's stood right by me. She was as big a part of this game as I was, and I'll always be thankful."

And then there was a whirlwind tour of eating and drinking sites in Manhattan, turning heads everywhere he went. And receiving the key to the city, doing the talk shows, and the stacks of telegrams congratulating him. But the triumph had no carryover for the team. In the end, the Yankees did not have what it took to win the East, and Abbott himself ended the year 11–14 with a 4.37 ERA.

But that one game, that one day, would define his career. "I had an incredible experience living in New York, playing for the Yankees, to go through all of the things I did, including the no-hitter," he told *MLB.com* years later, when he returned to play in an Old-Timers' Day at Yankee Stadium. "The no-hitter was the highlight of my career. The specialness of it, I didn't know how lasting it would be when it happened. Everywhere I go, people talk about that game, how exciting it was. That makes me very proud."

Extra Innings

- Jim Abbott's parents went to watch a high school football game on the afternoon of September 4. They had recently moved and hadn't yet bought a new satellite dish to watch the Yankees. "We didn't know anything about it until the football announcers mentioned it in the sixth inning," Mike Abbott told the *Bergen Record.* "We're going to have to get another satellite dish."

- On May 29, 1993, while facing the Chicago White Sox, Jim Abbott had taken a no-hitter into the eighth inning when Bo Jackson broke it up with a single. Ron Karkovice followed with a home run. "I think no-hitters take a little bit of luck," Abbott said. Abbott himself picked up a good-luck charm just a few days before his September 4 masterpiece, from a one-handed seven-year-old girl named Jessica Morz. Abbott had spent some time talking with her before a game, and she had given him a Yankee troll doll and told him it would bring him good luck. Abbott not only had the troll doll in his locker on September 4, but also "I had on my lucky shorts, my lucky shirt, and my lucky jeans," he told the *Bergen Record.* "I mark the jeans with an X so I know which ones they are."

The day after the game, Abbott was given a trophy by the grounds crew. Frankie Albohn, head groundskeeper, presented the pitcher with the pitching rubber, which they dug out of the mound and had the entire team sign. Albohn himself also was missing a hand.

September 3, 1995: Oakland at New York

Races Wild

In which the wild-card race is enlivened by one player's special day

Every baseball game is made up of moments determined by chance—by the wind, the way the ball bounces, the turf—and by the interaction of thousands of individual decisions, what pitch to throw, whether to swing away, whether to jump for the ball or play the carom. Sometimes all the breaks go the right way, for a day, or for a season, for a player, or for a whole team. We have an expression for this phenomenon in baseball: lightning in a bottle.

When Tony Fernandez came to the Yankees in 1995, it looked like the Yankees might just be able to catch it. In 1994, the team was the strongest it had been in decades, but the strike-shortened season and the cancellation of the playoffs and World Series meant that group would never be tested. In 1995, Fernandez looked to be one of the strongest additions to the roster. A native of the Dominican Republic, Tony had debuted with the Toronto Blue Jays in 1983. During his first eight years in Toronto, he won four Gold Gloves and was a three-time All-Star. In 1986, he set a new high-water mark for hits in a season for a shortstop with 213. After a series of short stints with the Padres and Mets, he was traded back to the Blue Jays in 1993, just in time to help them to a World Series championship—the right place at the right time. The Yankees hoped he would be in that situation again when they brought him to New York.

"I remember him coming to the Yankees and I thought he was going to be the perfect fit for us and put us over the top," recalled Paul O'Neill. "He was really known for his fielding, but offensively he could do a lot of things. He knew how to hit—a lot of people forget what a good hitter he was." That may be because Fernandez recorded the lowest offensive numbers of his career (.245 batting average, .321 on-base percentage) in his year in New York. As he struggled for traction, so did the Yankees, only beginning to pick up the pace as the race to the playoffs heated up. Fernandez began to hit, and so did O'Neill, and even team captain Don Mattingly, who had suffered an eye infection early in the season and whose power in recent years had been sapped by a back injury. After years of tinkering with his stroke, Mattingly discovered a stance that would allow him to swing without hurting himself. Going into September, the Yankees went on a winning streak, notching their fifth straight on September 2, with a win over the A's that put them one game back in the wild-card race. (In 1995, Major League Baseball added a new layer of playoffs known as the Division Series for each league, after realigning the leagues to each have three divisions and one wild-card winner.) By beating the A's, they evened their record at 59–59 and stayed ahead of Oakland, who were three back in the race. One more win and they could not only sweep a wild-card rival, they also could possibly move into a tie with Seattle.

But the A's, who counted among their number the slugger Mark McGwire, former Yankee Rickey Henderson, and future Yankee Scott Brosius, were not about to be brushed aside without a fight. Both teams arrived at Yankee Stadium the next day, ready to battle. David Cone faced Oakland's Steve Ontiveros. In his nine seasons in the majors, Ontiveros had never developed into a dominant, front-line starter. He enjoyed probably the best season of his career in 1994 as a swing man for the A's, sustaining a 2.65 ERA through 115 innings, 13 starts, and 27 appearances, but as a starter exclusively in 1995 his ERA was above 4.00. Cone, on the other hand, had made star turns with the Mets, Blue Jays, and Royals, winning a World Series in 1993, the Cy Young in 1994, and had become a "rent an ace" with a reputation for being a big-game pitcher. The Yankees picked him up from Toronto in July for their stretch run, but Cone had stumbled in late August.

But pitching was not to be the story on this late summer afternoon. Cone got off to a momentary good start when he fanned the pesky leadoff man, Henderson. But Stan Javier followed with a single, stole second, and scored immediately on a Brent Gates single. Cone then caught Geronimo Berroa looking and induced a ground out from Terry Steinbach to end the inning.

The Yanks came right back against Ontiveros. Wade Boggs kicked off the rally with a triple, and Bernie Williams doubled to bring him in. He advanced to third on a deep fly from Paul O'Neill, and when Darryl Strawberry grounded out, the fleet-footed Bernie scored. That was two runs, and they almost had more, but after Dion James walked and Don Mattingly singled, Mike Stanley hit into a force play for the third out.

The one-run lead lasted exactly two outs, when Mike Bordick homered in the top of the second to tie the game at two. The A's jumped ahead again in the fourth, when Berroa hit an inside-the-park home run to start the inning. Steinbach followed with a double. José Herrera bunted, and although Cone fielded the ball, the pitcher had no chance to throw Herrera out, while Steinbach moved to third. Craig Paquette brought him in with a sac fly, and it was 4–2 A's.

Tony Fernandez answered this time. With two out and Mattingly on first, he hit a home run into deep right field to tie the game. Randy Velarde walked, and Boggs followed with a ground-rule double, meaning Velarde had to stop at third, where he was ultimately stranded. But even this momentum would not last, as Cone could not keep the Athletics down, this time his own pitching victimizing him. With one out, Javier walked and stole second, moving to third on a ground out. On his way to walking Berroa, Cone threw a wild pitch that allowed Javier to score and the pitcher found himself again looking up at a deficit, now 5–4. Javier—who had come up with the Yankees and was the son of longtime St. Louis Cardinal second baseman Julian Javier—was pumped up. "[This is] the most emotional game I've played in."

The Yankees' hitters went back to work. O'Neill and Strawberry led off with back-to-back singles. James and Mattingly both flew out to left, but Stanley, the Yankees' power-hitting catcher, doubled, and both men on base came home. Up came Fernandez. Just a single would score Stanley, and that's what Tony tallied. Randy Velarde followed with another base hit, moving Fernandez to third and driving Ontiveros from the game. A's manager Tony LaRussa went to Rich Honeycutt, one of his best men in the bullpen. Boggs, who had already tripled and doubled in the game, knocked Tony in with a single. But Honeycutt allowed no more to score, stopping the bleeding at 8–5 Yankees.

"They kept scoring runs for me," Cone later said admiringly. "But I couldn't hold them down. It makes for a long, miserable afternoon." Cone wanted to go out and pitch a 1-2-3 at that point, but things did not work out that way. He walked the leadoff man, Herrera. Paquette singled. Bordick lined out to Fernandez and Brosius struck out, but flamboyant, mouthy, free-spirited Rickey Henderson came to the plate. Cone could not keep Henderson contained—an RBI single followed, and it was 8–6 Yankees. "I can't remember an inning where they didn't score," Cone told reporters after the game. "Or where I wasn't working from the stretch."

In the seventh, Cone was finally driven from the game when Berroa doubled with one out. Bob Wickman relieved him, stranding Berroa where he was with two quick ground outs. Berroa was incredulous about the fast action. "That was the wildest game I played in my life. It was so crazy, it was a game where you had to concentrate hard to the last out." But Wickman would not be so effective in the eighth. Paquette singled to start the inning. Wickman caught Bordick on called strikes, but instead of Brosius, he now had to face pinch hitter Mark McGwire. Wickman tried to brush the burly slugger off the plate but hit him in the elbow with a pitch. McGwire had to leave the game, and former Yankee Mike Gallego ran for him. Henderson, up next, grounded to Fernandez, but was too speedy to be doubled up. That put men on the corners and two out. Here Wickman fell apart, surrendering three successive singles, to Javier, Gates, and Berroa, and the lead. "It was the team's day until I came in and blew it," Wickman said. It was his eighth blown save of the year. Fernandez tripled in the bottom of the frame but was stranded.

The Yankees were still down 9–8 when they batted in the bottom of the ninth facing Oakland's bullpen ace, future Hall of Famer Dennis Eckersley. Fernandez needed only a double to complete the cycle, Boggs a home run. Fernandez was up first, and he did it—doubled—representing the tying run. Velarde sacrificed him to third, bringing Boggs to the plate. Boggs had been oddly criticized for hitting for average and not power throughout his career, but he certainly had the strength to put the ball over the wall. If he could hit a home run here, it would be a game-winner, and both men would have hit for the cycle. But just a fly ball would bring in the tying run. Boggs connected on an Eckersley fastball; the ball sailed into deep center . . . caught. Fernandez scored.

Manager Buck Showalter now called for his closer, John Wetteland, to stop the A's in the tenth and give the Yankees a chance to win it in the bottom of the inning. Wetteland had struggled at times in the season, though his recent appearances had been solid. But his first batter was Henderson, who had a 2–2 count when he homered into the right-field seats off a fastball. "It sounded good off the bat," Wetteland said. "It is a pretty awful sound, but more than hearing it, you feel it in your gut." Wetteland called the home run "heart-wrenching," prompting the *New York Times* to conclude, "he could have just as easily been talking about the season the Yankee bullpen has had thus far." It was the 20th game overall that the bullpen had lost. The Yankees were not able to get to Eckersley this time, and they lost the longest game of the season, 4:27, by a score of 10–9. Between the two teams there had been 33 hits but only one that made the difference.

After the game, Fernandez was philosophical about having caught lightning in a bottle for himself while doing his best for the team, too. "Anyone who does it [hits for the cycle] has to feel some satisfaction," he said. "But it would have been nicer if we won the game."

Extra Innings

- "Almost every player has a night when after two or three at-bats you have a chance to hit for the cycle. Usually you have to hit a triple or a home run, and usually you don't do it. It's a pretty special feat from a hitter's standpoint."—Paul O'Neill

- The previous Yankee to hit for the cycle, 23 years earlier, Bobby Murcer, was at the Stadium, announcing the game for the television broadcast.

- On September 3, 1995, three young Yankees got called up from Triple-A Columbus for the remainder of the season. Pitcher Joe Ausanio, outfielder Ruben Rivera (cousin of pitcher Mariano Rivera), and a young infielder named Derek Jeter. "Why doesn't anyone remember Tony Fernandez anymore?" asks Ausanio today. "Two words: Derek Jeter. From when we first came up, you could just see the talent. He was already a leader."

- Tony Fernandez broke his arm during spring training in 1996 and did not play the entire year, but the team awarded him a 1996 World Series ring anyway.

43

October 8, 1995: New York at Seattle

Seattle Slew

In which the captain excels but a pitch goes Strange

With the revised postseason format introduced in 1995, four teams from each league would make the postseason—the leaders of the East, Central, and West Divisions, and a wild card. The Yankees had their eyes on the wild card for most of the season, but to become the first wild-card entry in American League history, they had to win 11 of their last 12 games to keep up with both California and Seattle. They did. On the opposite coast, the Seattle Mariners had climbed an even steeper hill, coming from 11.5 games out on August 24, only to tie the California Angels on the final day of the season and force a one-game playoff to determine the division winner. (The loser of the playoff would not only lose the Western Division, but be eliminated from the wild card as well.) Thanks to some clutch hits by future Yankee Luis Sojo and the pitching of Randy Johnson, the Mariners came out on top 9–1 and advanced to face the Yankees in the first ever American League Division Series (ALDS).

The best-of-five series was slated to begin in New York for two games, and then switch to Seattle for the remainder of the games. It would be the Yankees' first postseason appearance in 14 years, and the first for team captain Don Mattingly. "It has taken participation in 1,785 regular-season games for Mattingly to get here," read an editorial in the *Newark Star-Ledger*. "No active major leaguer, and no Yankee, has played more games without reaching the playoffs." And although the M's would not be able to use their ace, Johnson, in game one, the Yankees knew Seattle would be a formidable opponent. The M's had beaten them six out of seven games in the Kingdome and held a 9–4 advantage in the season series.

Cone pitched the Yankees to a win in game one, though it was a high-scoring adventure to get there. "He's not going to pitch a shutout every time," philosophized Mattingly, who went 2-for-4 with an RBI in the 9–6 win. The next night rookie lefthander Andy Pettitte went for the Yankees against Andy Benes, a native of Mattingly's hometown, Evansville, Indiana. "I was in seventh grade when [Donnie] was in high school," explained Benes. "I never really watched him when he was in high school, but I followed him when he was a Yankee in the early times. I think he deserves the opportunity to play in the postseason. It's ironic that we're playing against each other in the postseason. We're bitter enemies now." Neither starter earned a decision in the game, which was eventually won in the 15th inning by a dramatic walk-off homer from Jim Leyritz.

With the Yankees up 2–0, they needed to win only one of the three games scheduled for the Kingdome to advance to the next round. Seattle manager Lou Piniella went with Randy Johnson to stem the tide. The six-foot, ten-inch lefthander, nicknamed the "Big Unit," was the most dominant pitcher in the American League at the time. In game three he struck out Mattingly three times, while Donnie's counterpart on the Mariners, Tino Martinez, hit a two-run homer and knocked in three runs in the 7–4 Seattle win. The next night Mattingly had four hits and the Yankees had built a 5–0 lead, but Seattle took game four as Edgar Martinez, the American League's leading hitter, batted in seven runs. The Mariners felt that their comeback against the Angels in August was just a prelude to the magic that would carry them through the Yankees. The Yankees felt that they had a date with destiny to keep, a birthright to reclaim. Every game in the series so far had been a roller coaster, "pure unadulterated theater" in *Newark Star-Ledger* columnist Jerry Izenberg's words, and like a grand piece of Shakespeare, it would take the full five acts to unfold the drama.

In game five, Showalter went with Cone, whose cold-blooded mound presence he hoped would chill the Mariners' offense, while Piniella went back to

Andy Benes. "It's the ultimate to be in the stopper's role," Cone told reporters before the game. "I can live with the ups and downs. I've had enough of them in my career. I look on the positive end that this is a once-in-a-lifetime opportunity." That afternoon, Showalter held an early batting practice for some of his young rookies, such as Derek Jeter and Jorge Posada (Posada was on the postseason roster as the number-three catcher, Jeter was not), but gave the afternoon off to his veterans. Before the game, he addressed the team as a group. When asked by reporters what he planned to talk about, Buck would not, or could not, say. "I can't use the 'Don Mattingly has never been to the postseason,' line again," was all he said.

The concrete-walled Kingdome echoed with fans' cheers from the moment the Mariners took the field, "Refuse to Lose" banners hanging from the upper deck. Both Cone and Benes came out dealing, Benes striking out two, and Cone getting two easy flies and a pop-up in the first inning. Benes sat down three Yankees in a row in the second as well, but Cone allowed back-to-back singles to Edgar and Tino Martinez, then dug his hole deeper when a wild pitch sent them to second and third. Cone did not want to allow even one man to score. He came back to strike out Jay Buhner, Luis Sojo, and Dan Wilson.

In the third, the Mariners drew first blood when second baseman Joey Cora hit a two-out solo homer. In an eight-year major league career to date, Cora had hit only seven home runs. Cone shook it off and retired Ken Griffey Jr. to end the inning with a fly to right.

The Yankees shook it off, too. With one out, Bernie Williams drew a walk, and Paul O'Neill answered Cora's blast with one of his own. "I had seen [Benes] in the National League so I'd had an opportunity to face him. Having an idea of a pitcher from another league, it's like you had your own scouting report," O'Neill recalled. "I knew the way Seattle pitched me at the time, and if you hit the ball hard to right field it was a home run in the Kingdome. At the time it was a huge hit for the team. You get a lead, and you start counting the outs until you get to the next round." But the one-run lead didn't last long. The Mariners tied the score in their half of the inning when Tino doubled and Buhner brought him in with a base hit that shattered his bat but reached over the infield.

With the score tied, Cone and Benes dueled another inning, letting nothing through until the sixth, when the Yankees jumped ahead again. Again with one out, Bernie walked, followed by walks to O'Neill and Ruben Sierra. With the bases loaded, up came the captain, Don Mattingly. Donnie delivered a double that brought in two runs, to make it 4–2 Yankees. "That was as crucial an at-bat as we had all year and Donnie was the guy you wanted up there," said O'Neill. "He was a great clutch player and it's just a shame he didn't get 150 postseason at-bats." Benes stifled the rally, though, getting Mike Stanley to pop up and Tony Fernandez to fly to left. "I thought the big inning was the sixth inning," Showalter told reporters later. "We felt coming in we didn't want to play a close game in this ballpark, and we weren't able to open it up in the sixth." A two-run margin would have to do.

After allowing a leadoff double to the so-far-unstoppable Edgar Martinez, Cone responded by striking out the side in the bottom of the sixth. The Yankees were back to counting the outs. In the top of the seventh, they tried to add to their lead. With two out, Bernie Williams walked for the third time, bringing O'Neill to the plate. Piniella lifted Benes in favor of lefty closer Norm Charlton. "I faced Norm a lot and I knew him well because he was in Cincinnati when I was," O'Neill remembered. Piniella, of course, had been Cincinnati's manager at the time. "Lou knew he had good luck against me." O'Neill hit a fly to left, and the threat was over. Cone came back with another 1-2-3, with two more strikeouts. Six outs to go.

But in the eighth, the "Refuse to Lose" M's rose again. With one out, Junior Griffey hit his fifth home run of the series, turning on a Cone fastball with his distinctive lightning-quick stroke and sending the ball into the second deck in right. Cone then retired Edgar but lost Tino to a walk. This would be the moment for a manager to call on his bullpen ace to close the door. But Showalter had seen his bullpen fail too many times that season, and that series, to have faith in them. His most effective reliever to that point in October was rookie *starter* Mariano Rivera, who had not given up a run in 4⅔ innings, but who knew if that was lightning in a bottle or not? "It certainly speaks volumes about the confidence, or lack thereof, that Buck had about his bullpen," said Michael Kay in his analysis of the game, "that the only guys up were [starters] Rivera, Pettitte, and McDowell throughout the whole game, and that tells you all you need to know how this bullpen deserted the Yankees in this series." With two out and one man on, Showalter stuck with Cone.

Jay Buhner followed with a single, and a young Alex Rodriguez was sent in to pinch-run for Tino. Piniella also sent a pinch hitter to the plate, Alex Diaz. Cone pitched him carefully—too carefully—and he walked to load the bases. Now Cone faced a second pinch hitter, Doug Strange in for Dan Wilson. Cone had one of the most dizzying arrays of pitches any pitcher had ever been graced with, but he went to a three-ball count on Strange. "When the count went to three and one," Strange told the *Seattle Post-Intelligencer*, "I got the take sign and I think they saw it. Donnie went to the mound to talk to Cone, who must have known I wasn't going to swing because he threw me a fastball right down the middle."

Jim Kaat, who was broadcasting the game for the Baseball Network, remembered the full count well. "I would say to me one of the most disappointing pitches that whole year was when he threw Doug Strange a 3–2 breaking ball, and walked a run in." The score was tied. Strange himself reported that the forkball down and in was usually a pitch he would swing at, but for some reason, this time he didn't. "To me it was such a picture of the game today," said Kaat, "where you go by the scouting report and you don't deviate instead of just trusting your stuff and saying, 'I'm David Cone and he's Doug Strange, a .200 hitter. I can get him.'"

Cone did not get him. The forkball bounced, and Strange walked in the tying run. "It takes some guts to go with that pitch," Cone told reporters later. "If I make that pitch, then we go to the ninth with a one-run lead. I didn't make the pitch."

Showalter went to Rivera then, and he caught Mike Blowers looking to end the inning. Cone had thrown 147 pitches on the night. Should Rivera, or someone, have come in sooner? "Wetteland had lost his stature," said Kaat. "But that's the mentality of playing for the Yankees. When you have an owner like George, you know, he wants the Yankees to go 162–0, which will never happen. So if you blow a few saves late in the year, they no longer have confidence in you." Wetteland had given up a grand slam earlier in the series.

The Yankees tried to make it a moot point. Facing Charlton in the ninth, Fernandez doubled and Randy Velarde walked. Piniella did not have anyone else he trusted in his bullpen either, so he went back to his ace, Randy Johnson. The Big Unit came in and struck out Boggs, then got Bernie Williams and Paul O'Neill to pop up in the infield.

In the Mariners' half of the ninth, the scene was replayed. This time Rivera gave up the leadoff hit, a single to Vince Coleman, and Cora bunted him to second. Griffey was intentionally walked, and so with two on, Showalter also went to a veteran starter in the bullpen, Jack McDowell. "Black Jack" had a 10–1 lifetime record against the Mariners and was 6–0 at Safeco Field, though never in relief. McDowell struck out Edgar Martinez and got Rodriguez to hit into a fielder's choice. This one would be decided in extra innings.

In the tenth, Johnson struck out the side, but though the Mariners had two hits in the bottom half, they did not score. So when Mike Stanley led off the eleventh with a walk, Showalter played for one run. Pat Kelly went in to pinch-run, and Tony Fernandez sacrificed him to second. Randy Velarde singled and Kelly scored, Velarde taking second on the throw to the plate. Jim Leyritz, the hero of game two, then batted for Boggs but was called out on strikes. Switch-hitting Bernie Williams was then walked intentionally, bringing the lefty

O'Neill up against the Big Unit. O'Neill, too, was called out on strikes, "but I remember thinking, we had beat Randy Johnson," O'Neill recalled. "We had beat their best. We had gotten the lead, and that's when you start thinking you're going to the next round—and suddenly they snatch it from you."

Joey Cora led off the bottom of the inning against McDowell, who he knew would be tough to hit. Mattingly was playing in, so Cora, who had been thinking about bunting, swung away. But after three pitches and two strikes, Mattingly backed up a few steps, and Cora decided it was worth it to try dragging a bunt toward first. "I wanted to get it past Jack. I know him, played with him, and he's not the fastest human being around," Cora told the *Post-Intelligencer.* The drag worked perfectly, and Cora had an infield single.

Griffey followed with a single to center, moving Cora to third. Then Edgar Martinez doubled, and it was all over. "I remember watching the ball going to left field, and watching Griffey running the bases, and knowing that we weren't going to get him out," O'Neill said. "Watching the game slip away from us. My wife was pregnant at the time. All the wives went on the trip and I can still see the outfit she had on, one of these beautiful maternity outfits. It brought such bad memories she never wore it again."

Griffey sprinted from first, egged on by his teammates leaping from their dugout, mimicking third-base coach Sammy Perlozzo, who was sending him all the way. Junior slid into home and was immediately crushed under a dog pile of ecstatic players. Another pile formed on Edgar, who had batted .571 in the series, at second base. "The balconied press box actually shook in the pounding pandemonium," wrote Bob Finnigan in the *Seattle Times.* "[A] Mariner public-relations man announced, '4.19.' It was either the time of game or a Richter scale measure of the madness."

The Yankees left the field amid the raucous celebration with as much dignity as they could. But in his office in the visitors' clubhouse, Buck Showalter broke down in tears. He and Piniella had just played a week-long chess game, and in the end, Buck had lost. "I have never seen better baseball, better played or better battled," said Piniella afterward. "It's a damn shame someone had to lose it because there was no loser on that field." Wetteland had remained in the bullpen, the decision to stay with McDowell forever to be second-guessed. Or maybe the Mariners' magic or momentum or mojo was just not to be stopped (though the Cleveland Indians actually would beat the M's in the ALCS).

"That's what hurts," Wade Boggs told reporters. The veteran third baseman, who had been with Boston for so many years, had enjoyed his time with the Yankees and wanted to return for another year, but his contract was up. "You go around and hug guys and you don't know if you're ever going to see them again. You walk out knowing you may never see them again. That's the tough part of this business."

As things would turn out, Boggs would be back in 1996, along with Cone, Wetteland, O'Neill, Rivera, Pettitte, Bernie Williams, and Derek Jeter. But Showalter would be shown the door, and another man chose to walk away. "Donnie kind of left it up in the air before the season," O'Neill recalled of Mattingly's retirement plans. "But on the way back he was talking to a lot of people on the plane. That is a long plane ride when you lose a series and have to fly back all night. With that feeling in your gut, it's a long flight, and I told my wife, this might be the last time we see this guy here. I think he knew that was the end of it."

O'Neill was right. Don Mattingly retired after the 1995 season. He had batted .417 in his one trip to October, but the thought of facing another long season full of back pain and subtle wrangling with the front office was more than he could contemplate. He had won the batting title in 1984, the MVP Award in 1985, and led the league in hits in 1986. He had proven himself in October. It was time to go home.

Extra Innings

- During the series, the Mariners' Ken Griffey Jr. was asked whether he would be tempted to play for the Yankees, as his father had, when his contract with the Mariners ran out. "I'll never play for Steinbrenner or in New York," was Griffey's response. "Steinbrenner was tough on me and [my brother] Craig when we were kids. One time Dad brought us into the dugout, and they threw us out. I don't forget things like that, and I never will."

- Only four times before in league championship playoffs had pitchers both started and relieved in the same series. In this first ALDS, two pitchers did it on the same night, in the same inning, when both Jack McDowell and Randy Johnson were used as relievers in the ninth inning of game five.

- Matttingly's number 23 was retired by the team four years later. After a period away from baseball except for periodic trips to spring training as a special instructor, Mattingly returned to the Yankees as hitting coach in 2004.

- Two of baseball's most recognizable stars in the ensuing decade were present for this series: Alex Rodriguez, who had played 48 games for the Mariners, and Derek Jeter, who played 15 for the Yankees. Rodriguez was on the postseason roster and figured in the games, but Jeter was not. The following season, both players took over at shortstop for their respective teams, starting a debate on which was better at that position. The debate finally ended in 2004, when Rodriguez came to the Yankees and moved to third base.

44

May 14, 1996: Seattle at New York

Dr. No

In which a New York icon makes an improbable comeback

In the winter after the Yankees were knocked out of their first postseason in 14 years, the organization made some changes, which included the acquisition of Mariners Tino Martinez, Jeff Nelson, and Luis Sojo. Rookie Derek Jeter was given a shot at being the everyday shortstop. But two names familiar to New Yorkers from eras past also joined the team. The first was the new manager, Joe Torre, a Brooklyn native who had made his name as a player with the Milwaukee Braves, winning the MVP Award in 1971, and who had managed the Mets from 1977 to 1981.

The other also was an ex-Met, a former star whose light had dimmed through a series of addiction and health crises, Dwight Gooden, the onetime fireballer also known as "Dr. K." A former Rookie of the Year and a Cy Young Award winner when he was only 20 years old, Gooden had been forced to sit out the entire 1995 season, banned from baseball because of drug abuse violations.

Gooden struggled in the spring, but under Torre's direction he took a slot in the starting rotation when the team broke camp. In his first three starts he was awful, giving up 17 runs and losing his place as a starter. "I was struggling," Gooden remembered with a shake of his head. "They had put me in the bullpen, and they were thinking about sending me to Triple-A, or possibly releasing me." But David Cone was felled by an aneurysm in his pitching shoulder—repaired by surgery but putting Cone's season, and career, into question. Needing an arm to fill the innings, Torre and pitching coach Mel Stottlemyre gave Doc a reprieve. Gooden could hardly believe his good fortune. "You go from walking in every day not knowing if your locker is still going to be there, wondering if you're going to play or if they're going to release you, to [being] back in the rotation." He was starting to get his stuff together, pitching seven scoreless innings in a start in early May. But he faced a dilemma as his scheduled start on May 14 approached.

"My father was really sick, and he was supposed to have surgery the next day," Gooden explained. "They had said he would probably make it, but it was an emergency surgery that he had to have because of his health." The elder Gooden was suffering from a heart condition, needing bypass surgery, and the son had planned to fly down to Florida to be with him in the hospital. "I was supposed to fly home. But when I thought about it, I thought my father would want me to pitch. I didn't call my mom that night or anything, I just decided to stay. I talked to Mr. Torre and Mel Stottlemyre and said, 'Hey, I want to pitch' and they said, 'What are you, crazy? Just go home and be with your family, it'll be okay.'" But Gooden had made up his mind. Torre, a manager whose knack for reading his players' hearts would be one of his most important qualities in leading these Yankees, stuck with him.

Before the game, Gooden told a reporter, "Whatever happens tonight, I'm dedicating this game to my dad. I want you to write that. This one is for him." In the bullpen, Gooden seemed nervous and distracted to pitching coach Mel Stottlemyre, but had an exceptionally live fastball.

The opponent that night would be the now-hated Mariners. "All of a sudden, Seattle were our rivals," said Paul O'Neill. "It wasn't Boston yet because they weren't that good, and Seattle was the team we had to beat." Ken Griffey Jr. wore the mantle of best player in the game at the time, he and many of the same players who had bounced the Yankees from the postseason in 1995 were back, and the bitter taste for the M's still lingered in the back of New York's throats. But starting for the Mariners was former Yankee Sterling Hitchcock, a lefty who knew them as well as they knew him. The Yankees would need a good start from Gooden to keep them in the game.

Gooden's battery mate was another new Yankee, Joe Girardi. An outstanding defensive catcher, Girardi was known for his game-calling skills and empathy with his pitchers. What he was not was the offensive force that previous catcher Mike Stanley had been, and some fans pooh-poohed the Girardi signing at first. Girardi remembered that day as a turning point in his time as a Yankee. "I had a touch of food poisoning that day," he recalled. "But you never want to sit out a game with the Yankees because you never know when something special might happen. Every day you put on the pinstripes and walk out into Yankee Stadium there's a chance for something great."

Girardi's upset stomach was nothing compared to what was churning in Gooden's mind. "He had a heavy heart that day over his father being hospitalized," Girardi remembered. But as he warmed up his pitcher in the bullpen, Joe realized some other things as well. "He was known as a fastball pitcher, of course. But he always had a great curveball, and as he aged he used it more. That day, his breaking ball was unbelievable."

So unbelievable that Doc could not finish off his first hitter of the evening, Darren Bragg. He had Bragg down 0–2 but couldn't quite nip the corner to get that called third strike. Bragg stared at all four pitches and walked. The next batter could have been Gooden's undoing, as young Alex Rodriguez smoked a line drive into center. Bragg took off from first, certain to score on a double or even a triple from the speedy A-Rod. But Gerald Williams, playing center for the Yankees that day because Bernie Williams (no relation) was down with a stiff calf, was speedier. He ran down the ball for the out, just pulling it in as he reached the warning track, at a flat-out run with his glove stretched as far forward as possible. When he stopped his momentum, Williams then threw to his cutoff man, Jeter, who tossed the ball to Tino Martinez at first base to double off Bragg. Two outs, no one on. Then came Griffey; he walked. And Edgar Martinez lined a ball hard, but O'Neill in right field ran that one down, too. Inning over.

Hitchcock had an easier time of it, retiring Wade Boggs, Girardi, and O'Neill on fly balls and putting Doc back on the hill. The second inning was a little easier—only one walk, the rest routine pop-ups and grounders. In the third, with two out, another walk, this one to A-Rod. But Gooden's control was returning, and when he blew a high fastball past Griffey, who just stared at it, for called strike three to end the inning, the crowd roared.

Gooden was regaining his control of his pitches, but his emotions were another matter. His mind was racing. "The first couple of innings I was okay, but after the third inning I would come in, and go in the tunnel [from the dugout to the clubhouse], and think, Is he going to be okay? Did I do the right thing? Then it would be three outs and I had to go back out on the field. I would go back out on the field and pitch, and then come back in. One time [team trainer] Steve Donahue came down in the tunnel and I was crying because I didn't know if I did the right thing. Then it was right back out there, pitching."

But with so much going on in his mind, Gooden's arm took care of itself. "My thoughts weren't really on pitching." Gooden recognized the irony of the situation. "In some ways it was the best thing that could have happened to me at that time, because if I didn't have all that going on, on the mound I'd be thinking, 'Okay, I gotta do well because I'm getting released' or 'I'm getting sent down,' and putting a lot of pressure on myself. With all the things in my mind [about my father], I just went out and whatever Girardi put down, I just threw it. So I was able to just go out and let it happen instead of worrying about how to do this or that." Girardi had gained Gooden's trust and respect in the few months they had worked together. "The thing I liked about him was if you were messing around, he'd fire the ball back to you real hard, you know, 'Let's get in the game.' He'd never let you slack down no matter what the score was or what was going on. He was a leader out there on the field."

Doc threw what Joe put down, and it worked. In the fourth, the Mariners went down in order, then again in the fifth. But in the sixth the door opened a crack for Seattle when Bragg hit a hard grounder to first. The ball took a bad hop and bounced off Tino Martinez's arm and into the box seats.

The entire Stadium froze while official scorer Bill Shannon studied the replay on the press box TV monitor. After a long minute Shannon ruled the play an error on Tino. Shannon later said, "No matter how hard the ball was hit, it was still a three-bouncer off the first baseman's chest." As "E-3" flashed on the screens, the crowd exploded with cheers.

With the ball going into the seats, Bragg was awarded second base. He moved to third on a ground out, bringing Griffey to the plate. The Yankees' infield moved in to cut off the run. Griffey worked the count to 2–2, then stared at a curve that broke too far inside for a full count. Girardi called for the fastball, outside corner. Junior swung right through it, corkscrewing himself in the batter's box, strike three. It was only Dr. K's third K of the game, but the second time he had gotten Griffey. The infield moved back. Edgar then lined another one, this one an easy play for Williams in center, and the threat was over. "He wasn't dominating people the way he used to," O'Neill remembered. "He didn't just blow people away, so to pitch a no-hit game at that time of his career, he really *pitched.*"

The Yankees rallied after the close call. Boggs and Girardi started the inning off with singles, and although O'Neill grounded out, Seattle manager Lou Piniella elected to walk Ruben Sierra intentionally to set up the double play and go after the lefty-swinging Tino. But on the first pitch, a hanging breaking ball, Tino got a ball in the air, a sac fly to center that scored Boggs, and Jim Leyritz followed with a single to bring in Girardi. That was all for Hitchcock, and Mike Jackson squelched the rally when Gerald Williams lined right to short. But now the Yankees had two runs, a tiny bit of breathing room, and the crowd was beginning to get excited.

So was Gooden. "The next thing I know, it's the seventh inning." The crowd seemed louder than usual as he took the field, and Gooden looked around the Stadium as the noise grew. "I look at the scoreboard and I had a no-hitter going. I thought, 'Man, this can't be happening.'" He hardened his resolve. "So when I went back out there, every pitch I threw, I threw as hard as I could for the last three innings."

Jim Kaat noticed the difference from the television broadcast booth, where he was working the game. "When Doc got through about four innings, I remember saying, 'Well, there's something special in the air here tonight.'" But Kaat felt Gooden's situation so precarious, both in the game and in his career, that he couldn't bring himself to overcome the old dugout superstition. "I made a mistake there from the broadcaster's standpoint. Even though there's the old superstition that you never say anything [about] a no-hitter, as an announcer you should always keep the audience informed of what is going on. To see Doc at that stage of his career, it was so fragile . . . I just didn't say anything and I should have." As Gooden took the mound in the seventh, Kaat saw how much he was pushing, which is usually not a recipe for success in baseball.

But Girardi kept him focused, and kept Gooden's energy in check. "One of the great things about Joe as a catcher is he had a way to see what you had that day, and make sure he got the most out of your abilities. If you were good locating the fastballs down in the zone, breaking balls behind in the count, whatever worked." In the seventh it was ground out, ground out, fly out. In the eighth it was fly out, ground out, and another called strike three, with the Mariners' best hitters coming up in the ninth, Alex Rodriguez, Ken Griffey Jr., and Edgar Martinez.

"Everything really is just leading up to the ninth inning in a no-hitter," said Paul O'Neill, who appeared in five no-hitters, three of them perfect games, in his career. "I don't know how many times you see a no-hitter broken up in the ninth inning. That's really when it all starts—those are the three big outs." The crowd began to chant "Let's Go Doctor" as Gooden took his warm-up tosses. When he was done, he asked the home plate umpire for a new ball. He received it, and then A-Rod stepped into the box.

Doc had him down 1–2 before a tiring Gooden threw three misses away, walking him. Now it was Junior, who hadn't hit the ball all night. This time he did, a slow grounder that Tino had to range far toward second for. "I was watching the play and thinking 'nice play' and then suddenly, 'uh-oh.'" Gooden realized he needed to get over there to cover first, but his feet moved like they were stuck in clay. "I was thinking to myself, 'C'mon, man, get over there' but I knew I would be too late." Tino, preparing to flip the ball, also saw that Gooden would never get there. In midmotion, he dove for the bag, his glove just beating Griffey's foot for the first out.

Now it was Edgar's turn to stand in as the tying run at the plate. With two strikes on him, he, too, walked, and Jay Buhner stood in as the go-ahead run. Gooden's first pitch to "Bone" was wild, and A-Rod and Edgar moved to second and third. Piniella sent in a pinch runner for Edgar while Stottlemyre visited the mound. A fly ball, or even a deep grounder, could score a man; a single could tie the game. Girardi was thinking "strikeout." With the count 2–1, Gooden painted the outside corner for a called strike, and Buhner fanned on the next pitch, the old high heat. "He just reared back and threw it by me," Buhner marveled.

One out to go, and Paul Sorrento dug in. Torre mulled over the idea of walking the lefty to get to catcher Dan Wilson, a righty, but ultimately scrapped the idea. "I didn't want to get involved with his game. It was Doc's game." Gooden went after Sorrento, the first pitch a curveball that Sorrento half swung at and missed. Then he looked at two more balls. "And I threw him the worst breaking ball of the whole game. I just hung it, right there [above the belt]," Doc recalled. "And he popped it up! If he hits that one out, not only could the no-hitter be gone, but the whole game, too." Sorrento took that big cut, but popped the ball up, and there was Jeter, the take-charge rookie, calling off everyone and squeezing it in his glove.

"Everything came flooding in," Doc remembered of that moment as he leaped up on the mound, waiting for the pop to come down. "Everything from making it, to my struggles. I was thinking back to my worst moments. Everybody and everything was going through my head. My wife said 'I've never seen you like that before,' and I said, 'Well, I never threw a no-hitter before.'"

Doc was engulfed by his teammates. They lifted him on their shoulders as he roared, his face contorted with emotions. The center-field scoreboard read "The Doctor Is in the House," and the announcement board out on the Major Deegan Expressway proclaimed "Oh My Gooden-ness!" After all the rough roads that Gooden had traveled, from leading the league in strikeouts when he was only 19 years old to being out of baseball when he was 30, through the party-hearty Mets and rehab clinics, to have it come to a peak at Yankee Stadium, of all places, was almost beyond belief. "That was definitely the highlight of my career," according to Doc. "Mr. Steinbrenner gave me the opportunity to jump-start my career again, and to do it in New York. For him to take that chance on me, signing me without ever sending anybody to see me throw. He just said, 'Hey, come and see what you can do.' So to do what I did, and do it there, was the best thing that could happen to me."

"Almost two years to the time he was out of baseball, the Doctor is in," wrote Bob Finnigan in the *Seattle Times*. "Doc Gooden, who dropped himself out of the game in 1994 and almost out of life, took this city and maybe the country back to when he was the best pitcher of them all."

After a curtain call for the cheering crowd, and the gauntlet of media interviews, and the multiple congratulations from his own teammates and even opponents such as Griffey, Gooden phoned his family in Florida and learned from his sister Betty that his father, Dan, was still stable, awaiting the surgery.

"Tell Dad I did this for him," Gooden told Betty.

"You just get down here and tell him yourself."

Next morning, Doc got on his flight to Tampa. As the 727 flew out of

LaGuardia Airport, Dan Gooden went into the operating room for four hours of surgery.

Joe Girardi philosophized about the coincidence. "Sometimes you think maybe God has a plan for these things, and to go through that at that time in his life, with his father in the hospital . . . who knows? Maybe it was something that would help them get through that, seeing what his son did." When he arrived in Tampa, the doctors told Dwight that his father did know what his son had done; he heard the news. When they were able to speak, "I gave him the ball and the tape of the game. We talked a little bit and I told him we'd watch the tape of the game at home," Doc remembered. "But unfortunately he never came home." Although the bypass surgery was successful, health complications kept Dan Gooden in the hospital for the rest of his life.

Gooden finished up the year 11–7 with a 5.01 ERA. He pitched another four years in the majors after 1996, traveling through Cleveland, Houston, and his hometown Tampa Bay Devil Rays before ending up back with the Yankees in 2000, in a swing role. That year he started and won the first game of a split-stadium doubleheader with the Mets, the first time he had appeared at Shea Stadium since being released by them.

In 2001 he took a position as an adviser-coach with the Yankees' organization in Tampa, where he works with pitchers every spring training and advises young players in the system to avoid making the mistakes he did. He still has the game ball from that night in May, as well as the videotape. "I still have not had the opportunity to watch the tape," he said when interviewed in the spring of 2004. "I'm sure someday I'll watch it with my kids."

Extra Innings

- In the no-hitter, Doc threw 134 pitches, only 74 for strikes. Gooden went on to win seven of his next eight starts. The Mariners, meanwhile, got 40 hits in their next two games.

- The closest Dwight Gooden came to a no-hitter in previous starts was in 1984, while pitching for the Mets. He held the Chicago Cubs to one hit on September 7. He also carried two no-hitters into the eighth inning while with the Mets.

- No Met pitcher has ever hurled a no-hitter. But two former Mets have done so with the Yankees.

- In 2004, another member of the Gooden family joined the Yankees. Outfielder Gary Sheffield is Dwight Gooden's nephew, Dan Gooden's grandson. Sheffield was assigned Gooden's old number with the Yankees, 11.

45

October 23, 1996: New York at Atlanta

King of the Comeback

In which the first of a long line of elite closers is broken by Yankee magic

Nineteen ninety-six was supposed to be the year that the Atlanta Braves steamrolled to a world championship, as the dynasty built on outstanding starting pitching and deep talent, which had taken them to the postseason every year since 1991 and which had won it all in 1995, was supposed to carry on. The script would have called for them to win the first two games of the World Series, and then come home to win two more to cap off the victory in the final game ever played at Fulton County Stadium before its demolition.

Things did not work out that way, thanks to the grit and determination of a team from the Bronx that had its own story of destiny to write. Coming off the bitter first-round elimination in 1995, the Yankees of 1996 were determined to reclaim their heritage as baseball's kings. With Doc Gooden's no-hitter early in the year, the fans began to believe there was something special brewing. Although the most beloved Yankee of a generation, Don Mattingly, had retired, a new scion of pinstriped pride had taken root, Derek Jeter. Jeter had been born in New Jersey, and though his parents raised him in Michigan, his dream had been to grow up to play shortstop for the New York Yankees. Unlike millions of other American boys with that dream, Jeter actually realized it.

The Yankees finished the season 92–70, four games ahead of the wild-card-winning Baltimore Orioles. After the Yankees disposed of the Texas Rangers in the American League Division Series, the Bombers faced the Orioles in the American League Championship Series, which the Yankees won in five games to send Joe Torre to his first World Series. No one had played in or managed as many games without getting to the big dance as Torre (4,722 total as player and manager), who, teary-eyed with emotion, could only sum up what it was like for him by saying, "It's big."

But Atlanta did win the first two games of the World Series in New York. They were the more experienced, more powerful team, with better pitching and bigger stars. In the first game they pummeled the Yankees with home runs, two by Andruw Jones, a 19-year-old phenom from Curaçao who, on Mickey Mantle's birthday, broke Mantle's own record for being the youngest player to homer in a World Series, homering in both of his first two at-bats. The Braves won, 12–1, behind John Smoltz. The next night, they switched to small ball, chipping away one run at a time to a 4–0 shutout for Greg Maddux. Torre, ever the calming influence since coming to the Bronx, had told George Steinbrenner before the second game that he didn't think the team was focused, the time off after beating Baltimore had hurt them, but not to worry because they were going to go down to Atlanta, sweep all three games there, and come back to the Bronx to win it on Saturday. George had his doubts, and so did every sportswriter and commentator in the country. The Braves had been picked to win, and it looked like the Series was going to be a rout.

David Cone changed that. He faced Tom Glavine, the third of the Braves' three aces, a lefthander in the mold of Whitey Ford. Cone carried with him three burdens that night. One, the knowledge that no team had ever come back from three games down to win a World Series; two, the ever-present concern over the medical miracle that had replaced the aneurysm in his arm just five months before; and three, the memory of game five against Seattle and the bounced ball four to Doug Strange on which New York's fate had turned.

But Cone was up to the task. The Yankees staked him to a one-run lead in the first inning, and helped him erase two hits with a nifty 3-6-3 double play. Bernie Williams reached on an error and came across with an unearned run in the fourth. Cone gave the Braves nothing after the first, only one little hit in the fifth, until the sixth inning. Here he committed the cardinal sin of walking the pitcher, Glavine, to lead off the inning. With the bases loaded, one out, and Fred McGriff ready to step into the batter's box, Joe Torre came from the dugout to talk to his pitcher.

Joe Girardi joined them on the mound. "Joe Torre always said that Cone was the toughest pitcher for him to read. You always ask them how they are feeling and they always say they're fine, but you can usually tell by a guy's body language if he's telling the truth. Not with Coney." Torre got nose to nose with Cone and tried to impress on him the gravity of the situation. Could he really get out of the jam? Girardi said nothing while Cone argued that he was fine, that he'd take care of things. "Joe had to make a decision there," Girardi remembered. "One thing that was always great about Joe was that he had confidence in his players. His decision was to let Coney get out of the mess on his own."

Torre had been reading Cone's face as much as his words. "He had that look in his eyes that I hadn't seen in a while. The thing was, I didn't really want to take him out of there, but I wanted to hear him say it. If he had hesitated, I would have taken him out. But he didn't."

Cone did get McGriff, a pop-up that held the runners. But with a 2–0 lead, Cone walked a fine line, literally, painting the corners trying to get Ryan Klesko, a power hitter who could have made it 4–2 with one swing, taking the count full, and then sneaking a pitch right in. . . . This was no Doug Strange breaking ball, but a slider that probably did catch the corner. Unfortunately for Cone, it was called ball four, and one run crossed the plate. Cone held his hands up as if to say "Where was that?" to the umpire. But that was all the Braves would get. Cone would earn the win in the eventual 5–2 victory, which set up game four as a contest for the ages.

The Yankees needed to win at least one more game to send the Series back to the Bronx, and if they could win this one, they would pull all even in the Series and could forget the two crushing losses they had suffered at the outset. To do it, they needed their starter, Kenny Rogers, to give them at least five good innings. Rogers had struggled with his confidence and his control late in the season, and in the postseason was far from the man who had pitched a perfect game for Texas in 1994. In the ALDS he gave up five hits and walked one, lasting only two innings, and in the ALCS hung in for only three innings, giving up four runs, five hits, two walks, and a home run. The Yankees battled back to win both of those games, but Rogers' October ERA came to 10.80. The Yankees had considered leaving Rogers off the World Series roster, citing his balky shoulder, and going with a three-man rotation of Cone, Jimmy Key, and 21-game-winning rookie Andy Pettitte. But Torre ultimately decided that would have weakened all three men—the entire chain, not just one link. So Rogers would start game four.

His opponent was Denny Neagle, who had the best year of his career with Pittsburgh that year, posting a 3.03 ERA in 27 starts before coming to the Braves in midseason to fill out the back end of the rotation after Glavine, Maddux, and Smoltz. Steve Avery had filled that role, but had gotten hurt in August, and Pittsburgh had needed to make a move. Neagle was delighted to arrive in Atlanta in time to finish the season and play in his first World Series. A lefty with a goofy personality and a good fastball, Neagle started the game with back-to-back strikeouts of Tim Raines and Derek Jeter. The only Yankee to reach base in the first three innings was Rogers, who singled with two outs and was stranded.

If only Rogers had pitched as well as he had hit. Although the Braves had gone down meekly in the first on three ground balls, Fred McGriff greeted Rogers with a home run to lead off the second. Unnerved, Rogers issued back-to-back walks to Javy Lopez and Andruw Jones as he "seemed to become even more deliberate and herky-jerky, as if his shoulder, or body, or psyche, had tightened up" (*New York Times*). Jeff Blauser lay down a suicide squeeze bunt. Lopez had already crossed the plate by the time Rogers snatched it up, but Cecil Fielder had come in for the ball as well. Mariano Duncan, the second baseman, did not make it over to first in time, and Blauser was awarded a single. Neagle then bunted the two men over, and they were quickly brought in by a double from Marquis Grissom. The Braves were back to their tomahawking, relentless ways, and led in the game, 4–0.

When the next inning began, only the third, with base hits from Chipper Jones and McGriff, Torre faced the inevitable and pulled Rogers. "Starter Kenny Rogers was even worse than his most bitter detractors could have feared," reported the *Atlanta Constitution.* Fortunately for the Yankees, relief pitching was the one area where they outshone the Braves. Time and again this October, the bullpen had earned wins in games that starters had blown. On came Brian Boehringer, who allowed Jones to score on a sac fly, but caught Andruw staring at strike three and Jermaine Dye popped to short. 5–0 Atlanta.

Boehringer restored a semblance of order to the Yankee universe as he set the Braves down in order in the fourth with two strikeouts and a grounder. He was lifted for a pinch hitter, who was in turn replaced by David Weathers to pitch the fifth. The portly, hangdog Weathers struck out Mark Lemke, but Chipper Jones walked. As Weathers went to work on McGriff, he was called for a balk, and with first base now open, McGriff was intentionally walked. Weathers then struck out Lopez, and had only Andruw Jones to retire to escape the jam. But the pride of Curaçao lined a ball down the third-base line. Charlie Hayes dove to his right for it and the ball sailed off his glove, scoring Chipper and leaving two in scoring position. But Dye grounded out. The Braves' rally had added only one more run, to make the score 6–0.

If the Yankees were going to have any miracles, they would have to start happening soon. Rookie Derek Jeter, whom the Yankee Stadium masses had taken to as something special, came to the plate to face Neagle. Jeter's inside-out swing habitually took the ball to right field. Neagle fed him a pitch away and Jeter popped it up. Dye, McGriff, and Lemke all ran toward the foul territory in right. Dye, coming in on the ball, had the best bead on it until he ran to his left to avoid umpire Tim Welke. The wind, or divine intervention, blew the ball to the right at the last moment, and although Dye lunged flat out and got a glove on it, the ball fell in the grass. Welke raised his arms to signal foul. Given new life, Jeter punched a single into right on the next pitch.

In his breakout year of 1995, Bernie Williams had become the Yankees' most patient hitter. In the five postseason games with Seattle, he had walked seven times. So it was no surprise to see him walk here, bringing "Big Daddy" Cecil Fielder to the plate. Fielder had come to the Yankees at the trading deadline from Detroit, as New York had sought a slugger to beef up the lineup for the pennant race. Fielder laced a ball into right that bounded on the grass. Dye was having a tough inning, as the ball skipped up and handcuffed him, then got by him, allowing both Jeter and Bernie to score, Cecil to second. Charlie Hayes followed with a single that scored even the slow-moving freight train that was Fielder. The lead had been cut in half, and Atlanta manager Bobby Cox made a move. On came Terrell Wade to face a resurgent Darryl Strawberry. Yes, the same Darryl Strawberry who earlier in the year had been out of Major League Baseball and playing for an independent league team in Minnesota, hoping for another chance. George Steinbrenner had offered the same helping hand to Darryl that he had to Straw's old Mets teammate Dwight Gooden. Darryl retained his lightning-quick, scythelike stroke, his intimidating power at the plate.

Wade walked him, forcing Cox to bring on Mike Bielecki. There were still no outs. Bielecki had never been an overpowering starter or reliever, and was nearing the end of his career. In Atlanta Cox and pitching coach Leo Mazzone had used him judiciously, though, and in 75 innings of mostly relief work, he posted his second-lowest career ERA of 2.63. He had not yet been scored on in October, and had struck out nine men. Bielecki added three more to that tally, punching out Duncan and pinch hitters Paul O'Neill and Tino Martinez. Torre had nearly emptied the bench, only to come up empty himself. Jim Leyritz went in to catch now that Girardi was out of the game, and Jeff Nelson came on to pitch.

Cox stuck with Bielecki, and sent Rafael Belliard in to play short for defensive purposes. Although Jeter worked out a walk, Bielecki again sent the Yankees back with nothing. Braves' fans again began to dream of wrapping up the Series at home the next day.

But two innings out of Bielecki were enough for Cox. In the eighth, he called on Mark Wohlers, the Braves' fireballing closer, the man who had been so instrumental in the Braves' 1995 world championship. He had remained dominant in 1996, saving 39 games, striking out 100 men in 77⅓ innings. He was known for throwing 100 miles per hour on occasion and had surrendered only eight home runs all year. Like Bielecki, he had not yet been scored on in the postseason.

Charlie Hayes stood in. Wohlers rocked back and fired, and Hayes got just a piece of the ball, a swinging bunt up the third-base line. Chipper watched and waited for it to roll foul; it never did. Hayes was on with an infield single. Strawberry followed with a late swing on a Wohlers pitch, lining a single to left. Mariano Duncan, who had only one hit in the Series, then took his hacks against the hard-throwing Wohlers. The ground ball to Belliard was made for a double play, but Belliard was handcuffed—the ball bounced off his hands and fell at his feet. He picked it up in time to get the out at second, but Duncan was safe at first, and Hayes had moved to third.

The next man up was "the King," Jim Leyritz, whose fifteenth-inning home run in game two of the 1995 ALDS had sent Yankee fans into delirium, and who also had hit a big one in the Yankees' pennant clincher against Baltimore. Leyritz had come up in the Yankee system in 1990, and had never played one set position. In 1996 he was ostensibly the backup catcher, but he also played first, second, third, left, and as DH. A self-described "dead fastball hitter," Leyritz dug in against Wohlers, figuring he would see some heat. He did, a 99-mile-an-hour fastball, and fouled it straight back. Wohlers came back with a slider instead; another foul. Leyritz spun the bat in his hand like a baton after every pitch, then stepped in, hands raised high, and rotored the bat slowly as he waited for the next one.

Wohlers dealt his pitch, but it wasn't the hundred-mile-an-hour fastball. It was a little slower, with a little bit of a hump in its flight path, a hanging slider. Leyritz hung back a fraction of a second and then tattooed the ball. Andruw Jones climbed the wall in left center, but the ball was far out of his reach, a three-run homer that tied the game at six. Leyritz roared as he circled the bases, the Yankees pouring out of the dugout to greet him.

Wohlers retired the next two men on ground outs, and the inning was over, but it was a new ball game. He stayed on to pitch the top of the ninth, and the Yankees loaded the bases against him with three little singles. But with two out, Mariano Duncan hit a dying quail into right, a little bloop job that could have scored two if it fell in. But Dye was there, lunging in, and meeting the ball in midair with his glove for the third out.

By this time Mariano Rivera was in the ball game. Rivera had been the Yankees' "secret weapon" all year, the nearly unhittable setup man who got the ball to closer John Wetteland day after day. Rivera set the Braves down with a minimum of fuss in the eighth, and got Grissom to pop up to start the ninth. But Mark Lemke, who had been tagged with the nickname "Little October" with the 10 hits he tallied in the 1991 World Series, then notched the 63rd postseason hit of his career, a single. Rivera then went after Chipper Jones, but was missing high in and above the strike zone. Chipper walked, and Torre brought on another of the bullpen's mainstays, tall Australian Graeme Lloyd. Although Lloyd had been booed when his performance had suffered in the regular season because of bone chips in his elbow, in October he had yet to give up a run. Lloyd got a 6-4-3 double play from McGriff, and the game moved to extra innings.

Now the managerial chess match moved to the endgame. Cox did not have many options left. Wohlers was done; on came Steve Avery. A tall lefthander, Avery was a starter who was pushed out of the spotlight by the Braves' three aces, and in the postseason had been pushed clean out of the rotation. His night started off promising, with two quick outs, but then he walked Tim Raines. Jeter then pulled a rare ball to the left side, a single, and Raines stopped at second. Cox elected to walk Bernie Williams intentionally.

Torre, too, was running out of options. Bench coach Don Zimmer told the *New York Times*, "We were out of players. We were discussing things like whether we would have to use David Cone to bunt. All we had left at the end was Wade Boggs." Torre had reserved Boggs for pinch-hitting duty, for just such a spot where a contact hitter with a superb batting eye could make a difference. Boggs hit for Andy Fox. Boggs had been known throughout his career for taking pitches until he saw a pitch he liked. Avery threw strike one, then Boggs fouled one off. The count went to 1–2. Boggs kept waiting for a pitch he liked. He never got one, unless you count ball four, which forced in a run.

That was it for Avery, who was replaced by Brad Clontz. In a double switch, Cox also brought Klesko on to play first base. The next man to bat was Charlie Hayes. He knocked a soft liner to Klesko, who booted it. Lemke picked it up in time to make the throw, but Clontz had not covered first. Jeter scored on the error, an all-important insurance run. Straw struck out, but the fate of this game would now be in the hands of the bullpen.

Lloyd stayed on to face the lefty Klesko and struck him out. Then it was John Wetteland's turn. Wetteland, who had lost Buck Showalter's faith, never lost Joe Torre's, even though he was a "heart attack" closer. He had saved 43 games that year for Torre, but he had a tendency to give up hits and walk a tightrope every time he went out. What made Wetteland (and Torre) special was that Wetteland never let the seemingly imminent doom bother him. So when he gave up a single to the first batter he faced, the unstoppable Andruw Jones, it was par for the course. As it was when Dye launched a fly to deep left, which Tim Raines hauled down just short of the wall for the second out.

Terry Pendleton had the same idea, similar result—this time Raines ran hard for the ball and somersaulted after he caught it sinking on the warning track. Game over, and the Yankees had won it. They had come back from six runs down, and they had come back from two games down. The championship spirit that was ignited in Atlanta would burn brightly not just for two more games, as the Yankees captured their first world title since 1978, but also for years to come as a new dynasty of pinstripe dominance began.

Extra Innings

- Game four set a new record for the longest World Series game in history, at four hours, 17 minutes.

- In all the World Series games the Yankees had played in the history of the team, they had never come from behind by such a large deficit (six runs) to win a World Series game. Only three other times in World Series history had a team previously overcome a deficit of six or more: Philadelphia in 1929, Brooklyn (over the Yankees) in 1956, and Toronto in 1993.

- "Geez, you would think those guys get tired of bailing [Rogers] out. But they do. They keep doing it."—George Steinbrenner, on his bullpen in game four, where the six relief pitchers used in the game combined to give up only four hits. (Rogers gave up five in two innings.)

- Graeme Lloyd earned the win in the comeback game and became the first Australian to win a World Series game.

May 17, 1998: Minnesota at New York

Imperfect Man II

In which history repeats itself in grand fashion

In 1982, David Wells graduated from Point Loma High School in Southern California, where he dreamed of following in the footsteps of another Point Loma alum, Don Larsen, who grew up to pitch a perfect game for the New York Yankees. As a high school player, Wells was named conference Player of the Year, but found himself drafted by a major league franchise far from his home: Toronto. He reached the Blue Jays in 1987, and by the mid-nineties found himself on the move, through Cincinnati, Detroit, and Baltimore. But the place Wells was destined to end up was the House That Ruth Built, where his folk hero was not Larsen but Ruth himself. In 1997, Wells became a Yankee and lobbied for the team to allow him to wear Babe Ruth's number 3. Ruth's number remained retired, as Wells was given number 33 instead, but Wells bought a game-used Ruth cap at a memorabilia auction for $35,000 and wore it in a start at the Stadium until manager Joe Torre told him to take the ill-fitting hat off. "Boomer" felt Ruth was a kindred spirit, not only a lefty pitcher with an expanding waistline but also a hard-drinking, party animal who could excel on the field no matter what excesses he indulged in. On May 17, 1998, though, Wells found himself in the company of Larsen once again.

The rubber-armed lefty took the mound that gray day against the Minnesota Twins. The Twins had won the world championship in 1991, but by

1998 were mostly stocked with young, inexpensive players—talented, but not seasoned—led by a few choice veterans such as Paul Molitor, who was wrapping up his Hall of Fame career. Before the game, manager Tom Kelly spoke optimistically to reporters, praising his team's excellent round of batting practice that morning. "The Twins apparently left their hits in the batting cage," wrote La Velle E. Neal III in the *Minneapolis Star Tribune.*

In his previous start, Wells had given up a huge lead to the Texas Rangers, which led to Torre questioning his concentration. But today, Wells had all his pitches working, including a cut fastball and a looping "twelve-six" curve, and the Yankees gradually built him a lead—or at least, Bernie Williams did. In the second, Bernie doubled, and came home on a passed ball and a wild pitch. In the fifth, he hit a solo homer to make it 2–0. In the seventh, he doubled again, scored on a Darryl Strawberry triple, and Straw came in when Chad Curtis singled. The four runs would end up being more than Wells needed.

What Wells would need was some solid defense. Although he struck out 11, Boomer was known as a pitcher who gave up hits because he always threw strikes, allowing batters to make contact. In the seventh he faced Molitor, a man who had already racked up over 3,100 hits in his career and who had a .400 career average against Wells. Boomer was behind in the count 3–1 and he knew if he threw too good a strike, Molitor would not miss the opportunity to hit the ball hard. But if he threw one too wide, the walk would ruin the perfect game. Wells painted the black, got the called strike, and then came back with another pitch just a hair farther out. Molitor couldn't take the chance that it would be the same spot. He swung and missed, strike three.

Wells couldn't strike them all out, though, and every time a ball rolled to the right side, some fans would gasp. Chuck Knoblauch, who had come from the Twins in a much-ballyhooed trade before the season, had been experiencing throwing yips at second base. Just the day before, he had committed two throwing errors on routine plays and had observers all over the league scratching their heads. But Chuck handled his chances flawlessly, including the one hard hit ball of the afternoon, the only ball that looked like it might be a hit all day.

The near-hit came in the eighth inning, when Ron Coomer lined a 2–1 pitch past the mound toward second. In a split second, Chuck took one step back to knock the ball down on the short hop. With the slow-footed Coomer running, he had plenty of time to pick the ball up and make the out. "When he hit it, I thought, 'That's going to center field,'" Wells said.

Otherwise, the Twins looked helpless. As early as the third inning, broadcasters were joking about the possibility of the perfect game. "You could sense it," said Jim Kaat, who had television announcing duties that day. "From early on you could tell the Twins had a very inexperienced lineup. You just had a sense as he was going through those early innings that he could do this. I mean, you never *predict* a perfect game, but we talked about it early on and, lo and behold, it came true." Kaat, who was an excellent pitcher with a long career himself, and a former Yankee, truly enjoyed watching Wells that day. "Boomer is my favorite pitcher to do a game for as an announcer. He doesn't make it complicated. He throws a lot of strikes and he's very predictable. You can always read his emotions. And when he's pitching well, you get a lot of fly balls to right field."

In fact, starting off the ninth inning, Jon Shave popped up a ball to right, though it took seven pitches to retire him. The crowd was so loud, they were making Wells nervous. "I was hoping the fans would just kind of shush a little," Wells told reporters. "They got to me. They made me a little nervous. They got me pumped up. When they start screaming, you want a punch-out. When you don't get it, you feel like you let them down." Four pitches later, Wells got the punch-out on the next batter, Javier Valentin. That left only Pat Meares between Wells and perfection. On Wells's second pitch, Meares hit a fly ball to right, where Paul O'Neill was waiting for it.

"It wasn't a real tough play," O'Neill remembered. "It was a real easy fly ball, just like you want it to be." O'Neill squeezed the ball in his glove as Wells shouted, squeezed his eyes shut, and gave a few chainsaw pumps with his fist toward the ground. Soon he was swallowed up by O'Neill and his teammates. "As I went in to the mound at the end, I remember jokingly asking him, 'Do you want this ball?' like it was nothing. I'm sure he still has it now."

Fellow pitcher David Cone also sought out Wells in the on-field celebration. He turned Boomer to face the scoreboard in left field and told him to take in all those zeros. "In baseball's most storied setting, the New York Yankees' David Wells threw the book—the history book—at the Twins on Sunday," wrote Scott Miller in the *St. Paul Pioneer Press*.

It was the second perfect game in Yankee Stadium history, after Larsen's, and the fifteenth perfect game in major league history. Yankee PR assistant Arthur Richman phoned Larsen—an old pal—at his home, and the old pitcher offered his congratulations to Wells. "We've never met," Larsen later told George Vecsey of the *New York Times*. "I'm sure we will—probably at some bar."

Wells found his locker surrounded with well-wishers, including comedian Billy Crystal, who joked, "I came in late. What happened?"

Ultimately Wells did the town in the style that he loved, partying in Manhattan's hottest nightspots with some teammates, from midtown to

Chinatown, but the meaning and the magnitude of the perfect game still hadn't sunk in after a few days. "This kind of accomplishment is too far-fetched for me," he concluded.

But not too far-fetched for the Yankees. O'Neill felt the game was one more "little boost" for a club that had just won 24 out of 29 games. "O'Neill and his teammates are beginning to wonder whether this is an omen, particularly considering that the last no-hitter for the Yankees was pitched by Dwight Gooden in May 1996, when the Yankees went on to win the Series," wrote Ellen Chase in the *Newark Star-Ledger*. Omen or no, the Yankees did go on to have a magical year, tallying 114 regular-season wins and setting a new all-time total with 125 wins as they went on to win the division, the pennant, and then beat the San Diego Padres in four straight in the World Series.

Extra Innings

- Wells also set an American League record for the most batters retired consecutively, at 38. He had sat down the last ten in a row he faced on May 12, all 27 men on May 17, and the first batter of his next start, on May 23. The previous American League record, 33 batters, was shared by Steve Busby (Kansas City, 1974) and John Montagne (Seattle, 1977). The major league record is 41 batters, set by San Francisco's Jim Barr in 1972.

- On September 1, 1998, Wells pitched perfectly through two outs in the seventh inning against Oakland, but then gave up a single to Jason Giambi. The Yankees won the game anyway, 7–0.

- Wells's perfect game was the fourth time in their 37-year existence that the Twins were no-hit, and the second time they were victims of a perfect game. Catfish Hunter—who also starred in pinstripes—beat them 4–0 on May 8, 1968, when he pitched for Oakland.

- The day of Wells's perfect game was "Beanie Baby" Day at Yankee Stadium. Some of the paid crowd came only to grab the hot collectible and leave. Within 24 hours of Wells pitching the perfecto, the souvenir stuffed toys were going for as much as $500 in online auctions.

- David Cone and Luis Sojo helped Wells through the perfect game by joking with him in the late innings. "I think it's time to break out your knuckleball," Coney told him. "I don't think we've seen your best stuff yet." None would admit to using the words "no-hitter" or "perfect game," though.

- The perfect game was Wells's 219th career start but only his fourth shutout!

Just Deserts

In which a medical miracle and a dose of old Yankee magic reward a pitcher's patience

After the magic of the 1998 season—with the team's record-setting 125 wins from April through October, David Wells's perfect game, and World Series sweep of the Padres—1999 might have seemed like a letdown. But Yankees fans everywhere rode the wave of the team's dominance from April all the way through a memorable rematch in the World Series with their old foe, the Braves, this time sweeping them four straight. Every day at the ballpark it seemed like a new hero emerged, and the whole summer was like one long victory party, even while tinged with sadness over the passing of Joe DiMaggio and Catfish Hunter.

On July 18, one old champion came back to the Stadium to be part of that shining summer. Yogi Berra, after 14 years of self-imposed exile from the Stadium after his unceremonious firing in 1985, made peace with George Steinbrenner and returned for "Yogi Berra Day," where he was lauded with praise and gifts, and reunited with an old battery mate, Don Larsen. Larsen threw the ceremonial first pitch to Yog', who borrowed Joe Girardi's glove to catch it.

"Maybe Yogi Berra left a little magic on the glove," began the story that ran in the *Seattle Post-Intelligencer* the next day. Or perhaps it was Larsen's doing. "Moments before the first pitch, Don Larsen went to the mound and shook David Cone's hand," read the game story in the *New York Daily News.* "Neither of them had any way of knowing what was about to rub off." Because the events that were about to unfold would challenge even the most naive Hollywood moviegoer's suspension of disbelief.

That day David Cone took the mound for his 344th start of his major league career, a career that had seen him win 20 games in 1988, when he was a young buck with the Mets, and repeat the feat as a wily veteran in 1998 with the Yankees—the 10-year gap between 20-win seasons itself a record. He had won the Cy Young Award as a Kansas City Royal and a World Series ring as a Toronto Blue Jay. Back in 1991 he had once struck out the side on nine pitches, and twice had captured the National League strikeout crown. He had been both the toast of the town and a staple of the tabloids in New York. He once tied a National League record by striking out 19 men in a game. He had three times taken no-hitters into the eighth or ninth innings, only to have them marred by a lone hit. He had been on the mound the night Seattle had bumped New York from the postseason in 1995.

And he also had suffered a potentially life-threatening aneurysm in his pitching shoulder in 1996, a problem that might have even dated back to the 147 pitches he threw that night in Seattle. "On the plane ride back, I'm talking to Donnie, and it hit me. I almost couldn't lift my arm over my head," he told the *Daily News*. Half a year later, the aneurysm was diagnosed. At the time, no one was even sure he would pitch again, but after an arduous rehab process, he was cleared to make a start against the Oakland A's on September 2, 1996. The Yankees' team physician, Dr. Stuart Hershon, reportedly told Cone before he took the mound, "Remember, only a few innings. Don't try to throw a no-hitter or anything." But Cone, like Ruth and Reggie and the great Yankees before him who performed best when under pressure and full of emotion, didn't heed the advice. As he told Jack Curry of the *New York Times* the day before the game, "This is going to rank up there with any game I've ever pitched. World Series. The All-Star game. Anything."

And it did. Cone no-hit the Athletics for seven innings, and then he reached his pitch count. Joe Torre told him he had thrown 85 pitches after seven, and it was time to hit the showers. The Yankees, whose 12-game lead over the Orioles had been cut to two, needed Cone healthy for the entire pennant race and postseason more than Cone needed to toss two more innings. "Coney made a sacrifice there, sacrificing a personal goal for a team goal," catcher Joe Girardi later said. Cone himself said all the right things in the press, agreeing with the decision to save his arm for the starts to come. But some saw tears in his eyes as he told them, "I'll never wonder if this could have been my last opportunity to throw [a no-hitter]."

Cone's comeback included the crucial game three win in the World Series that year, and then 20 wins in the team's then-record 114 in 1998. Nineteen ninety-nine had been good for the team and for Cone, who was 9–4 with the second-lowest ERA in the league at 2.65 going into his start on July 18.

The opponents that day would be the Montreal Expos, in New York for what was then looked on as a novelty—interleague play, regular-season games between American and National League teams that would count in the standings like any other games. The Expos, too young to have seen Cone when he was with the Mets, had no idea what to expect from this mound artist. Then again, with David Cone, no one ever knew what to expect.

"There was a day when I went to warm him up in the bullpen, and he threw me out after three pitches because he said he didn't want me to see how bad his stuff was that day. So you never knew what you were going to get with him," Girardi recalled. "His arm slot always depended on what felt right to him on a given day. Sometimes he would just make up arm angles to get a better feel." Girardi recalled both the day and Cone's temperament. "It was a real hot day that day. Coney's face gets real red on a day like that and it looks like his face is going to explode. And he always had to go off on somebody anyway. He would always need to let off steam before a start." Girardi, used to Cone's ways, would usually make himself the one to bear the brunt of the outburst. Normally, hot, humid weather would help to loosen the muscles and tendons in Cone's arm. But maybe it was a little too hot—Yankee infielder Jeff Manto had to be treated in the hospital for heat exhaustion before the game. That day, Cone worked hard in the bullpen warming up, trying to find that right combination of arm action and angle to let his pitches flow.

He didn't find it, but the Expos didn't know that. Wilton Guerrero struck out to start the game. Terry Jones hit a liner into right that Paul O'Neill dove for and caught. "So early in a game, a play like that seems nice, but not really important," O'Neill said. "But later on, it becomes important." Rondell White followed with a fly that went all the way to the warning track in left, but no farther. Ricky Ledee caught up to it routinely, and the first inning was over.

On the mound for the Expos that day was a young Javier Vasquez, who would himself become a Yankee much later in his career. Vasquez started off his day hitting Chuck Knoblauch with a pitch, but then retired the Yankees easily, sending Cone back out into the 98-degree heat.

This time Cone struck out Montreal's best hitter, Vladimir Guerrero, and retired José Vidro and Brad Fullmer on ground balls. The Yankees wouldn't go down so easily. Vasquez retired Tino Martinez on an easy comebacker but then walked Chili Davis. Not wanting to do the same to Ricky Ledee, he threw a strike that caught too much of the plate, and Ledee sent it sailing up into the top deck in right for two runs. Vasquez then hit Scott Brosius, and Girardi followed with a double, scoring Brosius—though Girardi was then caught at third for the second out. Knoblauch walked, and Jeter followed with another homer into the hot air, this one to center, well over 400 feet and into the Yankees' bullpen. O'Neill then grounded out, but it was 5–0 Yankees.

Cone came back from the wait during the rally and struck out the side. But the heat and humidity reached a peak of its own, and rain began to fall. Just another little stroke of fate. "You know, in the first and second inning, his stuff wasn't great," Girardi said. "But we had a half-hour rain delay. It wasn't that long, maybe thirty minutes, but with a guy like Coney at that stage of his career, you have to think, is it worth it to send him back out there? But he was doing what it took to stay warm, he played catch in the tunnel, and when the rain delay was over, his stuff was twice as good as it had been before."

Cone was helped by facing a young team who swung early in the count, but he also knew he had to keep his pitch count down. "He had already thrown an extra 50 pitches, trying to find that arm slot where it didn't hurt," according to Girardi. Now that he had found it, "he was filthy. His fastball was good, the splitter was good, and he had a breaking ball that started out behind the right-handed batter and broke over the plate." The Expos flailed. It took Cone only seven pitches to retire them in the fourth, starting an early buzz in the Stadium crowd, who had seen Wells's perfecto just 14 months before.

Cone was even more virtuosic than Wells in his masterpiece. Cone did not even go to three balls on a single batter the entire game. Between innings, he made a beeline for Joe Torre's office. "I didn't speak to him at all," Girardi recalled. Neither did his other teammates—they never got the chance to flout the old taboo against mentioning the no-hitter. But in Torre's office, the radio was on, and as early as the third inning, radio broadcasters Michael Kay and John Sterling were talking about the possibility of a perfect game. "I'm not a big believer in jinxes, but I heard 'perfect game' about 100 times yesterday for four or five innings," Cone told Bob Raissman of the *Daily News.* "Believe me, there's nothing to that jinx because I heard it and it didn't work." Chili Davis, at least, did try to lighten the mood when he took a catcher's glove out before the seventh and warmed Cone up while Girardi got his gear on. "He was a minor league catcher," Cone recalled. "He said, 'C'mon, you can throw harder than that. I was a catcher! Don't be afraid to just let it rip.'"

In a strange parallel to Wells's perfect game, the hit-that-almost-was came in the same inning, the same situation, to the same fielder. With one out in the top of the eighth, José Vidro hit a hard grounder through the right side. But Chuck Knoblauch—whose throwing lapses never went away all the time he was in New York—ran all-out to his right, backhanded the ball, screeched to a halt on the outfield grass, and nailed Tino's glove at first for the out. Cone followed that with a strikeout to end the frame, and walked off to a thunderous ovation. "You can't help but feel the emotion of the crowd. I could feel my heart thumping through my uniform."

The Yankees scored another run in the eighth on a Paul O'Neill double and a Bernie Williams single. But no one wanted to see a long rally at that point. When Chili Davis came to the plate with two men on and grounded into a double play, the crowd cheered. Ricky Ledee grounded out to end the inning, and everyone came one step closer to the answer to the question Could Cone really do it? With all the unbelievable subplots, Yogi, Larsen, two shoulder surgeries in four years, the sacrificed no-hitter in Oakland, could David Cone write his own chapter in the history books?

He started the inning with a strikeout, getting Chris Widger on three sliders in a row. The crowd, which had not sat down since Cone took the mound for his warm-up tosses, roared on every strike. "It's a game I would have loved to have watched if I didn't have to hit in it," Widger later said.

A pinch hitter came on then, lefty-swinging Ryan Maguire. Cone twirled a slider. Maguire made contact, but not good contact, and hit a sinking liner into left, the sun field on a July afternoon. Ledee came charging in, eyes behind dark shades, and everyone could see he had lost the ball. But his trajectory and the ball's met, and Ledee opened his glove shoulder high and scooped it out of the air as he ran—awkward, but caught. "It was interesting to see Coney's eyes as Ledee tried to find it," Girardi remembered. "He would come right out and say, 'If you dropped that ball, I would have killed you.'" But Ledee made the grab and that left only one Expo for Cone to kill.

It was Orlando Cabrera, who had foreseen the moment as early as the sixth inning. "I started thinking, 'If he throws a perfect game, I'm going to be the last out,'" Cabrera told reporters. He thought his one chance to get off the hook would be for someone ahead of him in the lineup to hit a ground ball to Knoblauch, who had made 16 errors already that season. "I've read about Knoblauch's problems throwing the ball to first base, and then when he caught that ball [of Vidro's] and made the perfect throw, I was like, 'Oh, well, we're done.'" Cabrera had a 1–1 count when he swung at a fastball and popped it up in the infield.

Cone pointed at the ball in the sky, the fierce look he had worn in his eye all day replaced by disbelief. As the foul ball settled into third baseman Scott Brosius's glove, Cone grabbed his head and fell to his knees.

"Don Larsen in '56, David Wells in '98, David Cone in '99!" shouted John Sterling on the radio. The center-field scoreboard flashed "It's Déjà vu All Over Again!" As Cone began to crumple, stunned and drained, he was caught by—who else?—his catcher, Joe Girardi. Girardi had only a few seconds to act. He grabbed Cone in a bear hug and heaved himself backward, pulling Cone on top of him, just before the rest of the team engulfed them.

"I remember from the '96 World Series, being at the bottom of the pile was scary," Girardi said. "And I knew if we were going to win in the World Series again, we needed this guy. I knew I had to protect him. I had a whole inning to think about it."

Eventually a limp Cone was extracted from the pile and paraded on his teammates' shoulders to the dugout. It had taken only 88 pitches to record all 27 outs, only three more than he had thrown that night in Oakland, but he looked as if the entire 13-year big league journey had been traveled in one day. "It makes you stop and think about the Yankee magic, and the mystique of this ballpark," Cone said, when he could.

The other man besides Cone being sought by the media in the afterglow of the feat was, of course, Don Larsen. He had intended to leave in the seventh, but couldn't pull himself away when he saw what unfolded. "I'm just glad I got a chance to see one," Larsen said of the perfect game. "I didn't see mine."

"[This game] will be remembered as the payoff for every obstacle Cone has overcome over the last decade-plus to establish himself as one of this town's most beloved and respected adopted sons," wrote Peter Botte in the *New York Daily News*. Tim Brown of the *Newark Star-Ledger* was even more direct. "Every once in a while, something like this happens to someone who deserves it, who gets it, who has it coming."

Girardi and Cone's teammates agreed. "I think guys were as happy for him as they could be for any player. He had the ultimate respect from his teammates, and as a player that means the most. You don't always get respect from other sources—the media, the fans, the front office—but what means the most to you is the esteem of the other players." Former Yankee David Wells, now pitching for Toronto, phoned Cone to congratulate him, then considered flying into town to help him finish off some of the bottles of Dom Perignon that were arriving from other old friends and teammates.

"You have to believe something was at work there," Girardi said. "After all that he had been through, and all that he had given up for the team, he truly deserved it. He was so creative and he knew how to pitch. He was the most fun to catch of any pitcher I can remember."

"I didn't know if I'd ever get another chance. Going into the latter innings, I said, 'This is it. This might be my last chance to do something like this,'" a relieved Cone said when trying to sum up the day for reporters. "I've been close a few times, so I took solace in the fact that maybe this was my day. I just didn't want to let it get away."

Extra Innings

- Yogi Berra received some great gifts from the Yankees in honor of his return, including a car, a trip to Italy, and an audience with the Pope. Yogi also was able to bring three generations of Berras back to the Stadium. "I've got five granddaughters, and they all want to meet Derek Jeter," he told the *Daily News.* In addition to Don Larsen, teammates Phil Rizzuto, Whitey Ford, childhood pal Joe Garagiola, and other baseball dignitaries joined the Yankees in saluting old number 8.

- Not only was July 18 Yogi Berra Day, it also was manager Joe Torre's 59th birthday.

- David Cone was the second-oldest man, at 36, to throw a perfect game. Cy Young did it in 1904, when he was 37. Randy Johnson, at 40, eclipsed Young's mark with his perfecto in 2004.

- Paul O'Neill is the only player to participate in three perfect games on the winning side. Not only was he on the field for both David Wells and David Cone's perfectos, he also was part of Tom Browning's perfect game while he was with Cincinnati.

- After the perfect game, the National Baseball Hall of Fame and Museum in Cooperstown, New York, requested either the cap or the jersey David Cone wore during the game. They also wanted a game ball. Cone sent the pitching rubber.

- One of Cone's congratulatory phone calls came from actor Kevin Costner, whose film *For Love of the Game* featured Costner as a pitcher who pitches a perfect game in Yankee Stadium. The film hit theaters just two months after Cone's perfecto. When asked how he felt about both Wells and Cone pitching perfect games during the time the film was in production, Costner said it was great, it made his film seem more believable.

- Expos manager Felipe Alou was asked when he thought Cone had a chance to pitch a perfect game. "When I wrote down the lineup and saw that we didn't have anybody who had faced him," said Alou.

- Joe Torre was present for all three perfect games in Yankees history. As a 16-year-old spectator he had seen Larsen's while rooting for the Dodgers. Don Zimmer was there in 1956, too, on the Dodgers' bench. Both men watched Wells and Cone from the Yankees' dugout. Zimmer was the only man in uniform for all three games.

48

October 14, 2000: New York at Seattle

Rocket's Red Glare

In which Roger Clemens proves he is a Yankee and a champion

The Yankees of 2000 were a team on a mission. Their goal: win a third World Series in a row and validate all speculation that this team might be a "dynasty." After racking up a mediocre 87–74 record and "backing in" to the postseason, losing 14 of their final 17 games of the season, the Bronx Bombers looked like they might be on their last legs.

But October brought new life to the Yankees, who stumbled through the ALDS with the Athletics—literally—as a late-inning pratfall by Luis Sojo at second base broke the tension on the team that had been building throughout the losing streak. That and an offhand comment by A's third baseman Eric Chavez before the deciding game five lit a fire under them: "I mean, they've won enough times," Chavez said confidently, unaware that his interview was being shown on the scoreboard while the Yankees took batting practice. "It's time for some other people to have some glory here . . . they had a great run." The team's stalwart veterans, such as Paul O'Neill, Tino Martinez, and Chuck Knoblauch, bristled at the suggestion they were over the hill. The Yankees beat Oakland 7–5 that night and moved on to face the Mariners.

The teams split the first two games at Yankee Stadium, then flew to the West Coast for the second time in a week. In Seattle the Yankees no longer had the Kingdome to dread. The M's October run of 1995 had touched off an epidemic of baseball fever that built them a new, high-tech, retractable-roof home, Safeco Field. The Yankees thrived in their first game at Safeco as Andy Pettitte allowed only two runs in 6⅔ innings, while Tino Martinez and Bernie Williams hit home runs. With Mariano Rivera entering the game with a 4–2 lead in the eighth, he earned both the save and finally surpassed Whitey Ford's postseason 33-inning scoreless streak. The Yankees tacked on four more runs in the ninth to cap it off. The 8–2 win prompted Buster Olney to conclude in the *New York Times* that "the deeper the Yankees move into October, the more they look the way they usually do this time of year, confident and relaxed, on track like the D train moving steadily through the Bronx."

The next day, the Mariners looked to even things up at two games apiece, but to do it, they would have to get through Roger Clemens, at 38 years old one of the prime suspects for the critics crowing that the Yankees were too old to pull it off one more time.

Clemens had come to the Yankees saddled with a reputation as a guy who didn't handle playoff pressure well, earning only three wins in 14 postseason starts. The reputation was not entirely deserved, but had its genesis in his years with Boston, when Clemens's hot temper got him tossed early from a 1990 ALCS contest against Oakland, and a much-debated blister injury forced him from the mound in the World Series in 1986. More recently, Oakland had beaten him twice in the previous week, and in 1999 in Boston the Red Sox had drubbed him, 13–1. But '99 was the same postseason where the Rocket had pitched the World Series clincher in a dominating performance against the Atlanta Braves; only a hamstring, tweaked when he hustled to cover first, kept him from the complete game. Some would say that was the night he became a Yankee. Could Roger rebound from the ALDS losses in 2000 the same way?

The Mariners found out quickly, yes. Throwing 96 mile-an-hour heat right from the very first pitch, Clemens struck out the first two batters he faced. Then he walked Alex Rodriguez, an expected outcome when two pitches in a row knocked A-Rod back off the plate when they came in chin high. Clemens sent a message to the M's best hitter, and their entire lineup, with those pitches: "I am dangerous and I dare you to hit me." Seattle manager Lou Piniella was incensed, but Clemens ignored the chatter from the benches. He then induced the ever-dangerous Edgar Martinez to pop up harmlessly in the infield.

With Paul Abbott on the hill for the Mariners, Piniella had his pitcher throw over Jorge Posada's head when he came up in the next inning. "If he wants to throw at our guys, we'll throw at his guys, period," Piniella said. But John Hirschbeck, umpire crew chief, had no intention of letting a beanball war break out, and he went to the mound to talk to Clemens before the bottom of the inning. Clemens remained implacable—his message had already been sent—and told Hirschbeck not to worry. In the second inning he hit 98 on the radar gun and powered through the M's lineup.

No Mariner came close to scoring in five innings, but the Rocket was burning through his fuel quickly. A few pitches began to sail in that inning, as if he were beginning to tire. But changing his undershirt, as he customarily does between innings when he pitches, Clemens noticed on the television in the clubhouse that he had not allowed a hit. Perhaps it was the realization that he was pitching a no-hitter, something he had never accomplished in his long career, or perhaps it was the fact that the Yankees put some runs on the board for him (Jeter hit a three-run shot), but "Roger put the hammer down after that," according to José Canseco, then a Yankee.

"Armed with a sizable lead, [Clemens] began establishing complete command of his breaking pitches, mixing his splitters and sliders," Olney wrote. And he was not out of gas. "Clemens's first pitch to David Bell in the sixth inning registered at 99 m.p.h." Clemens himself would later say he had his "best splitter of the year. It was really dancing and doing everything I had to do, and once I had that with my velocity, it's fun."

In the seventh, the Rocket started off Al Martin with a high fastball, then went to a sinker down and in. Martin golfed a liner over first. "I was just able to get my hands around," Martin said. Tino Martinez leaped as high as he could and the ball just ticked his glove as it went on by, into the right-field corner for a double. The no-hitter was gone, but not Roger's focus. Here was A-Rod at the plate and Edgar on deck again. Martin was stranded at second as Clemens struck out both men, then walked John Olerud, but retired the side as Mike Cameron fanned as well.

Two more strikeouts in the eighth, and two more in the ninth, and Clemens had not only pitched a one-hitter, the complete game, and put his team up 3–1 in the series, he also had tied the record for strikeouts in a nine-inning championship series game at 15, set by Livan Hernández in 1997. Clemens threw 138 pitches in the performance and walked only two.

"As a Texan, Roger Clemens is straight from the Western movies, the hired gun brought in to restore law and order," wrote George Vecsey in the *Times*. "Up to last night, Clemens lacked that one signature game, the epic beating in the public square that established his control of the general populace . . . but last night's brutal stomping of the Mariners . . . was the reason the Yankees imported Clemens in 1999." Gary Graves in *USA Today* evoked a different film genre, science fiction: "On those nights when the Rocket is in another orbit, the New York Yankees simply sit back and enjoy the ride."

Clemens himself admitted it might have been his best game ever. "Tonight was special," he said. "The ball was jumping out of my hand."

Extra Innings

- During the 2000 ALCS, David Justice broke the record for most appearances in postseason games. The previous record had been held by none other than Reggie Jackson, at 84 games. Justice, like Reggie, came to the Yankees after being a proven postseason performer elsewhere, and helped the team to a world championship with timely power hitting. Justice retired after the 2002 season, having appeared in 112 postseason games (30 division series, 46 league championships, and 36 World Series games).

- Clemens had mowed down the Mariners early in his career, setting a new record on April 29, 1986, when he fanned 20 M's in a game. The Rocket also has racked up 21 regular-season wins against the Mariners, the most by any opposing pitcher.

- Only two pitchers ever struck out more men in a postseason game, and only three others equaled Clemens's 15-strikeout performance. Clemens is the only man to strike out 15 in a nine-inning ALCS game.

17	Bob Gibson	St. Louis Cardinals	1968 World Series
16	Kevin Brown	San Diego Padres	1998 NLDS
15	Sandy Koufax	Los Angeles Dodgers	1963 World Series
15	Mike Mussina	Baltimore Orioles	1997 ALCS (extra-innings loss)
15	Livan Hernández	Florida Marlins	1997 NLCS

49

October 13, 2001: New York at Oakland

The Play

In which hope flares again in a grieving city

In September of 2001, baseball took on a significance for the city of New York and the United States that it had not held since World War II, when Franklin Delano Roosevelt wrote to the Commissioner of Baseball, Kenesaw Mountain Landis, to urge him to keep baseball operating during wartime. "I honestly feel that it would be best for the country to keep baseball going," Roosevelt wrote in what was nicknamed the "green light letter." During the war, the President reasoned, ". . . . everybody will work longer hours and harder than ever before. And that means that they ought to have a chance for recreation and for taking their minds off their work even more than before."

But in 2001 it was not work, but terror that the people needed respite from. After the terrorist attacks that destroyed the World Trade Center and devastated lower Manhattan, New Yorkers did not have much to lift their spirits, and all major sports went on a brief hiatus. When games resumed, the Mets rose up with inspiring play for a few days, but ultimately it was the Yankees who would carry the hopes of the city into October.

It was a heavy load, and in the first two games of the division series against Oakland, the team looked exhausted and old. On October 11, one month after the tragedy, the second game of the series was delayed for half an hour as a live broadcast of President George W. Bush played on the Yankee Stadium DiamondVision, delivering the news that military action in Afghanistan had begun. The game was marked by moments when it looked like the Yankees were on the verge of breaking through, only to fall back—the crowd rising to cheer, only to look around and see tears on people's faces. The prevailing feeling throughout the city was that the luck had run out and bad times had come.

The Yankees went into Oakland for the third game of the series facing elimination. No team had ever lost the first two games of a five-game postseason series at home and come back to win three in a row. Derek Jeter described being down 0–2 as "the worst scenario you can be in." Murray Chass in the *New York Times* nearly eulogized when he wrote "The end of their three-year run as . . . champions is nigh."

The Athletics were a familiar foe, both from regular-season meetings and the previous year's ALDS. In many ways the A's formula for success emulated the Yankee model, combining great starting pitching with patience at the plate. There the resemblance ended. In 2000 it had looked like the young, light hearted A's might finally knock the stolid, businesslike Yankees from their throne, but the series had slipped away from them after the Yankees rediscovered how to laugh after Luis Sojo made a pratfall on his own shoelaces.

There was no laughing this time. After being smothered by the first two of the A's "Big Three," Mark Mulder and Tim Hudson, the Yankees would face Barry Zito, possibly the toughest of the trio. The free-spirited 23-year-old sported the best left-handed curveball in the game, a "twelve-six" he could drop in for a strike and a variation he could wing toward a left-handed batter that would break over the plate. Zito's ERA since the All-Star break was a stingy 1.32. Not since the days of Vida Blue, Catfish Hunter, and Ken Holtzman did the A's have three starters of such high caliber, and behind those three aces they became a dynasty, winning the World Series three years running, from 1972 to 1974.

To get there this time, they'd first have to knock off the current dynasty, though, and a man who had come to the Yankees in search of a ring himself, Mike Mussina. Mussina had been the Yankees' big free-agent acquisition heading into the season. A right-handed control pitcher who had been Baltimore's undisputed ace, the Moose had tired of the Orioles' continual "rebuilding." Mussina, who graduated from Stanford in only three years with a degree in economics, had full command of five pitches. He could thread a needle with a four-seam fastball, cut it in on left-handers, sink a two-seamer, throw a straight change, and also baffle hitters with a knuckle curve, each pitch delivered with the identical arm motion. And Mussina was peaking at the right time. He always maintained that after reaching 200 innings in a season, his control and strength were at their best. At Fenway Park late in the season he had come within one pitch of a perfect game.

The Yankees expected a low-scoring game, and Joe Torre benched two of his lefties, David Justice and Paul O'Neill. O'Neill had announced early in the season that he planned to retire, and Torre contemplated the possibility that Paulie, the man he described as "the glue for this club," might spend his last game as a Yankee on the bench. "It's obviously something I didn't want to do," Torre explained. "But I think we needed a change." He inserted Shane Spencer into right field in O'Neill's place, and Randy Velarde as the designated hitter.

The game started off, as so many games in the Yankees' championship run from 1998 to 2000 had, with Chuck Knoblauch leading off. Knoblauch's career had started hot out of the gate, winning Rookie of the Year honors in 1991 as well as being an instrumental part of the Minnesota Twins' "worst to first" World Series victory over the Atlanta Braves that year. By the mid-nineties, however, like Mussina he was chafing under an abstemious owner, and as the Twins cut salary, he was traded to New York. A small man with a small strike zone, Knoblauch was known for being a pest at the plate, working counts and forcing pitchers to exhaust their repertoire to get him out. He also was usually among the leaders in being hit by pitch each year.

But Knoblauch had developed a mental hitch about making the throw to first base almost as soon as he arrived in New York. The hiccups would seem to disappear for months at a time but always return. By the end of the 2000 season, Torre found himself using Knoblauch as the DH instead of in the field. When the throwing woes resurfaced in spring training of 2001, Knobby converted to left field and Alfonso Soriano, a shortstop prospect whose advancement was blocked by Derek Jeter, was switched to second base. Knoblauch turned out to be a fine outfielder, using his excellent speed and very strong arm to rack up eight outfield assists before the league learned not to run on him. But the change in position did not ease his mind enough for his hitting to improve, and Chuck had his worst year at the plate, hitting only .250, his on-base percentage dropping to .339 (from a career average of .385).

Knoblauch hung in against Zito, eventually grounding a ball to short, where Miguel Tejada booted it. The leadoff man had reached. Torre elected to play small ball, and with the power-hitting Soriano coming up, he put on a bunt play. Soriano popped the bunt in the air and it blooped easily into Jason

Giambi's glove at first. Derek Jeter came next, but popped the ball into right. Zito then faced Bernie Williams. On two strikes, he snapped off one of his overhand curveballs, an unhittable pitch. Bernie swung and missed, and Knoblauch was stranded.

Fortunately for the Yankees, Mussina could match Zito pitch for pitch, or even do him one better. After inducing leadoff man Johnny Damon to ground out, and Tejada to ground to third, he faced the reigning MVP and one of the toughest sluggers of his day, Jason Giambi. Giambi was known for his incredible eyesight as well as his lefty power stroke; he had walked 129 times in 2001. Mussina dropped his own big curve in for strike one. Then he placed a fastball on the inside corner under Giambi's hands. Then he gave him one low and away that nipped the outside corner: good morning, good afternoon, and good night, Giambi was gone on three pitches.

Thus the gauntlet was thrown down on the pitchers' duel, and the hitters on both teams looked lost for several tense innings. In the bottom of the fourth, Mussina seemed to lose his edge. Tejada led off the inning with a wallop that Knoblauch hauled in on the warning track. Giambi then smoked a ball to right for the first hit of the game. Jermaine Dye followed with a hot grounder that eluded Derek Jeter's dive to his right. Jeter had been hobbling on an injured hamstring as well as playing at double-play depth, and the ball scooted through.

With two on, one out, Eric Chavez came to the plate. To this point in the series, the A's had scored most of their runs on the long ball. They were 0-for-20 with runners in scoring position. Mussina fed him a fastball in and Chavez took a big cut, just a tad early, and fouled it deep down the right-field line. Jorge Posada came out of his crouch to visit Moose on the mound. The next pitch also was in, but Chavez grounded it to first. Tino Martinez whipped it to Jeter for the force at second base, but there was no chance to turn a 3-6-3 double play. With men on the corners and the Coliseum crowd chanting to the rhythmic beat of snare drums, Jason's younger brother Jeremy Giambi stepped in. Moose was breathing hard, but no emotion showed on his face as he pitched. The younger Giambi hit the ball hard, but right at Soriano, who juggled the ball briefly before slinging it to first for the out.

The A's momentum was momentarily squelched but it remained to be seen if the Yankees could grab it. Leading off the inning was Tino Martinez, one of the lefties still in the lineup. He fouled off Zito's first pitch, but was far from impatient in the batter's box. Tino proceeded to take the next three pitches in a row, all balls in different locations. Then he fouled off another pitch to run the count full. And another. Zito showed no outward sign of frustration, but the at-bat had dragged out considerably. Another foul. Tino had now seen everything Zito had to offer, and on the next pitch, the eighth of the at-bat, he lined the ball hard into center. Unfortunately, Johnny Damon was right there to snare it, but it was the hardest hit ball off Zito all night, and perhaps the next batter could benefit from all those pitches Zito had thrown.

Jorge Posada did. He took a ball. Ramón Hernández, the A's catcher, called for a pitch inside, but this time Zito's control or focus failed him. He left the ball over the middle of the plate, and Posada crushed it into the seats in left. It was the first lead the Yankees had managed against the A's in 76 innings, dating back into the regular season. "It was a fastball that should have went in and it didn't," Zito said after the game. "The fastball to both sides of the plate is something that I need to establish, to make my speed work. And the fastball in was definitely a good pitch for me tonight, [just not that one]."

Sensing vulnerability, the Yankees tried to jump on Zito. Shane Spencer smacked the very next pitch to left for a double. Randy Velarde, who had been with Oakland the season before, also tagged hard the first pitch he saw, but again Damon grabbed the liner for the second out. Brosius followed with a routine fly to Damon and the threat was over.

A standard dugout joke is to say to a pitcher after the team has scored one, "Well, there's your run." Mussina had been pitching all year with crummy run support, among the lowest in the league, and the joke was no longer funny. But he was determined to make that one run stand up. He retired the next eight men in a row, with some help from his fielders. Brosius made a sparkling leaping grab from the infield grass to snag a Damon liner, and Knoblauch ended the sixth with a long run from left center to grab a Giambi foul with a feet-first slide onto the third-base warning track. But with two outs in the seventh, Jeremy Giambi stroked a single with the lefty-hitting Terrence Long coming to the plate.

Moose started Long with a changeup away, which Long looked at for a strike. Then he swung through a fastball, strike two. Moose came back with a fastball away but did not get the call, 1–2. Then a curveball away, again missing and evening the count at 2–2. He tried to nip the outside corner again, but Long fouled it off. Finally Moose tried to come inside on Long, who turned on the pitch. He pulled the ball just fair inside the first-base bag, and the ball bounded into foul territory and the Yankees' bullpen. Spencer raced into the corner to grab it while Jeremy Giambi was rounding the bases.

Spencer unleashed a throw that sailed high over the head of Alfonso Soriano, his cutoff man on the first-base line, and over the head of Tino Martinez, his secondary cutoff man. Ron Washington, the A's third-base coach, was waving Giambi home while Hernández, the on-deck batter, motioned him down for a slide. The ball bounced about five yards beyond the first-base bag toward home plate and probably would have slowed and jogged off line. But Derek Jeter, racing across the infield, intercepted the ball on one bounce in his bare hand, pirouetted toward home plate, and threw a shovel pass into the glove of Posada just in front of the plate. Posada swept the tag back just in time to swipe Giambi's leg before his foot hit the plate. Giambi was out, Derek Jeter had just added another clip to his highlight reel of October moments, and New Yorkers everywhere began to think that maybe miracles could still happen. "The Yankees needed rescuing tonight, and it was as if Superman swooped down and saved the day," wrote Buster Olney in the *New York Times*.

When speaking about the play later, Jeter insisted in his usual self-deprecating manner that he hadn't done anything special. "I'm supposed to be there," he said in response to media incredulity. "My job is to read the throw, if there's going to be a play at third, to be the cutoff man to third [or] the plate." He credited bench coach Don Zimmer with hatching the idea in spring training, but Joe Torre explained that what happened wasn't quite the way the Yankees practiced it in March. "When we have him as a trailer, he's not quite working that way. We like a more conventional throw, but he was in a position where he had no choice. The kid has great instincts, and that was obviously the play of the game."

Zito set the Yankees down one-two-three in the top of the eighth, but the Yankees had begun to count the outs. Torre brought Mariano Rivera into the game to get six. "I made up my mind early, before the game started, that if we got in a situation like that I'd use Mo for two innings," Torre said. "Moose was sensational. He only threw 100 pitches. But they hit a couple of balls hard in the seventh inning, and 100 pitches in a game like this is more like 140, because every single pitch you throw means something." Mariano faced two pinch hitters to start the eighth. Olmedo Saenz flew out harmlessly to right, but backup catcher Greg Myers, a left-handed hitter, came up. Rivera's cutter often saws off the bats of lefties, but in this case, although Myers broke his bat, he muscled the ball up the middle, just over Mariano's leap. That prompted a quick mound visit and Mo righted the ship, popping up Johnny Damon. Tejada lined the ball hard to left, but Knoblauch grabbed the sinking liner against his stomach.

There would be no insurance runs for Mo to work with in the ninth, either. Mark Guthrie replaced Zito but was just as tough, setting down Jeter, Bernie, and Tino in order. As Guthrie breezed through the ninth, Andy Pettitte began taking some to the mitt in the bullpen. Was it just his day to throw, or was there a possibility he might come into the game? We'll never know for certain. Mariano faced the heart of the A's order: the elder Giambi, Dye, and Chavez. He started with a fastball up and in at 93 miles per hour. The next pitch Giambi grounded weakly to Soriano. Dye smacked a ball into right center, a double, though, and Chavez came to the plate representing the winning run. Perhaps Mariano sensed the eagerness in the young hitter. With two strikes, he fed him a high fastball and Chavez took a massive cut at it—late—for strike three. Jeremy Giambi came up then with one last chance to redeem himself, but Mo would have none of it. He induced the same weak grounder Jason had begun the inning with, and the Yankees had survived to play another day.

The Yankees did become the first team to lose the first two games of a five-game series at home and come back to win all three. By game five, the funereal atmosphere of the Stadium was gone, replaced by a jubilation that would carry the Yankees all the way through a championship series with Seattle and three incredible World Series games where a new miracle seemed to occur each night, including back-to-back games extended with game-tying home runs in the bottom of the ninth off sidearmer Byung-Hyun Kim. Ultimately the Yankees succumbed to the Diamondbacks in Arizona, but for a brief time they had brought joy and light back to the city in its darkest time.

Extra Innings

- When baseball resumed play after the September 11 shutdown, the Mets and Yankees wore FDNY and NYPD hats during batting practice. Joe Torre chose a Port Authority Police cap, but traded it in during the Oakland series for a gift from Yogi Berra: a cap reading "It Ain't Over 'Til It's Over." To keep with the theme, though, Joe had one of the clubhouse boys sew an NYPD patch onto the side of the cap.

- Jeter's highlight reel continued in game five of the ALDS as he tumbled into the stands to snare a foul pop off the bat of Terrence Long in the late innings. During the division series Jeter also surpassed Pete Rose's record of 86 postseason hits, prompting Joe Torre to do a double take. "You say, 'Well, that's got to be a mistake, this kid has only been around a few years,' and you realize his whole major league career has been postseason."

50

October 16, 2003: Boston at New York

The Curse Lives

In which fate brings together old rivals and makes new heroes

For those who believe in fate, the year 2003 had one meaning. It was the year the New York Yankees waited 100 years to meet the Boston Red Sox in game seven for the pennant. The Red Sox had waited 102. The rivalry between the teams stretched all the way back to the founding years of the Yankees, when Ban Johnson's favoritism for the American League's New York City franchise deprived Boston of some players in lopsided trades. The lopsidedness only increased in the 1920s, when the infamous sale of Babe Ruth to the Yankees marked the end of Boston's era of dominance and the start of New York's.

In addition to the pennant races that took place before divisional play, the two teams had met in two playoff situations. In 1978, of course, they played that tie-breaking single game at Fenway Park, so infamous for Bucky Dent's fly ball over the Green Monster. In 1999, the Red Sox won the expanded "wild card" berth into the postseason, and after beating the Cleveland Indians in a wild best-of-five division series, faced the Yankees in the American League Championship Series. The Yankees of 1999 still carried the momentum of their previous year, when they rolled to an American League record 114 regular-season wins and barely broke stride on their way to their third world championship in four years. They swept the Texas Rangers, holding them to a single run in three games, and then polished off the Red Sox in five games.

In the Red Sox' lone win in that series, Roger Clemens had matched up with Pedro Martinez at Fenway Park. Clemens had been lauded as Boston's savior in the 1980s, a young fireballer who in 1986 won the Cy Young Award and the league Most Valuable Player Award, went 24–4 and carried the Sox into the World Series with a win in game seven of the ALCS against the Angels. But 1986 ended in heartbreak for Boston, and Clemens's role in it was overshadowed by a ground ball that went through first baseman Bill Buckner's legs. Like so many star players for the Sox, Clemens was eventually run out of town, general manager Dan Duquette remarking that he was in "the twilight of his career." Clemens went to Toronto, where he won two more Cy Young Awards, and in the spring of 1999 suddenly found himself the subject of a blockbuster trade. The Yankees' popular, rubber-armed lefty

David Wells, second baseman Homer Bush, and reliever Graeme Lloyd went to Toronto, and Clemens went to New York in search of one thing, a World Series ring.

At first it was hard for the New York fans to accept Clemens—who had always been an American League East rival—as one of their own, an impression that was not helped when Clemens melted down facing Pedro in game three of the 1999 ALCS. Overhyped and emotional, Clemens allowed the crowd to get to him and the Red Sox knocked him out in the third inning. The Rocket gave up five runs on six hits including a home run, opening the door for an eventual 21-hit, 13-run romp. Pedro, meanwhile, after a heroic relief appearance in the deciding game of the division series, pitched seven shutout innings that day, thus fully assuming the mantle of Boston's new savior.

In 1999 Pedro also would earn his second Cy Young Award, lead the league in ERA (2.07), wins (23), winning percentage (.852), and strikeouts (313). But questions about his durability and health plagued him throughout his stay in Boston. Would his shoulder give out as his brother Ramon's had? Should his pitch count be limited to 100 pitches per start? The "best pitcher in baseball" spent stints on the disabled list every season, but when he was on his game, he was nearly unbeatable.

But one pitcher cannot a savior be. After the Yankees knocked off the Sox in '99, they swept the Atlanta Braves in the World Series, Clemens pitching the clinching game in a gutsy performance against John Smoltz. When Clemens came off the field after tweaking a leg muscle while covering first base, the Yankee Stadium crowd showered him with thunderous applause. He told reporters after the game, "I finally know what it feels like to be a Yankee," and he was finally accepted as one.

Over the course of the next few years the rivalry between Boston and New York heated up, as new ownership took over the Red Sox with a commitment to keeping the team competitive. In 2003 the Sox made it to October as the wild-card entry again. While the Yankees were warming up by beating the Minnesota Twins, Boston dropped the first two games of their division series to the Oakland A's. But for once the Red Sox had forged a team with clubhouse unity and did not buckle under pressure. New owner John Henry was a believer in exploiting inefficiencies in the system, and he had charged wunderkind general manager Theo Epstein with the task of stocking the team with players who could put up monster numbers without monster salaries. Epstein had assembled a cast of affable, hardworking no-names such as Bill Mueller, Kevin Millar, Todd Walker, and David Ortiz to fill out the roster around the stars such as Nomar Garciaparra and Manny Ramirez. Millar had been on his way to Japan after the Florida Marlins had sold the rights to him before the Red Sox called. Bill Mueller ended up winning the batting title, contending with teammates Ramirez and Walker for it much of the season.

Millar and Ortiz in particular helped to loosen the clubhouse atmosphere with their jocularity and friendly attitudes, and the influx of new blood meant a team that was not burdened by "the curse" of past years' expectations. The Red Sox rode a roller coaster throughout the year, including their usual quota of heartbreaking, bizarre losses, but always bounced back with optimism and enthusiasm. Millar coined the slogan "Cowboy Up" for the team, and when they found themselves down two games to none and facing elimination by Oakland, he instigated a curse-breaking round of head-shavings in the clubhouse. Even manager Grady Little submitted to the razor, as did general manager Theo. (Nomar begged off losing his hair, for his wedding to soccer star Mia Hamm was slated for November.) The Red Sox accomplished the nearly impossible, coming back to beat the A's three games in a row to set up their destined date with the Yankees.

The two teams had butted heads all year. The Red Sox sported the most explosive lineup in the American League and ended the season with the highest team batting average (.289), most hits (1,667), extra-base hits (649—a new all-time major league record), and runs scored (961). They even broke the all-time record for slugging percentage set by the 1927 Murderers' Row Yankees (.491 vs. .489). The Yankees, meanwhile, had the best aggregate of four starting pitchers with Roger Clemens, Andy Pettitte, Mike Mussina, and David Wells. Both teams had their difficulties solidifying their bullpens, though. Pedro and Grady Little suffered through many no decisions, blown saves, and late-inning losses in the early months of the year. The Yankees had lost Steve Karsay to injury for the year and searched for months for adequate setup men, at one point taking on Armando Benitez. While the closer for the Orioles and later the Mets, Benitez was widely derided by Yankees fans for his tendency to crumble under pressure. With the Yankees he did not turn out to be much better, but the season suddenly began to look much brighter when Benitez was traded to Seattle in exchange for righthander Jeff Nelson. Nelson, a six-eight Texan with red hair, a big mouth, and a wicked slider, had been a bullpen mainstay during the Yankees' championship run from 1998 to 2000 before he left for Seattle as a free agent. The Sox eventually found reliable setup men in righty Mike Timlin and lefty Alan Embree, who returned from the disabled list.

The first six games of the ALCS featured more subplots than a daily soap opera, each episode more gripping and twisted than the last. Game three, at

Fenway, featured a round of head-hunting by Pedro, a bench-clearing brawl in which septuagenarian bench coach Don Zimmer rushed Martinez and was thrown to the ground, and a bullpen fracas in which a Red Sox employee and Nelson came to blows. What a contrast between Pedro's histrionics, jawing and gesturing at Jorge Posada in the Yankees' dugout, and Roger Clemens, an "intimidation pitcher" if ever there was one, taking the mound calmly and pitching effectively and without undue emotion, in the same ballpark where a few years before he had been rattled right off the mound, and in 1990 had famously erupted at an umpire. The Yankees beat Pedro that day and also beat the Sox' number two starter, Derek Lowe, in both of his starts.

The man they couldn't seem to beat was Tim Wakefield. Wakefield was a true knuckleball pitcher, who often threw as much as 85 percent knucklers in a game. He also was the Red Sox with the longest tenure, having come to the team in 1995 as a minor league free agent, and by 2003 was seventh on the Sox' all-time appearances list for pitchers, creeping up on Clemens, Bill Lee, and Cy Young himself. He also had tallied his 100th win as a Sox, putting him in the company of Smoky Joe Wood, Luis Tiant, and of course Clemens and Young. In his time with Boston, Wakefield had been asked to start, close, be a swing man, spot start, and mop up, sometimes all in the same month. With the low-stress action the knuckler put on his arm, though, Wake could do all that without pain or worry. In 2003, with backup Doug Mirabelli assigned to be his personal catcher, Wakefield spent the season in the rotation, going 11–7 with a 4.09 ERA. Not exactly lights out, until it came to the Yankees in October. Wakefield was the game one starter—Martinez and Lowe both having pitched in the final game against Oakland—and held the Yankees to two runs while the Red Sox walloped three homers at Yankee Stadium for a 5–2 win. In game four the Red Sox' normally explosive offense was held to three runs—but Wakefield held the Yankees to two, again. When the Yankees' offense finally did break through, scoring six runs in game six, the Sox logjam let loose as well, winning the game 9–6. Nomar Garciaparra, who had been struggling, went 4-for-5.

So each team struggled for dominance, so closely matched that they had split the season series 10–9 (Yankees), and each had scored 24 runs in the ALCS; there could be no other fate than for it to come down to a winner-take-all elimination game. Not only that, but for it to be a matchup of "Cy Young versus Cy Old," as Martinez faced Clemens, the first ever matchup of Cy Young Award winners in a game seven situation. "It's a high-wire act," said Torre of the night's drama in his pregame press conference. "It's always that way when you play the Red Sox, but when you realize it's October and the winner of this game goes to the World Series, that drains you. It's fun. It really is fun, but you don't know it's fun until it's over with."

Game seven came on a chilly Thursday night in New York City. A water main break in nearby Washington Heights snarled traffic, and some players had to be helped in with police escort. One of them was Jason Giambi, who arrived to find himself dropped to seventh in the batting order. Not because he was late, but because he had been pressing. "Jason has been struggling," manager Joe Torre explained to the press corps. "He just feels a great deal of responsibility. I just sense that he's taken on more than any one person needs to take on and I just thought I'd drop him in the lineup." Shaking up his lineup had been a Torre method since the 1996 World Series, and it often worked wonders to spur an offense. "Of course, I'll probably find him [up] with the bases loaded twice," Torre added wryly. "But that's the way it goes."

As if there were not already enough drama associated with the game, how about the fact that Roger Clemens had announced his retirement prior to the season? For several months he had been in pursuit of his 300th win, and every place the Yankees played became a stop on the Clemens farewell tour. If the Yankees did not win this game, this would be his good-bye to Yankee Stadium as well. He took the mound for his warm-up pitches after his customary trip to Babe Ruth's monument, where he would wipe a little of the sweat off his own brow onto the Babe's before every start. The Stadium was primed, packed to the rafters as always in October with cheering, screaming fans.

Clemens dealt a strike to leadoff man Johnny Damon, and the din became a roar that did not abate during the half inning. The Rocket was reaching 94 miles per hour on the radar gun with regularity. Although Todd Walker, the Sox' slugging second baseman, singled to right, Clemens retired Nomar and Manny on harmless flies to right.

When Pedro came out of the Red Sox dugout, the booing from the crowd was intense and sustained. He walked slowly at first, his face expressionless but his gait stiff. Then he broke into a jog and took his place on the hill. He held his bright red glove in front of his face as he set himself for his warm-up pitches. In game three he had thrown far too many curveballs and his velocity was low, not the Pedro that people hoped to see. He had spent time on the disabled list with a sore shoulder earlier in the year, but insisted that his arm did not hurt.

He began the game throwing softly, dropping in a 71-mile-per-hour curveball and getting two quick strikes on Alfonso Soriano before missing with three straight balls. Soriano was a bright and rising star for the Yankees, a lithe, mahogany-skinned Dominican who had converted to second base (from shortstop) when Chuck Knoblauch had been moved from the position. Soriano could sometimes be brick-handed in the field, but even with his free-swinging ways, his hitting was too good to do without. In 2001 he had nearly been World Series MVP, and in 2002 had almost become only the fourth 40–40 player in major league history. (He hit 39 home runs and stole 42 bases.) But in 2003 his weakness seemed to be an inability to lay off pitches low and away. Pedro threw a pitch at 89 miles per hour, low and away, and Soriano missed it; one out.

Next up was Nick Johnson, in every way Soriano's opposite. The pasty-faced, barrel-chested Johnson was a slick fielder and the ultimate in patience at the plate. Pedro's second pitch to him was up and in, eliciting boos and gasps from the crowd. He walked him on five pitches, the last of which appeared to get away from him, prompting Joe Buck to state on the Fox television broadcast, "We have yet to see anything resembling a good fastball from Pedro Martinez."

But Pedro, for all his prowess as a fastballer, had always had a lethal circle change and curve, and was always a smart pitcher. He busted Derek Jeter inside and got a weak pop to first for the second out. Bernie Williams swung at the first pitch late and just got a hot grounder past the dive of Bill Mueller into the opposite field. But with a full count on Hideki Matsui, Martinez suddenly found some zip, pouring a 93-mile-per-hour fastball over the plate that Matsui popped up to center.

Clemens was not so lucky in the second. After getting David Ortiz out on a fly to center, Clemens faced Kevin Millar. Millar rapped a ball into the gap in right center that Bernie Williams cut off to hold Millar to a single. Up next was Trot Nixon. Nixon, a Durham, North Carolina, native, had been picked by the Sox in the first round of the 1993 draft. A left-handed batter, he had joined the big club for good in 1999 but found his ability to hit left-handed pitching often questioned. In 2003, with manager Grady Little's faith behind him, he had a career year, hitting .306 with 28 home runs.

One thing that was never in question was Nixon's ability to hit Clemens. In regular-season play he was 13 for 35 (.371), with seven walks and three home runs off the Rocket. Roger missed the strike zone with his first two pitches and then left one up in the zone—the ball disappeared into the right-field bleachers, and the thousands of Red Sox fans who had made the trip could suddenly be heard cheering. Clemens did not let it bother him. He came back to strike out batting champ Bill Mueller on a splitter that dove sharply down. With two out and two in, Jason Varitek came to the plate. He lined a shot into right field, digging for second to test platoon outfielder Karim Garcia's arm. Garcia's arm was strong—as it turned out, too strong—and he overthrew second, allowing Varitek to slide in easily. Now Clemens faced the pesky Johnny Damon. He thought he was out of the inning as a ground ball went to third base.

In midseason the Yankees had traded for third baseman Aaron Boone, who was run out of Cincinnati when his father was let go as manager. Since coming to the Yankees, Boone had slumped, playing solid defense but looking lost at the plate. Instead, playing third that night was Enrique Wilson, a utility infielder for the Yankees who, defying all logic, seemed to have Pedro's number. In his career, Wilson batted .500 against Martinez, and in the 2003 season he was 7-for-8. Wilson also was normally quite sure in the field, but this time he scooped up the grounder and threw a tailer that bounced on the first-base line and into the camera well by the Yankees' dugout. Varitek was granted home, bringing in an unearned run. Clemens escaped further trouble when Walker grounded to first.

Martinez went back to work, inducing Jorge Posada to pop up to center, then coming back from a 3–0 count on Jason Giambi to strike him out with high heat. Enrique Wilson lofted a high pop into left, almost out of play, but Manny Ramirez tracked it down in foul ground. Pedro still didn't look like the Pedro of old, but the result was the same: no runs, no hits, no errors, no men left. Clemens followed with a one-two-three of his own, throwing a cut fastball to some batters, but Pedro was even more settled into a groove now, getting pop-ups to center from Garcia and Johnson and striking out Soriano for the second time.

When Clemens came out for the fourth inning, he threw one pitch to Kevin Millar, who walloped it out of the park. Behind the plate, Posada pounded his glove in anger as Millar made contact, knowing it was gone the moment he hit it. In the Yankees' dugout, pitching coach Mel Stottlemyre picked up the bullpen phone, and Mike Mussina began to warm up.

Mussina, ever a model of consistency and implacability on the mound, had been told by Torre and Stottlemyre that he might be needed during the game. "[Mike]'s a professional," said bullpen coach Rich Monteleone. "He knew we were drained down there in the bullpen. But Mel had said, you know, we'll only bring you in to start an inning."

But Clemens then walked Nixon, prompting a long visit from Stottlemyre to the mound. The next batter was Mueller. Two times in the series Grady Little had put on a hit-and-run play, only to run into a strike-'em-out, throw-'em-out double play. This time, though, it worked to perfection, Jeter moving over to cover second and Mueller shooting the ball right through the vacated hole. Now there were men on the corners and no outs. This time it was Torre who came out of the dugout. "When I took Roger out, it was no shock to him," Torre told reporters later. "He knew, obviously, that he wasn't as good as he normally is or wanted to be." Clemens left to an ovation much like the one he had garnered back in 1999, although this time the situation was more dire.

Mussina had made 400 appearances as a pitcher in his career to that point, none of them in relief. For years he had been a victim of poor run support in Baltimore, and his first year in New York he had also. Against Minnesota in the ALDS he had been the hard-luck loser as well, prompting him to comment, "I can only control 60 feet, 6 inches," a comment some in the media took as a criticism of his teammates but that few teammates did. He faced Varitek with his usual aplomb, bending down for a peek at the runner on first as he came set, then controlling 60 feet, 6 inches masterfully. Varitek struck out on a tight knuckle curve. Jeter visited the mound before Damon's at-bat. Damon, a known speedster, could be hard to double up, but the infield did not play in to cut off the run; they played at double-play depth. Moose put two quick strikes on Damon, who then hit a hard one-hopper right to Jeter, who crossed the bag himself and nipped the runner at first. Moose pumped his fist and shouted in a rare display of emotion. "If they get a couple of runs there, it's huge. He did a tremendous job," said Monteleone of his temporary charge.

But if there was a swing of momentum, the Yankees could not capitalize on it. Although Matsui doubled with two out, Pedro had struck out Williams with a 94-mile-per-hour heater, and when Posada grounded to first, Martinez was out of the inning quickly. He had thrown almost 60 pitches but appeared to be getting stronger as time went on, regaining his velocity and mixing his pitches without hesitation. Mussina allowed two hits in the fifth, but stranded the two men harmlessly.

Jason Giambi led off the fifth. He had not batted as low as seventh in any lineup since July 1999. Now he stood in against Pedro, waggling the bat in the fashion of his mentor, Mark McGwire. Giambi guessed that Martinez might start him with a changeup. He guessed right, waiting on the pitch and then driving it to deep right center, into the bleachers. The Stadium crowd came to life again, drowning out the celebratory music and Giambi's own teammates' congratulations. Pedro came back to get Wilson on a fly to left and to strike out Garcia and Soriano—Sori for the third time. But a crack had appeared in the armor, and Joe Torre could be seen with a small, very small, smile on his face in the dugout. "Against Pedro, anytime you can break through initially, I think that's what sort of opens the door," Torre explained. "[Giambi] was responsible for us to get that feeling again, that 'We can do this.'"

Mussina returned for a one-two-three, aided by a stellar defensive play from

Wilson and a strikeout of Nixon on a split-finger fastball. Pedro cruised through the bottom of the sixth as well, striking out Jeter. The top of the seventh brought lefty Felix Heredia out of the bullpen. The night before, Heredia had been brought in to face Damon lefty-on-lefty with the bases loaded and the game tied, but had walked him. This time he faced Damon again, and this time all he threw were strikes. Damon managed to foul one off, but then swung at a fastball away for strike three. Heredia retired Walker on a pop into foul territory on the third-base side and then gave way to Jeff Nelson, who faced Nomar Garciaparra.

In his earlier stint with the Yankees, Nelson had often aggravated Torre and Stottlemyre for relying too much on his slider and not using his fastball to set it up and get ahead in the count. But Nelson knew the slider was his best pitch. He threw all sliders to Nomar, four in a row to make the count 2–2, and then a fifth, which broke into the left-handed batter's box as Nomar flailed at it to seal the strikeout. It was time for the seventh-inning stretch.

At Yankee Stadium, after the tragedies of September 11, they instituted a tradition of singing "God Bless America" in addition to "Take Me Out to the Ball Game." In the regular season the song was prerecorded, but in the postseason it was done with great pomp and circumstance, sung nightly by "The Irish Tenor" Ronan Tynan. In the 2003 postseason in particular, the moving sound of the Stadium crowd singing in unison with the soaring vocals seemed to have an invigorating effect on the Yankees—or perhaps an enervating one on the opposing pitcher, who had to stand for five extra minutes before warming up. For whatever reason, the seventh inning had become the hot offensive inning for the Yankees at the Stadium. They had scored seven runs in the seventh there in October, more than any other inning. The crowd buzzed with anticipation, but Matsui grounded to second on the first pitch, and Posada flew harmlessly to center. That brought Jason Giambi to the plate. This time no changeups—Pedro buzzed Giambi at 93 and 95 miles per hour. Same result, though, as Giambi connected with a 2–2 fastball and sent it into deep center, his third home run in two days, cutting the Boston lead to two runs. Wilson followed with a single when Kevin Millar's feet went out from under him as he fielded the ball, and Garcia another as the crowd taunt-chanted "Pe-dro, Pe-dro." Mariano Rivera, perhaps the best closer of all time and certainly the best postseason pitcher of all time, began to warm up in case the Yankees took the lead. Pitching coach Dave Wallace made a visit to the mound to break up the rhythm of the inning, but standing in the batter's box was Soriano. Alfonso was ready for his fourth strikeout of the night, which ended the rally.

The eighth inning opened with Nelson on the mound and Manny Ramirez at the plate. He went to 3–0 on the league's second-best hitter, and then Manny squibbed a ball toward third. Wilson gloved it quickly and threw in one motion, an excellent play to nab Manny at first. With lefthander David Ortiz coming up, the Yankees drew another ace, David Wells (who was back with the Yankees for another tour of duty after Toronto and the Chicago White Sox). Unfortunately, Wells hung a curveball on his first pitch, and Ortiz banged it into the right-field seats. Wells reacted with an emphatic and easily readable expletive, but retired Millar and Nixon easily. The Yankees were chasing three runs again, and they were running out of time.

Pedro came out to start the eighth, but statistical wisdom and the method the Sox had used to "preserve" his health for years dictated that he never threw much beyond 100 to 110 pitches. Only five times in 2003 had he pitched the eighth inning. Mike Timlin and Alan Embree were warming in the Boston bullpen. In the postseason the bullpen had been stellar, with a combined ERA of 1.17 and opposing batters hitting only .173 against them. Neither Timlin nor Embree had given up a run, Timlin only one hit. But they were spectators as Pedro kept at it. He faced Johnson first, who turned in a seven-pitch at-bat, though he popped up to short. Next came Jeter. He had a big cut at the first offering for strike one, then fouled another for strike two. Pedro went for the kill with a high fastball, but Jeter got the bat head behind it and laced the ball into right field. With his inside-out swing, the ball hooked away from Nixon and went over his head, a double.

As Bernie came to the plate, Boston's bullpen was ready, both the righty Timlin and the lefty Embree taking occasional tosses but mostly standing and watching the action. The metallic clanging of Freddie the Fan's spoon banging on his good-luck pan echoed above the buzz of the Stadium crowd. Bernie worked the count to 2–2. Pedro threw his 115th pitch of the night and Bernie served it into center, Jeter scoring easily.

Grady Little came out of the dugout, and every observer of the game, from the youngest fans to the most jaded reporters, knew he was going out to get his ace and turn the game over to the bullpen before things got out of hand. Grady was on the mound for fewer than ten seconds before he patted Pedro on the shoulder . . .

And returned to the dugout without him. Tim McCarver, while announcing the game on Fox TV, called it "the most blatant situation for a second-guess in this series." But Pedro had asked to stay in, and the manager respected him. He was still hitting the mid-nineties on the radar gun, had seemed to get stronger as the game went on. And both Pedro and Grady had been burned in bullpen meltdowns many times that season, though not recently. Pedro stayed in to try to be the savior Boston had always wanted him to be, to mint a championship team the way the Yankees of 1996 were minted when Joe Torre left David Cone in to face Atlanta with a precarious two-run lead, and he won the game. Isn't this what they were "preserving" his arm for in all those 100-pitch starts over the years?

Matsui stepped into the box. The "rookie," playing his first year in the American major leagues, had been Japan's biggest star on Japan's highest-profile team, the Yomiuri Giants. With his calm batting stance, a shrug of his front shoulder keeping him relaxed, Matsui had faced situations like this before. A home run would tie the game, but all year Matsui had eschewed big power numbers in favor of fundamental baseball, moving the runner and racking up RBI (106) and hits (179). Pedro had him down 0–2 and Matsui turned on an inside pitch. It bounced just fair inside first and then up into the fans for a ground-rule double, moving Bernie Williams to third, a lucky hit but not lucky enough to bring the runner home.

It would take Posada to provide that, muscling a flare into center field that just dropped in the middle of the converging center fielder, shortstop, and second baseman. Bernie and Matsui scampered home as Yankees poured out of their dugout, shouting and waving them in. Jubilant pandemonium broke loose in the stands. Posada ran all the way to second, since no one was left in the neighborhood to cover the bag. The game was tied. With Giambi coming up with a chance to hit a third home run, Grady Little would not tempt fate any longer. This time Pedro took the walk to the dugout while Embree took the hill.

Lefty-on-lefty, Embree induced Giambi to fly out to center on a 97-mile-per-hour pitch that shattered the bat into several pieces. He then gave way to Timlin, but with Pedro out of the game, Enrique Wilson was lifted for pinch hitter Ruben Sierra. Sierra was intentionally walked, bringing up Karim Garcia. Garcia walked to load the bases, bringing Soriano to the plate for his fifth at-bat, his second with a chance to break the game open. This time Sori smashed a ball the opposite way, but Todd Walker left his feet in a full body dive to snare it and flipped to Nomar for the force at second.

And so to the ninth. Mariano Rivera came in to the strains of "Enter Sandman," a heavy-metal anthem the scoreboard operations crew had picked for him back when he had become the closer for the team in 1997. A tall, slim, soft-spoken Panamanian, Rivera could throw a variety of pitches, a four-seamer, a two-seamer, and a cutter, but for the most part whenever he came into a game, he threw the cutter. "I don't think there's ever been a pitcher who has existed with one pitch, one speed, one location, pitch after pitch, until

Mo," said former pitcher Jim Kaat, then a broadcaster with the Yankees. "Year after year. And they haven't been able to catch up to him." By 2003 he had racked up 283 saves, 582 strikeouts, and innumerable dribbling hits and bloops. His career ERA stood at 2.49 but in 2003 it was a career-best 1.66. In the postseason he was even better. Coming into this game, his postseason ERA was a minuscule 0.72 with 28 saves, 6 wins, and only 2 blown saves.

One other change took place for the Yankees. With Wilson lifted for a pinch hitter, a new third baseman was needed. And so Aaron Boone came off the bench.

Mo dealt his cutter with a deceptively easy motion, and the ball would suddenly explode upon the batter. On the third pitch of his at-bat, Mueller swung defensively and grounded the ball to second. Varitek also grounded the ball but through the hole at first. Damon was up there hacking, fouling off pitches, but grounded right to Boone, and Walker hit a looping liner that Soriano leaped to catch. Mo leaped on the mound in time with him, clicking his heels together in a rare show of excitement.

But Timlin retired the Yankees easily in the bottom of the ninth, and so the game went to extra innings. Mariano caught Nomar looking, got Manny to ground to second, and although Ortiz doubled, Millar popped up to short. The bottom of the tenth began at the stroke of midnight, and this time it was the man who had been the Yankees' nemesis the whole series, Tim Wakefield, on the hill. Wakefield, with his free and easy knuckler, could pitch several innings without a problem.

The Yankees had only three men left in their bullpen. José Contreras and Gabe White had been used several times in the series, including the day before, and were available only in an emergency. Jeff Weaver, a young starter who had lost his slot in the rotation to the veteran from Cuba, Contreras, also was available, but he had not pitched since September. Mel Stottlemyre told Andy Pettitte to go put on his spikes. If the Yankees didn't take it in the bottom of the tenth, Mo could go one more inning, but that would be all. Rivera had not pitched three complete innings since September 1996.

The Yankees did not score off Wakefield in the tenth. Matsui grounded to first; Posada lined into center, where Damon made a nice play on a ball hit right at him; and Giambi drew gasps from the crowd on one deep but foul down the right-field line before flying out to left.

Mariano came out for his third inning, and threw strike one, strike two, to Nixon. He had thrown 39 pitches to that point. His 40th, though, was way high, Posada coming out of his crouch to grab it. The next one was way inside, evening the count at 2–2. Posada banged his mitt as if to say "Stop fooling around." The next pitch poured right into the strike zone and Nixon just stared at it, caught looking. Bill Mueller didn't wait that long for a good pitch to hit. He hacked at the first one, squibbed it off the end of the bat, and was out on a ground ball to second. Then came Doug Mirabelli. He had entered the game in the ninth, after Varitek had been replaced by a pinch runner. Wakefield's personal catcher had come up with surprising hits at opportune times on several occasions during the season. Not this time. Looking completely overmatched, he had two strikes on him before he could react. He swung at the third, low and cutting away from him, and didn't come near it. Mo's three innings were done. Pettitte was on his way to the bullpen. And Wakefield was settling in for a marathon.

He threw his eight warm-up pitches and then faced Boone. Boone had hit only .254 for the Yankees during the regular season, and in the ALCS, he had gotten only two hits (.125). The third-generation major leaguer, younger brother to Seattle's Bret Boone, had never gotten his feet under him in New York.

One pitch later, they barely touched the ground. Wakefield threw a knuckler that spun over rather than skipping or dancing to the plate, and Boone put an entire season's frustrations behind one swing. He pulled the home run ten rows into the left-field seats, threw his arms up into the air, and floated around the bases. By the time he reached home plate, the team was there, leaping up and down with him. Mariano had run out to the mound, where he collapsed in hysterics, first-base coach Lee Mazzilli trying in vain to lift his limp form. Eventually third-base coach Willie Randolph helped to heave the drained closer upright, and he joined the hugfest going on all over the field. Joe Torre, as usual, cried. "For three innings, I was waiting for Manny to turn his back and see a ball go into the stands. It finally happened," Joe said. "This is the best. Taking nothing away from Paul O'Neill's teams or Tino's teams or Brosius, Knoblauch or Girardi, David Cone, Jimmy Key, John Wetteland, my first year, taking nothing away from those teams, to come here and play against the Red Sox, and play them 26 times and beat our rival like we did, it couldn't be more satisfying. This has to be the sweetest taste of all for me."

Wakefield had not even turned to look. As soon as his foot came down from his follow-through, before the ball had even reached the peak of its flight, he had started his walk to the dugout.

Boone found it hard to speak in complete sentences. "Great . . . silver lining . . . uh," he began as the television crews circled him. "Derek told me the ghosts would show up eventually." Clemens and Wells later rounded up Mel Stottlemyre for a pilgrimage to commune with those ghosts, taking a toast out to Monument Park to have a cold one with the Babe. "He's shining on us, he's looking down," said Wells, who had once bought an authentic game-worn Babe Ruth cap at auction and wore it in a game at the Stadium. "Why not give him a toast, man? He's the one that got us here. From 1918 till now—the curse lives."

Extra Innings

* Jinxed? The Boston grounds crew, in anticipation of the World Series, had already painted the World Series logo on the grass at Fenway Park before game seven took place.

* Boone's was the tenth walk-off home run in New York Yankees postseason history, dating back to Tommy Henrich's belt off Don Newcombe in the 1949 World Series against the Dodgers.

* Bernie Williams is the only Yankee to have hit two walk-off homers in the playoffs, both in extra innings and both in the opening game of a series. In the 1996 ALCS he did it to Baltimore's Randy Myers in the eleventh inning, and in the 1999 ALCS he did it to Boston's Rod Beck in the tenth inning.

* Did Andy Pettitte put his cleats on to pitch the twelfth inning, if necessary? "Oh, yeah. Andy was down in the bullpen. He had just gotten down to the bullpen when we won the game," said Rich Monteleone, Yankees' bullpen coach.

* Much to everyone's surprise, perhaps even his own, Roger Clemens unretired during the winter of 2003–2004, and returned to pitch for his hometown Houston Astros in the 2004 season. There he joined fellow Texan Andy Pettitte in the rotation. Pettitte and Clemens had become close friends during their tenure with the Yankees together, and when Pettitte signed with Houston to be closer to his own wife and kids, he lobbied Clemens to think about doing the same. Clemens then won his seventh Cy Young Award, at age 42 the oldest man to do so.

The 50 Greatest Games Ranked 1 to 50

How I Ranked the 50 Greatest

When I first set out to choose the 50 greatest games in the New York Yankees' history, I didn't think I would be ranking them. I considered more than 100 games, and one can make compelling arguments for each one of them to be included. As such, trying to arrange the games in some strict fashion, quantifying the "greatness" of each one, seemed like an impossible exercise. While I was writing the book, I created a Web site where fans could post their memories of great games and debate my choices. Ultimately, I chose 49 games myself and let the fans nominate and vote on number 50. (By popular vote, they chose Roger Clemens's one-hitter in the ALCS.) All the debate kept me thinking about the question of ranking. Some games were obvious candidates for the "Top 10," but could I say why? Historical significance? Excitement factor?

Baseball being a game that mixes statistical knowledge with intuition, I decided to combine a numerical ranking system with my own gut feelings to create the final rank. I assigned each game a score from 1 to 5 on nine different criteria:

- How well remembered is this game?
- What was this game's overall historical significance?
- Were any records set or broken, and how many?
- Did this game involve interesting characters in Yankee history or an interesting back story?
- Was this game part of a meaningful pennant race or postseason?
- Did this game involve bizarre twists of fate or unbelievable luck?
- Was the rivalry with the Red Sox a factor?
- What was the excitement level for the fans in the stands or those following the game at home?
- Was this game often nominated or voted for in my polls?

I then knocked points off for the games that had any ignominy, such as Ruth being caught stealing to end the game, and Andy Hawkins's no-hitter in which the Yankees lost, 4–0. The final phase then was moving some games up or down the list according to my purely subjective feelings that one game was greater than another. The game that scored the highest, Don Larsen's perfect game, scored a 32. Hawkins's negated no-hitter scored only 8.

   #1. October 8, 1956: Don Larsen's perfect game

   #2. October 1, 1932: Babe Ruth's "called shot"

   #3. October 2, 1978: Bucky Dent's home run

   #4. October 5, 1941: Tommy Henrich reaches on passed ball

   #5. October 16, 1962: Ralph Terry redeemed

   #6. October 7, 1952: Billy Martin caught foul pop

   #7. October 13, 2001: the "Jeter flip" game

   #8. October 2, 1949: DiMaggio's flu, still beats Boston

   #9. October 16, 2003: Aaron Boone's walk-off homer

 #10. October 8, 1995: Mattingly's swan song

 #11. June 29, 1941: DiMaggio passes Sisler on the way to 56

 #12. October 14, 1976: Chris Chambliss's sudden-death home run

 #13. September 20, 1961: Maris races Ruth to #59

 #14. October 23, 1996: Jim Leyritz's home run off Wohlers

 #15. October 10, 1904: Jack Chesbro's "wild pitch" game

 #16. October 6, 1977: Reggie Jackson's three-homer game

 #17. October 3, 1947: Bill Bevens one out away from World Series no-hitter

 #18. July 18, 1999: David Cone's perfect game

 #19. May 17, 1998: David Wells's perfect game

 #20. May 14, 1996: Dwight Gooden's no-hitter

 #21. October 4, 1955: Tommy Byrne game seven heartbreaker

 #22. July 12, 1951: Allie Reynolds's no-hitter vs. Bob Feller

 #23. October 14, 2000: Roger Clemens's one-hitter in ALCS

 #24. October 10, 1964: Jim Bouton wins 2–1 on Mantle walk-off

 #25. July 4, 1983: Dave Righetti's no-hitter

 #26. April 24, 1917: George Mogridge's no-hitter

 #27. September 4, 1923: Sad Sam Jones no-hitter

 #28. August 27, 1938: Monte Pearson's no-hitter, 10th consecutive win

 #29. October 13, 1960: Mazeroski's walk-off homer

 #30. September 28, 1951: Allie Reynolds's second no-hitter

 #31. September 4, 1993: Jim Abbott's no-hitter

#32. August 6, 1979: game after Thurman Munson's funeral

#33. October 9, 1977: ALCS rematch with Kansas City

#34. July 25, 1912: Bert Daniels hits for the cycle

#35. October 8, 1961: Whitey Ford breaks Ruth's scoreless innings record

#36. June 3, 1932: Lou Gehrig hits four home runs

#37. July 26, 1928: Yanks score 11 runs in the twelfth; Bob Meusel hits for the cycle (third time in his career)

#38. May 20, 1948: Joe DiMaggio hits for the cycle (second time in his career)

#39. September 30, 1984: Don Mattingly 4-for-5 to win batting title

#40. July 23, 1957: Mickey Mantle hits for the cycle

#41. August 29, 1972: Bobby Murcer hits for the cycle

#42. July 6, 1920: 14 runs in a single inning (set team record)

#43. October 5, 1921: first World Series game in Yankee history

#44. October 10, 1926: Ruth caught stealing to end World Series

#45. September 3, 1995: Tony Fernandez hits for the cycle

#46. August 1, 1937: Lou Gehrig hits for the cycle

#47. July 24 and August 18, 1983: the "pine tar" game

#48. July 19, 1940: Buddy Rosar hits for the cycle

#49. September 8, 1940: Joe Gordon hits for the cycle

#50. July 1, 1990: Andy Hawkins's no-hitter, but lost, 4–0

The "Other" 50 Greatest Games

The fifty games that weren't included . . .

April 30, 1903 The Yankees play their first game ever in New York, one small step for a team, one "giant" step for the American League. Jack Chesbro wins 6–2 over Washington.

August 16, 1920 Not a "great" game, but a historically significant one. Carl Mays hits Ray Chapman with a pitch, the only major league pitch to kill the batter. (Chapman dies in the hospital the next day, and the Yankees lose the game to the Indians, 4–3.)

September 26, 1921 Pennant race, Yankees beat Cleveland, 8–7, in the rain, behind a great long relief job by Waite Hoyt and a save by Mays. Ruth homers twice, and Yankees go ahead of the Indians by two games.

October 5, 1922 World Series game two, the Yankees play the Giants to a standstill, literally, as the game ends in a 3–3 tie when umpires call the game with 45 minutes of daylight still remaining. Every game of the series was at the Polo Grounds, since it was home to both clubs.

April 18, 1923 Opening day at the newly built Yankee Stadium, Ruth hits the first homer in the house that he "built" and leads the Yankees to a win.

October 15, 1923 Casey Stengel was an outfielder for the Giants in this World Series and hit the first Series homer in Yankee Stadium—an inside-the-park home run in game one—but ultimately the Yankees prevailed in six games, coming back to win 6–4 from 4–1 down in the clincher.

September 27, 1927 Ruth hits home run number 60 on the year, capping a feat that would stand as a record until 1961 and that was nearly beyond belief at the time.

October 5, 1927 World Series game one, in which the Yankees' "Murderers' Row"—possibly the greatest team ever—had beat Pittsburgh before the Bombers even finished batting practice.

September 9, 1928 Doubleheader sweep for the Yanks over the Athletics, 5–0 and 7–3. Game two was tied in the eighth before Meusel hit a grand slam to win it. New York had blown a long lead over the summer, at least

13 games, and Philadelphia had gone briefly ahead of them, but after the series in New York, the Yankees went on to win the pennant.

October 9, 1928   World Series game four, Ruth hit three homers in a game to sweep the Cardinals and get revenge for Alexander's defeat of them in 1926.

September 25, 1929   On the day that Miller Huggins dies of blood poisoning in a New York hospital, the Yankees are playing the Red Sox at Fenway Park and leading 7–3 when they hear the news. The Yankees immediately give up seven runs, but somehow manage to battle back to win the game.

October 2, 1933   Babe Ruth, rotund and known exclusively as a hitter for more than a decade, pitches for the final time in a major league game. In fact, he pitches the complete game and wins it 6–5! Against the Red Sox!

October 2, 1936   World Series game two, when Tony Lazzeri hits only the second grand slam in Series history. Yanks win, 18–4. It is still the highest-scoring game for a single team in World Series history.

October 6, 1937   World Series game one, the Yankees finally get to the Giants' Carl Hubbell, who beat them the year before in the opener.

July 29, 1938   Spud Chandler pitches 15 innings (!) as the Yankees beat the White Sox, 7–3. Chandler would retire in 1947 with the highest winning percentage (.717) of any pitcher with 100 or more victories.

October 2, 1938   World Series game two, Dizzy Dean, in his last stand with the Cubs, fends off the Yanks for 7 innings with junk, but they finally get him in the end.

July 3, 1939   On Lou Gehrig Day at the Stadium, the Iron Horse proclaims himself the "luckiest man on the face of the Earth." And then the Yankees had to play a ball game.

October 8, 1939   World Series game four, the "Lombardi snooze." In which DiMaggio scores the Series-clinching run in the ninth, after hitting a single, but the catcher gets knocked silly by Charlie Keller on a play at the plate, allowing Joe D. to come all the way around. Joe McCarthy also wins his tenth straight World Series game as manager.

October 5, 1949   World Series game one, in which Allie Reynolds outpitched the Dodgers' Don Newcombe, 1–0. Tommy Henrich hit a walk-off home run for the only run.

April 18, 1950   Opening Day, the Yankees faced the Red Sox, and after having beaten the Sox for the pennant on the final day of 1949, both teams were itching for a rematch. The Yankees had a huge comeback from down 9–0 to beat the Sox, 15–10, once again! (Also Billy Martin's major league debut; he had two hits in one *inning*.)

September 17, 1951 Yanks 2, Cleveland 1. DiMaggio scores the winning run on a squeeze bunt by Rizzuto—possibly the best bunter of his generation. Bob Lemon fields the ball and throws it in the stands in disgust, having no chance to catch Joe D. at the plate.

October 8, 1951 World Series game four, a rookie pitcher named Ed Ford (later known as Whitey) pitches a shutout in his first Series appearance, putting the "Whiz Kid" Phillies away. This is also the series where Mickey steps in the drain.

October 5, 1953 World Series game six, Billy Martin drives in the winning run to clinch the Series. He gets 12 hits and bats .500 in the Series.

September 30, 1956 Mickey Mantle wins the Triple Crown at age 24 with a .353 average, 52 home runs, and 130 RBI.

October 9, 1958 World Series game seven, in which the Braves try to beat the Yankees for the second year in a row, but the Yankees rise up and snatch victory in the deciding game seven. Joe Torre is at first base for the Braves in that game.

September 1, 1961 The Tigers come to New York only 1½ games behind in the pennant race. Whitey Ford faces Don Mossi but cannot go deep in the game because of injury, but three successive singles in the ninth inning by Bill Skowron, Elston Howard, and Hector Lopez give screwballing bullpen ace Luis Arroyo the 1–0 victory.

May 17, 1963 Against the A's, Mickey Mantle hits a game-winner in the ninth that hits the upper-deck facade, the closest a fair ball ever came to being hit out of the Stadium. (On the same day 39 years later, Jason Giambi would hit a walk-off in even more dramatic circumstances.)

October 2, 1963 World Series game one, the one-two punch of Sandy Koufax and Don Drysdale stymie the Yankees, who had won 104 games that year. But hey, Koufax struck out 15 in game one.

August 25, 1968 Bronx native Rocky Colavito becomes the only Yankee position player to earn a pitching win when he beats the Tigers in relief. Rocky also scores the winning run after a walk.

October 19, 1976 World Series game three. Do you remember Jim Mason? He came on for the Yankees as a defensive replacement, and hit a home run in the seventh. It was the Yankees' only homer in the Series, in which the Big Red Machine dominated, and it was the only Series at-bat in Mason's career.

June 17, 1978   Ron Guidry, in the most dominating season for a pitcher in his era, strikes out 18 batters and creates a new tradition at Yankee Stadium: the two-strike clap.

October 6, 1978   ALCS game three, against Kansas City, George Brett hits three homers off Catfish Hunter, but Thurman Munson's huge two-run shot in the eighth inning makes it a 6–5 Yankee win.

October 13, 1978   World Series game three, Graig Nettles puts on a clinic at third base, stifling the Dodgers and swinging the momentum to the Yankees after they had lost the first two games.

October 13, 1981   ALCS game one, some of the weirdest playoffs in history thanks to the strike, but Tommy John (he of the reconstructed elbow) pitches the Yankees to a 3–1 win over the A's.

October 6, 1985   On the final day of the season, ancient knuckleballer Phil Niekro wins his 300th game and he does it in pinstripes, 8–0 over the Blue Jays.

October 4, 1995   ALDS game two. In the fifteenth inning at Yankee Stadium, the King, Jim Leyritz, launches an uncanny postseason reputation with the game-winning home run against the Mariners.

October 9, 1996   ALCS game one, in which Derek Jeter is aided by an eager fan to a home run, but Bernie Williams is the one who hits the walk-off in the eleventh inning to beat the Orioles.

October 24, 1996   World Series game five, Andy Pettitte pitches a 1–0 gem against the Braves and John Smoltz to give the Yankees a 3–2 lead in the Series. This after having given up seven runs in game one.

October 5, 1997   ALDS game four. A dark moment in Yankee history, when Mariano Rivera gave up a home run to the Cleveland Indians' Sandy Alomar in Mo's first year as a big-time closer. The Yankees lost the series, but the team, and Rivera, returned the following year with a vengeance, and Rivera went on to become the best postseason reliever in history.

October 17, 1998   World Series game one, against the Padres. With a seven-run seventh inning, two Yankees find redemption for a misplay in the ALCS, as Chuck Knoblauch hits a three-run homer and Tino Martinez hits a grand slam.

October 26, 1999 World Series game three, in which two relative unknowns (Jason Grimsley out of the bullpen, and Chad Curtis, with two home runs) sink the vaunted Braves.

October 27, 1999 World Series game four, the day Paul O'Neill's father, Chick, passed away, and Roger Clemens dominated the Braves to clinch it.

April 23, 2000 In Toronto, Bernie Williams and Jorge Posada become the first teammates in history to homer from both sides of the plate in the same game. Jorge jokes to Bernie, "Let's make rings."

June 19, 2000 After getting beaten by a huge margin by the White Sox and losing ace Orlando Hernandez to injury, the Yankees come into Fenway Park and beat the Red Sox, 22–1, the most lopsided shellacking in the teams' history.

October 2000 World Series A Subway Series for a whole new generation of Yankee fans. The Mets end up sunk by two utility infielders. In game one, Torre plays José Vizcaino on a hunch, and he gets the game-winning hit in extra innings. In game five, the clincher, Luis Sojo hits a 25-hopper up the middle that seals the deal.

September 2, 2001 In Boston's Fenway Park, Mike Mussina takes a perfect game through 8⅔ innings and has two strikes on Carl Everett when Everett laces a clean single into right. Mussina's opponent that night is former Yankee David Cone.

October 30, 2001, and November 1, 2001 "Mystique and Aura" starring nightly, as the Yankees win two unbelievable World Series games at the Stadium, beating Diamondbacks' closer Byung-Hyun twice, and hitting game-tying or game-winning home runs off him two nights in a row.

May 17, 2002 After giving up three runs in the fourteenth inning to the Twins, the Yankees load the bases in their half, bringing new free agent acquisition Jason Giambi to the plate. In the pouring rain, Giambi hits a grand slam game-winner, the first Yankee to do it since—who else?—Babe Ruth.

June 13, 2003 Roger Clemens undertakes an odyssey trying to win his 300th game, traipsing his family and friends through Boston, Chicago, and elsewhere before finally nailing down not only win 300, but also strikeout 4,000, against the Cardinals.

Acknowledgments

This book would not have come about had my agent, Lori Perkins, not brought up the subject casually during lunch one day when I was in town to see a game at the Stadium. I owe her thanks for believing in me and for giving me many excuses to go to more ball games. Thanks also to my editor at Wiley, Stephen Power, for patience and fortitude and for thinking this book would be as much fun as I did.

The book also would have been much poorer without the support and help of the New York Yankees' Media Relations Department, especially Rick Cerrone, his Tampa staff Stephanie Hall and Michael Margolis, and the inestimable Arthur Richman, who was the first person to make me feel welcome in the dugout several years ago when I was on my very first Yankees-related writing gig. Thanks also to the legendary Tom McEwen, and to all the players and coaches who gave me their time and memories in interviews, letters, and e-mails, including Joe Ausanio, Yogi Berra, Jim Bouton, Tommy Byrne, Bert Campaneris, Jerry Coleman, Bucky Dent, Al Downing, Ryne Duren, Whitey Ford, Joe Girardi, Dwight Gooden, Ron Guidry, Reggie Jackson, Jim Kaat, Phil Linz, Elliott Maddox, Don Mattingly, Gene "Stick" Michael, Rich Monteleone, Bobby Murcer, Graig Nettles, Paul O'Neill, Willie Randolph, Mickey Rivers, Ralph Terry, Tom Tresh, and Roy White.

From the Columbus Clippers organization I had the help of Todd Bell and the outstanding hospitality of club historian Joe Santry—the most fun I ever had during a rainout.

Let's not forget Mom and Dad, who so conveniently lived driving distance from Yankee Stadium when I was a kid, and now from Legends Field in Tampa, where much of the "live research" for this book was conducted. I also must thank some dedicated Yankee fans who have lent both advice as well as their videotapes of games, including David, Jim F., Ron Hallsten, Dan "Knuckles" McCourt, Joseph Riccitelli, Shaky, Phil Speranza, and the gangs at *NYYfans.com* and the Behind the Bombers board of Allsports.com.

In the world of baseball research, history, and statistics, much of the keenest knowledge and most interesting facts are not necessarily found in the library but in the minds of the baseball enthusiasts I have met through the Society for American Baseball Research (SABR). I had input, fact-checking, research help, and moral support from the following folks: Zita Carno, John

Cizik, Rory Costello, Josh Davlin, John Docke, Bruce Fleming, M. Frank, Harvey Frommer, Bob Golon, John Guilfoyle, Charles Hollander, the indefatigable David Horwich, Jonathan Jacobs, Rich Klein, Carl Larsen, David H. Lippman, Brian Mac, Aniello "Neil" Massa, John Matthew IV, Vinny Natale, Bill Nowlin, William Puotinen, Frank Russo, Jeff Sackman, Ryan Schroer, Stuart Shea, Mark Simon, Victor Sloan, David Smith and *Retrosheet.org*, Steve Steinberg, Tom Stillman, Stew Thornley, Bob Timmerman, and Mark Wernick. Any errors remaining in the text are purely mine.

Notes on Research Techniques

For each game presented here, I began my research with newspaper game accounts. For each game I tried to read at least four different newspapers covering the event, two from the home team's city, and two from the visiting team's city. With the New York papers I often chose the dry but factual *New York Times*, and the more colorful *New York Herald Tribune*. I also read every account that was published in the *Sporting News* relating to these fifty games. For many postseason games, I also read the *Washington Post* and *Los Angeles Times* versions. Through these game stories I would try to re-create as accurately as possible a chronological series of events in a game. (I am also greatly indebted to *Retrosheet.org* for providing play-by-play records of many of the games.) All in all I read more than six hundred individual news stories from more than 40 different newspapers. But news accounts can carry one only so far, especially since they can sometimes be inaccurate (perhaps disturbingly often), or may fail to reflect changes in scoring decisions made after deadline. And play-by-play records can be ambiguous—a double that was nearly a home run and just missed clearing the wall is quite a different thing than a hot liner that shoots the gap. So where possible I supplemented my reading with books of baseball history, player biographies, magazine articles, and anything else I could find that might shed light on the game action or players involved.

My next step was to contact as many of the living players as I could. Some declined to be interviewed, but many had just as much fun talking baseball as I did, and their insights into what it was like to play in these games cannot be replaced by other means.

Finally, whenever possible, I listened to archives of radio broadcasts, or watched tapes from television. I wish I could have watched film or tape of every one, because I always found myself noticing things that no newspaper reporter, biographer, or player had bothered to mention previously. I believe it was the long-tenured *Washington Post* baseball writer Thomas Boswell who once wrote that baseball is a game that rewards attention. I have looked at these games as carefully as I could, and though trying to re-create the action is an inexact art, my attention has always been rewarded.

In researching baseball history, I quickly found that even seemingly authoritative sources can differ on the most basic data, including the spelling of players' names and numbers such as batting averages. Thanks to original research done by colleagues such as Bill Nowlin, I have made some choices in the text here that differ from *Total Baseball* and other sources. Among the "corrections" I have made thanks to Bill are spelling Bill Dineen's name with two n's, not three (*Total Baseball* lists him as "Dinneen," yet newspapers of his era preferred Dineen, as do relatives still living in his hometown of Syracuse, New York) and the omission of the nickname "Pilgrims" to stand in for the Boston American League team later known as the Red Sox. There do not seem to be references in contemporary sources naming the team the "Pilgrims" at all, and since this "fact," which one sees repeated in many history books, has been seriously called into question, I won't be one to propagate it.

The most difficult thing for any historian, of any subject, though, is always in reconciling the fact that multiple eyewitnesses will give differing—even conflicting—accounts of what they saw. Add the fact that human memory is fallible, and that many individuals may have a stake in how an event is remembered, and it becomes apparent that the debate over certain things—where did Ruth point? And what did he mean by it at the time?—will never be settled no matter how much research one conducts. Ultimately the stories that are the most compelling are the ones that can be debated, that people are still talking about a century or more after they happened. Repeating those tales while eating peanuts on a sunny day out in the bleachers, or huddled under the upper-deck roof during a rain delay, is what turns the events of history into lore, and lore into myth. I've done my best to uncover all the facts, but in the end what gives these stories their power is their status as lore. Remember that time when Mickey Mantle almost hit a ball out of Yankee Stadium? They say the ball was still rising when it hit the facade. . . . In reality, the Mick performed this feat as many as five times, and the ball was probably near its apex when it hit every time, but knowing that in no way diminishes the legend of Mickey Mantle for me. If anything, the reputations of my heroes have been burnished by all the newspapers I have read, all the people I have talked to, and the accomplishments they are measured by. Yes, Virginia, there really was a Mickey Mantle, a Babe Ruth, a Reggie Jackson. And that's what will keep me hooked on baseball, both the current game and the history: watching the news of today become the lore of tomorrow.

References

Books

Angell, Roger. *A Pitcher's Story: Innings with David Cone.* New York: Warner, 2001.

Baylor, Don, with Claire Smith. *Don Baylor: Nothing but the Truth.* New York: St. Martin's Press, 1989.

Berra, Yogi, with Dave Kaplan. *Ten Rings: My Championship Seasons.* New York: HarperCollins, 2003.

Bouton, Jim. *Ball Four: My Life and Hard Times Throwing the Knuckleball in the Big Leagues.* New York: Dell, 1970.

Bresciani, Dick, and the Boston Red Sox Public Affairs Department. *2002 Boston Red Sox Media Guide.* Boston: Boston Red Sox, 2002.

Cerrone, Richard, et al. *2000 Yankees Information & Record Guide.* New York: New York Yankees, 2000.

———. *2001 Yankees Information & Record Guide.* New York: New York Yankees, 2001.

———. *2002 Yankees Information & Record Guide.* New York: New York Yankees, 2002.

———. *2003 Yankees Information & Record Guide.* New York: New York Yankees, 2003.

———. *2004 Yankees Information & Record Guide.* New York: New York Yankees, 2004.

Creamer, Robert. *Stengel: His Life and Times.* New York: Simon & Schuster, 1984.

Eskenazi, Gerald. *The Lip: A Biography of Leo Durocher.* New York: William Morrow, 1993.

Frommer, Harvey. *A Yankees Century.* New York; Berkley/Penguin, 2002.

Golenbock, Peter. *Wild, High, and Tight: The Life and Death of Billy Martin.* New York: St. Martin's Press, 1994.

Gooden, Dwight, with Bob Klapisch. *Heat: My Life on and off the Diamond.* New York: William Morrow, 1999.

Grossman, Leigh, ed. *The Red Sox Fan Handbook.* Pomfret, Conn.: Swordsmith Productions, 2002.

Halberstam, David. *October 1964.* New York: Ballantine, 1995.

Holtzman, Jerome. *No Cheering in the Press Box,* 1st rev. ed. New York: Henry Holt, 1995.

Kahn, Roger. *October Men: Reggie Jackson, George Steinbrenner, Billy Martin, and the Yankees' Miraculous Finish in 1978*. New York: Harcourt, 2003.

Kubek, Tony, and Terry Pluto. *Sixty-one: The Team, the Record, the Men*. New York: Macmillan, 1987.

Larsen, Don, with Mark Shaw. *The Perfect Yankee*. Champaign, Ill.: Sports Publishing, 2001.

Luciano, Ron, and David Fisher. *Strike Two*. New York: Bantam Books, 1984.

Lyle, Sparky, and Peter Golenbock. *The Bronx Zoo*. New York: Dell, 1979.

Madden, Bill. *Pride of October: What It Was to Be Young and a Yankee*. New York: Warner, 2003.

Mantle, Mickey, with Mickey Herskovitz. *All My Octobers*. New York: HarperCollins, 1994.

Neft, David S., and Richard M. Cohen. *The World Series*. New York: St. Martin's Press, 1990.

Neft, David S., Richard M. Cohen, and Michael L. Neft. *The Sports Encyclopedia: Baseball 2001*. New York: St. Martin's Press, 2001.

Nettles, Graig, and Peter Golenbock. *Balls*. New York: Pocket Books, 1984.

Ritter, Lawrence S. *The Glory of Their Times: The Story of the Early Days of Baseball Told by the Men Who Played It*. New York: William Morrow, 1984.

Roth, Emil H. *Baseball's Most Historic Games: 1876–1993*. Denver: author, 1993.

Ruth, Babe, as told to Bob Considine. *The Babe Ruth Story*. New York: E. P. Dutton, 1948.

Seidel, Michael. *Streak: Joe DiMaggio and the Summer of '41*. New York: Penguin, 1988.

Shaughnessy, Dan. *The Curse of the Bambino*. New York: Penguin, 2000.

Smalling, Jack. *The Baseball Autograph Collector's Handbook,* 12th ed. Durham, N.C.: Baseball America, 2003.

Sobol, Ken. *Babe Ruth and the American Dream*. New York: Ballantine, 1974.

Stokes, Geoffrey. *Pinstripe Pandemonium: A Season with the New York Yankees*. New York: Harper & Row, 1984.

Stout, Glenn, and Richard A. Johnson. *Red Sox Century*. Boston: Houghton Mifflin, 2001.

———. *Yankees Century*. Boston: Houghton Mifflin, 2002.

Thorn, John, Pete Palmer, and Michael Gershman. *Total Baseball,* 7th ed. Kingston, N.Y.: Total Sports, 2001.

Tofel, Richard J. *A Legend in the Making: The New York Yankees in 1939*. Chicago: Ivan R. Dee, 2002.

Torre, Joe, with Tom Verducci. *Chasing the Dream: My Lifelong Journey to the World Series.* New York: Bantam Books, 1997.

Witty, David, et al., *The 2002 Kansas City Royals Media Guide.* Kansas City, Mo.: Kansas City Royals, 2002.

Zimmer, Don, with Bill Madden. *Zim: A Baseball Life.* Kingston, N.Y.: Total Sports, 2001.

Personal Interviews

Ausanio, Joe. Interview. By phone. February 4, 2004.

Berra, Yogi. Interview. Legends Field, Tampa, Fla. March 8, 2004.

Bouton, Jim. Interview. By phone. February 2, 2004.

Byrne, Tommy. Interview. Wake Forest, N.C. March 6, 2003.

Campaneris, Bert. Interview. Conine All-Star Golf Classic, Hollywood, Fla. February 9, 2004.

Coleman, Jerry. Interview. By phone. February 24, 2004.

Dent, Bucky. Interview. McCoy Stadium, Pawtucket, R.I. May 24, 2003.

Downing, Al. Interview. Legal SeaFood, SawGrass Mills, Fort Lauderdale, Fla. February 9, 2004.

Duren, Ryne. Interview. Lakeland Café, Land O'Lakes, Fla. February 16, 2004.

Ford, Whitey. Interview. Legends Field, Tampa, Fla. March 5, 2004.

Girardi, Joe. Interview. Legends Field, Tampa, Fla. March 1, 2004.

Gooden, Dwight. Interview. Legends Field, Tampa, Fla. March 9, 2004.

Guidry, Ron. Interview. Legends Field, Tampa, Fla. March 5, 2004.

Jackson, Reggie. Interview. Legends Field, Tampa, Fla. March 5, 2004.

Kaat, Jim. Interview. Conine All-Star Golf Classic, Hollywood, Fla. February 9, 2004.

Linz, Phil. Interview. Fort Lauderdale Stadium, Fort Lauderdale, Fla. February 7, 2004.

Maddox, Elliott. Interview. Coral Springs, Fla. February 9, 2004.

Mattingly, Don. Interview. Legends Field, Tampa, Fla. March 5, 2004.

Michael, Gene. Interview. Legends Field, Tampa, Fla. February 18, 2004.

Monteleone, Rich. Interview. Legends Field, Tampa, Fla. March 3, 2004.

Murcer, Bobby. Interview. Legends Field, Tampa, Fla. March 9, 2004.

Nettles, Graig. Interview. Legends Field, Tampa, Fla. March 5, 2004.

O'Neill, Paul. Interview. By phone. March 10, 2004.

Randolph, Willie. Interview. Legends Field, Tampa, Fla. March 8, 2004.

Rivers, Mickey. Interview. Legends Field, Tampa, Fla. March 3, 2004.

Terry, Ralph. Interview. By phone. January 29, 2002.

Tresh, Tom. Interview. Cracker Barrel Restaurant, Venice, Fla. February 17, 2004.

White, Roy. Interview. Legends Field, Tampa, Fla. March 5, 2004.

Web Sites

ASAP Sports. 1996–2004. ASAP Sports, Long Island, N.Y. <*www.asapsports.com*>

The Baseball Almanac. 2000–2004. Baseball Almanac, Miami, Fla. <*www.baseball-almanac.com*>

The Baseball Library. 2002–2004. The Idea Logical Company, New York. <*www.baseballlibrary.com*>

The Baseball Page. 1995–2004. Kirk Robinson and Dan Holmes, Cooperstown, N.Y. <*www.thebaseballpage.com*>

Baseball Reference. 2000–2004. Sean L. Forman, Philadelphia. <*www.baseball-reference.com*>

CNN/SI. 1998–2004. CNN Sports Illustrated, New York. <*www.sportsillustrated.cnn.com*>

Historic Baseball. 2000–2004. Historic Baseball, South Carolina. <*www.historicbaseball.com*>

MLB.com. 2002–2004. Major League Baseball Advanced Media, New York. <*www.mlb.com*>

National Baseball Hall of Fame. National Baseball Hall of Fame and Museum, Inc., Cooperstown, N.Y. <*www.baseballhalloffame.org*>

Retrosheet. 1996–2004. Retrosheet, Newark, Del. <*www.retrosheet.org*>

YankeeInfo.com. 2000–2004. YankeeInfo.com. <*www.yankeeinfo.com*>

YES Network. 2002–2004. Yankees Entertainment and Sports, New York. <*www.yesnetwork.com*>

Index

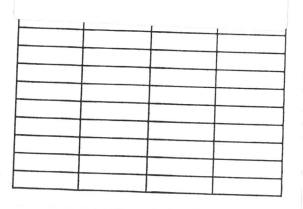